"Jennifer Hopper's investigation of age the political debate surrounding the Affordable Care Act provides a welcome exploration of the influence and limitations of presidential leadership within the media marketplace in the post-broadcast age. Her careful and thoughtful analysis offers a new understanding of framing efforts and effects and sheds light on how even in a complicated media environment the president retains powerful advantages for advancing his agenda".

— **Diane J. Heith**, *St. John's University*

"*Presidential Framing in the 21st Century News Media* does a wonderful job of analyzing President Obama's herculean efforts to use the wide range of modern media outlets to sell and then re-sell the Affordable Care Act. From the challenges over framing the original bill and whether to embrace the term Obamacare to marketing health insurance to young adults on "Between Two Ferns," this accessible and thorough book is a vital resource for students of political communication, journalism, the presidency and public policy".

— **Stephen Farnsworth**, *Professor of Political Science, University of Mary Washington & Former Chair, Political Communication Section, APSA*

PRESIDENTIAL FRAMING IN THE 21ST CENTURY NEWS MEDIA

The Patient Protection and Affordable Care Act came into existence at a time when the president's ability to lead the public was in question, political polarization had intensified, and the media environment appeared ever more fragmented, fast-moving, and resistant to control. Under such circumstances, how can contemporary American presidents such as Barack Obama build and maintain support for themselves and their policies, particularly as controversies arise?

Using case studies of major contests over how key elements of the Affordable Care Act would be framed, and analysis of how those frames fared in influential and popular U.S. news sources, Hopper examines the conditions under which the president can effectively shape public debates today. She argues that despite the difficult political and communications context, the president retains substantial advantages in framing major controversial issues for the media and the public. These presidential framing advantages are conditional, however, and Hopper explores the factors that help make presidential frames more or less likely to gain hold in the news today. More so than in the past, an element of unpredictability in this news environment means that in pursuing favorable messaging, the president and his surrogates may also generate some unintentional consequences in how issues are portrayed to the public. Presidential frames can evolve with unfolding events to take on new meanings and applications, a process facilitated alternately by supporters, opponents, and media actors. Still, media figures and political opponents remain largely reactive to presidential communications, even as some seek to publicize and exploit weaknesses in the administration's narratives. A close look at these recent cases casts new light on the scholarly debate surrounding the president's ability to persuasively communicate and challenges conventional wisdom that the 21st century media largely present an unmanageable news environment for the White House.

Presidential Framing in the 21st Century News Media engages with current events in American politics, focusing on the Obama Administration and the Affordable Care Act, while also reflecting upon the state of the American presidency, the news media, and the public in ways that have substantial implications for all of these actors, not merely in the present, but into the future, making it a compelling read for scholars of Political Science, Media Studies, Communication Studies, and Public Policy.

Jennifer Rose Hopper is Assistant Professor of Political Science at Southern Connecticut State University, where she specializes in the American presidency, mass media, and political communication. Professor Hopper teaches courses on U.S. national political institutions, including Congress, the presidency, and the news media, as well as courses focused on the broader political environment and studying political parties, interest groups, social movements, and public policy.

PRESIDENTIAL FRAMING IN THE 21ST CENTURY NEWS MEDIA

The Politics of the Affordable Care Act

By Jennifer Rose Hopper

Routledge
Taylor & Francis Group
NEW YORK AND LONDON

First published 2017
by Routledge
711 Third Avenue, New York, NY 10017

and by Routledge
2 Park Square, Milton Park, Abingdon, Oxon, OX14 4RN

Routledge is an imprint of the Taylor & Francis Group, an informa business

© 2017 Taylor & Francis

The right of Jennifer Rose Hopper to be identified as author of this work has been asserted by her in accordance with sections 77 and 78 of the Copyright, Designs and Patents Act 1988.

All rights reserved. No part of this book may be reprinted or reproduced or utilized in any form or by any electronic, mechanical, or other means, now known or hereafter invented, including photocopying and recording, or in any information storage or retrieval system, without permission in writing from the publishers.

Trademark notice: Product or corporate names may be trademarks or registered trademarks, and are used only for identification and explanation without intent to infringe.

Library of Congress Cataloging in Publication Data
Names: Hopper, Jennifer Rose, author.
Title: Presidential framing in the 21st Century news media : the politics of the Affordable Care Act / by Jennifer Rose Hopper.
Description: New York, NY : Routledge, 2017. | Includes bibliographical references and index.
Identifiers: LCCN 2016035087 | ISBN 9781138202368 (hbk) | ISBN 9781138202375 (pbk) | ISBN 9781315474137 (ebk)
Subjects: LCSH: Health care reform—United States. | Medical policy—United States. | United States. Patient Protection and Affordable Care Act. | Medicare—Public opinion.
Classification: LCC RA395.A3 H643 2017 | DDC 362.1/04250973—dc23
LC record available at https://lccn.loc.gov/2016035087

ISBN: 978-1-138-20236-8 (hbk)
ISBN: 978-1-138-20237-5 (pbk)
ISBN: 978-1-315-47413-7 (ebk)

Typeset in Bembo
by Swales & Willis Ltd, Exeter, Devon, UK

CONTENTS

List of figures   *viii*
Acknowledgments   *x*

1 Presidential Framing in the 21st Century News Media   1

2 What's in a Name? Taking Back "Obamacare"   17

3 The Politics of Framing Policy Substance: Tax or Penalty?   43

4 Bumpy Rollout, Faulty Framing: HealthCare.gov's Debut   65

5 Portraying Presidential Pledges and Dropped Plans   93

6 Of Socialized Medicine and Death Panels: Framing Contests over Health-Care Reform in Comparative Perspective   113

7 Conclusion   141

Appendix   *149*
Index   *155*

FIGURES

2.1 "Obamacare" in *The New York Times* and *The New York Post*, December 23, 2011–March 22, 2012 — 26
2.2 "Obamacare" and Policy Depictions in *The New York Times* and *The New York Post*, December 23, 2011–March 22, 2012 — 27
2.3 "Obamacare" and Policy Depictions on CNN and Fox News, December 23, 2011–March 22, 2012 — 28
2.4 "Obamacare" in *The New York Times* and *The New York Post*, March 23, 2012–June 23, 2012 — 30
2.5 "Obamacare" and Policy Depictions in *The New York Times* and *The New York Post*, March 23, 2012–June 23, 2012 — 31
2.6 "Obamacare" and Policy Depictions on CNN and Fox News, March 23, 2012–June 23, 2012 — 32
2.7 "Obamacare" on the Sunday News Shows, March 23, 2010–March 23, 2014 — 35
2.8 "Obamacare" Prevalence on Sunday News Programs, March 23, 2010–March 23, 2014 — 36
2.9 Changing Composition of "Obamacare" Users over Time on Sunday News Programs — 36
2.10 "Obamacare" Mentions and Policy Depictions on Sunday News Programs by Year — 37
3.1 Use of Framing Devices over Time in Print and on Cable News — 51
3.2 Actors Using Framing Devices over Time — 52
3.3 Proportional Use of Framing Devices over Time in Print and on Cable News — 54
4.1 Appearance of Presidential and Opposition Frames in News Outlets over Time — 80

4.2	"Obama's Katrina" Analogy in the Analyzed Coverage, November 11–25, 2013	83
4.3	Treatment of "Obama's Katrina" Analogy on Twitter, November 15, 2013	85
5.1	Overall Coverage of Frames across Analyzed Outlets, October 20, 2013–November 20, 2013	101
5.2	Daily Appearances of Frames in Analyzed Outlets, October 20, 2013–November 20, 2013	106
5.3	Appearances of "Obama as Lying" and "Defending Obama" Frames before and after November 7 Apology	107
6.1	Coverage of Kennedy's Health-Care Proposal, Week Following MSG Speech	120
6.2	Number of Articles in Which Medicare Was Treated as "Socialized Medicine" in *The New York Times*, 1962–1965	125
6.3	Treatment of ACA as "Socialized Medicine" by Month across News Outlets, August 2009–March 2010	128
6.4	Treatment of "Death Panels" by Month across News Outlets, August 1, 2009–March 24, 2010	132
6.5	Treatment of "Death Panels" Frame on Twitter, December 23–24, 2009	134

ACKNOWLEDGMENTS

Authors who say that books are large undertakings that rely on the support and help of many others are not exaggerating, as I have learned. Over the past few years I have incurred a number of debts to people without whom this book would not have been possible. Any errors or deficiencies in the pages that follow are solely my own responsibility.

Several of the chapters of this book were conceived initially as conference papers or journal articles, and I have been fortunate to have a number of discussants and anonymous reviewers provide me with valuable feedback and constructive criticism. Thank you to the *International Journal of Communication* for allowing an updated version of research originally published in that journal to appear here. William Adler, Ben Epstein, and Diane Heith were kind enough to look at drafts of portions of this book along the way and offer their keen insights and much appreciated advice. Christine Wade, Andrew Polsky, and Melissa Deckman have been tremendously encouraging of my scholarship and career over the past few years, and I would be remiss not to thank them for that. I would also like to express my gratitude to Washington College and Southern Connecticut State University for all they have done to support the writing of this work. The research librarians at the John F. Kennedy and Lyndon B. Johnson Libraries were an enormous aid in constructing Chapter 6.

The wonderful students I have had the opportunity to teach over the years also helped to spark and refine many of the arguments of this work. Gabrielle Tarbert, Claudette Erickson, and Alexandra Kurtz, in addition to being delightful to spend time with, provided immense research help and first-rate assistance with this endeavor.

I also want to acknowledge the team at Routledge and Taylor & Francis, for everything they have done to publish this book. From the first time that I met

Natalia Mortensen at a conference years ago, she was tremendously warm and encouraging in listening to my very early plans for this book, and I would like to thank her both for inspiring confidence in me to embark on this projects and for shepherding it towards its completion. One could not ask for a better editor with whom to work. Thanks are also due to Lillian Rand for being supremely helpful in leading me through the process, and skillfully addressing my questions and concerns along the way. I am also grateful for Gale Winskill's expert editing talents which quickly and dramatically improved the text.

I want to thank my parents for their love and for supporting me in everything I do: I would not be where I am without them. Thank you so much to my whole extended family and my amazing group of friends—your encouragement and enthusiasm has powered me through in every possible way.

This book is for my brother Tim, for making me laugh, reminding me why I love politics, and proving that the best people go to work for the Government. It is also for my brother Tommy, for being a huge source of strength and inspiration, and whose artistic eye and data-presentation wizardry aided me in creating the cover art and figures in this book. And this book is for Ian and his unwavering encouragement and support, and who makes every day and every accomplishment, big or little, full of meaning and love.

1
PRESIDENTIAL FRAMING IN THE 21ST CENTURY NEWS MEDIA

Presidents cannot always convince others to adopt their views on politics. One might expect, however, that at the very least they would be able to exert some influence over what their signature legislation is popularly called. Even the fiercest critics of the No Child Left Behind Act or the USA Patriot Act, for instance, typically still refer to the laws by their given positively oriented names, part of the rationale behind such strategic labeling in the first place. And yet, the Patient Protection and Affordable Care Act, the health-care reform policy President Barack Obama and his Administration invested tremendous political capital in passing through Congress in 2010, is widely referred to as "Obamacare," a nickname invented by the law's opponents. There is perhaps no greater affront to a president's ability to shape public debate than watching his critics' derisive moniker for his most significant policy reform spread like wildfire in popular discourse.

And yet, this reading of events is an incomplete picture of the forces at work in this story. It ignores the ways that the president and his team, by publically embracing the label "Obamacare," and working to recast it as a positive one, made their supporters more likely to do the same. This reading takes a short-term view of the meaning of political rhetoric, failing to recognize how words might evolve and take on new connotations in the long term. It neglects the role of the news media, a central linkage institution between citizens and government in our society, that took the president's use of "Obamacare" as a green light to use the term in its "objective" coverage, accelerating the proliferation of the name in public discussion. Remarkably, that the Affordable Care Act (which I will alternately refer to as the ACA) is known primarily as Obamacare is not, properly told, principally a story of the lack of control presidents have over how their messages are communicated, but also a tale of presidential *influence*.

It is not surprising that presidential influence over the ways we communicate about politics can be so difficult to discern clearly. Even presidents themselves express ambivalence about their ability to control the trajectory of such stories. In July 2012, nearing the end of his first term, and with voters' determination of whether he would receive another looming in the fall, President Obama sat down for an interview with *CBS This Morning* anchor Charlie Rose. Rose asked the president what lessons he had learned in his first term that he might use to "guarantee success" in a possible four more years. Seated next to his wife, First Lady Michelle Obama, the president responded:

> The mistake of my first term—couple of years—was thinking that this job was just about getting the policy right. And that's important. But the nature of this office is also to tell a story to the American people that gives them a sense of unity and purpose and optimism, especially during tough times. It's funny when I ran everybody said, "well he can give a good speech, but can he actually manage the job?" And in my first two years, I think the notion was, "well, he's been juggling and managing a lot of stuff, but where's the story that tells us where he's going?" And I think that was a legitimate criticism.
>
> *(Boerma 2012)*

A little over two years later, giving an address at Northwestern University, the president noted,

> There's a reason fewer Republicans you hear them running about Obamacare—because while good, affordable health care might seem like a fanged threat to the freedom of the American people on *Fox News*—(laughter)—it turns out it's working pretty well in the real world. (Applause).
>
> *(White House 2014)*

These quotes offer us two different pathways for understanding why interpretations of events counter to those preferred by the president might spread. Does this occur primarily when the president fails to be an effective storyteller, imbuing the American people with "unity and purpose and optimism" about what the government is doing, as Obama indicates in the first quote? Or rather, as the president relates in the second statement, do media outlets that convey the stories to the public about what is happening in the "real world" twist and distort those narratives to the president's detriment? That President Obama has expressed both of these views, highlighting his own communications shortcomings and the unfairness of the media landscape he faces, suggests the difficulty of untangling when and why presidents in the contemporary era are effective at framing their policies in news coverage; a central (though certainly not the only) channel for conveying these impressions to the public.

Reconsidering Presidential Framing and the News

To enhance understanding of the complex interactions among the U.S. presidency, White House opponents, and the news media that affect how we think and talk about politics, careful, detailed analyses of how the process unfolds in the present day are necessary. This book aims to shed light on these interactions by exploring how the presidency works to frame high-profile, contentious public-policy issues today, even as political foes and a daunting news landscape complicate those efforts. Through case studies of major contests over how key elements of the Affordable Care Act would be framed, and analysis of how those frames fared in influential and popular U.S. news sources, I examine the conditions under which the president can affect conversations about policy, perceptions of a program's provisions, and forestall controversy surrounding it. The chapters that follow trace presidential efforts to interpret events that have either been precipitated by or triggered a framing contest, as powerful interests opposed to the Administration have challenged the president's preferred understandings. These contests play out in a continually evolving news media environment consisting of a wide spectrum of outlets, from more traditional sources that have been around for decades (such as newspapers with national followings, and evening news programs on the major broadcast television networks) to newer forums (including partisan cable news programming and online formats), the latter of which can allow for unfiltered communication between political actors and citizens.

The central argument of the book is this: that despite the fragmented political and communications context of the early 21st century, the president retains substantial advantages in framing major controversial issues for the media and the public. Though many recent works in political science and media studies have emphasized the challenges of the contemporary media moment for any political actor seeking to shape the news, I put forth the concept of *presidential framing resilience*. This concept identifies the president as effective at spreading his or her preferred frames in a variety of media settings, old and new, and recognizes the staying power of those frames over time in the news, reflecting the office's power in political communication. In some ways, then, it urges a return to earlier theories of the modern American presidency which highlighted the president's tremendous ability to shape public debates and news narratives about U.S. politics. But whereas that ability has increasingly come into question—particularly on domestic policy issues—in today's far more complex news environment, presidential framing resilience seeks to capture what effectiveness in communication might look like in this distinctive media moment. The polysemantic nature of the term "resilience" is therefore useful in conveying the adjustability and fluidity of presidential frames as they are conveyed via the 21st century media; we can identify the president's message scattered across many news sources, but not necessarily strongly concentrated and uncorrupted in any single venue. Still, in the era of cable television and the Internet, that the president's frames are so prevalent and widespread is of great import.

This framing influence is conditional, however, and retaining these communications advantages is, in part, up to the president and his team. In the chapters that follow, I demonstrate the impact of presidential communication choices, by exploring the factors that help make presidential frames more or less likely to gain hold in the news. Deficiencies in the president's communications strategies can take several forms. He and his team can squander their frame disseminating abilities if they fail to construct convincing, coherent frames that comport with established news norms, if the frames do not provide sufficient political cover for supporters to adopt and echo them in public debate, and if their frames prove incapable of evolving credibly over time as circumstances require.

Further, several of my cases demonstrate that innovative tactics such as web-based communications do not just allow the president to bypass the legacy press to frame issues for his base, but can have important effects on traditional media coverage, albeit in some ways likely unexpected by the president's team. On the one hand, this can lead to what I term *presidential framing side effects*. More so than in the past, the incontrovertible element of unpredictability in this news environment means that in pursuing favorable messaging, the president and his or her surrogates may also generate some unintentional consequences in how issues are portrayed to the public. Mainstream news content is directly altered by the introduction of the presidential frame into the communication surrounding the policy, but some of these changes are side effects, incidental to the content and purposes of the initial presidential frame. The White House, then, has an intended result for its framing project, but the media's interaction with this frame produces coverage that is a direct by-product of the frame, yet *not* originally contemplated by the presidents and their surrogates.

Another example of the unpredictability of today's presidency-media-public system is a phenomenon I will refer to as *presidential frame refraction*. As presidential frames engage the attention of the news media, they may not be simply affirmed or rejected, but instead deflected from their original path, just as a ray of light through glass shifts direction as the density of the medium it travels through changes. Presidential frames evolve with unfolding events to take on new meanings and applications, a process facilitated alternately by supporters, opponents, and media actors. Thus the "resilience" aspect of presidential framing is complemented by the notion of frame refraction—the president's frames are spread widely in popular news sources, but in ways that are malleable, allowing others to alternately co-opt, rework, or challenge them.

A key takeaway of this book, then, is that even in today's daunting news landscape, media figures and political opponents remain largely reactive to the president's frames, even as some seek to publicize and exploit weaknesses in those narratives. Returning to his quotes above, then, President Obama was right in both respects; presidential leadership requires effective storytelling, and when the president falls short in this regard, the contemporary media can seem cruel indeed.

An Important but Little Explored Case

As we turn the page on the Obama presidency, a study of the Administration's framing of the Affordable Care Act is in order. Currently we have no detailed, systematic analysis of health-care reform coverage across a wide spectrum of major U.S. news outlets over a lengthy, consequential time period as the policy was debated, passed into law, challenged by opponents, and implemented. The ACA is perhaps the signature legislative achievement of the Obama Administration, yet is a policy with low levels of support and one that is little understood by Americans.[1] Scholars have demonstrated a strong relationship between the public's evaluations of health-care reform and Obama's job performance, frequently operating to the president's detriment (Jacobson 2011). In addition to congressional Republicans spearheading numerous votes to repeal the ACA, a conflict over defunding and delaying its provisions resulted in a federal government shutdown on October 1, 2013. Presidential framing of the ACA, then, reflects a "best test case" of the president's ability to shape news narratives and public debates in the contemporary era. If the president is able to exert an influence here, amid weak public backing, widespread misinformation regarding the law's fundamental provisions, and absent bipartisan support, it suggests that presidential influence would exist on other, less fraught cases in contemporary American politics. This subject matter aids our understanding of the dynamics of the relationship between the presidency and the media at a time when both institutions have undergone substantial change.

Additionally, presidential communication, media coverage, and health-care reform are important to study in their own right. Having survived several challenges in Congress and the courts, it appears the ACA will continue to shape American politics for years to come, meaning we should understand how and why impressions of the law have developed and evolved over time. The Pew Research Journalism Project (2010) declared the lead-up to the ACA as the first major, long-running policy debate that the press covered in a new media era marked by the participation of bloggers, social-media outlets, and increasingly influential cable news networks. At a time in which the landscape where presidential communication takes place is constantly shifting, we need detailed, comprehensive studies of how the American presidency and the media (and the disparate actors that now make up the latter institution) are adjusting to such changes.

While there are admitted limitations to focusing an inquiry on a single Administration, President Obama faced a media environment far different from that of even his immediate predecessor in office, George W. Bush. The popularity of social-media sites such as Facebook and Twitter dramatically increased, and politicians (including Obama) began to use these and other online formats to communicate with the public as a practice of everyday governance, rather than merely a campaign strategy. With each election cycle we gain new studies of how candidates have used the Internet and social media to reach potential supporters and turn out the vote, and yet little scholarly attention has been devoted to such strategies employed in the context of building and maintaining support for domestic policymaking. We need to give more consideration to how presidents encourage and sustain support for complex public programs and policies, and how these innovative tactics impact news coverage consumed by significant portions of the U.S. population. The traditional news media also underwent significant upheaval in this period, marked by the demise of many print outlets, fewer resources and staff cuts for even venerable "old media" institutions, and paywall model experiments for those seeking to survive in an Internet era. At the same time, a prestige press newspaper such as *The New York Times* remains an important source of original journalism, and the content of its political coverage ripples influentially throughout the rest of the media system.

Thus, while this study focuses on the Obama Administration and the Affordable Care Act, it reflects upon the state of the American presidency, the news media, and the public in ways that have substantial implications for all of these actors, not merely in the present, but into the future.

The Presidency, Public Leadership, and the Contemporary Media Environment

Presidents have long understood part of their role in American politics is to "tell a story to the American people," as President Obama put it, about who they are and where they are going. Teddy Roosevelt deemed the presidency a "bully pulpit," pioneering the role of the president to promote his policy preferences to the public (Gamm and Smith 1998). Woodrow Wilson theorized the president should be a leader-interpreter, intuiting the people's true desires and explaining them back to them (Tulis 1987). Modern presidents lauded for their rhetorical ability and persuasiveness, from Franklin Delano Roosevelt and his use of fireside chats to the "Great Communicator" Ronald Reagan, prioritized shaping the national agenda and using every available communication channel to convince the public of the wisdom of their views and decisions. The avenues for reaching the public have modernized and diversified with advancing technologies, from the industrial printing press to radio to television to the Internet, ever-broadening the ways that presidents and citizens can hear from each other.

Despite the modern presidency's emphasis on public leadership and persuasion, there is a great deal of disagreement in the scholarly literature about how effectively presidents can communicate their views to the public, particularly in a noisy, disjointed media setting in which they are frequently challenged by political opponents (Jacobs and Shapiro 2000; Kumar 2007; Cohen 2008; Eshbaugh-Soha and Peake 2011; Edwards 2012). Kernell's (1993) influential work on presidential "going public" and more recent, related research including studies of presidents "going local" (Cohen 2009); taking their messages on a "presidential roadshow" (Heith 2013); and successfully employing the bully pulpit, if only provisionally (Rottinghaus 2010) all demonstrate the importance to modern-day presidents of seeking to reach the public with their messages, and yet also the ways this has become trickier over time.

Many of these challenges derive from the modernization and globalization of the mass media, evident in the advent of cable television, the Internet, and social media. Whereas a prime-time televised presidential address in the 1960s would be seen by a high percentage of Americans confined to the content presented by the "Big 3" broadcast television networks, in November 2014, ABC, CBS, NBC, and Fox refused to give Obama an 8 p.m. time slot for an address on immigration for financial reasons—and even had they acquiesced, it is unclear how many viewers the president would have received given the seemingly limitless cable and online entertainment programming choices (Fuller 2014). Furthermore, scholarly studies present a mixed picture of whether the president can obtain supportive coverage for his frames in the news today. On the one hand, journalists rely heavily on official sources like the president, even as technological advancements have given reporters greater potential freedom to interpret events (Livingston and Bennett 2003). Some contend the contemporary press is only semi-independent, often unquestioningly passing on the preferred messages of powerful political elites (Bennett et al. 2007; Finnegan 2007; Hallin 1986). Past research has demonstrated that the president can at the very least set the public agenda and redirect the media's attention to particular issues (Cohen 1995; Lee 2014; Miles 2014). Farnsworth (2009) finds the president now acts as a "spinner in chief," using the White House's media dominance to foster his or her short-term political goals, if not always the long-term interest of the nation. Major (2014) finds the media privilege the president's framing of unilateral executive powers, thereby contributing to the growth of this independent authority. Entman's (2004) cascading activation model charts how framings of foreign policy issues can flow from the White House to the news media and ultimately to the public, with initial frames enjoying lasting power and those congruent with cultural norms transmitted most easily.

Yet these cases also indicate why we might expect Obama to fall short in the case of health-care reform; in contrast to foreign policy where the president faces fewer challenges to his authority, here we consider a domestic policy that encountered tremendous resistance and in which the president sought to dislodge some widely held negative impressions. Further, there is even a lack of scholarly consensus on the president's effectiveness in shaping news content on the same topic over the same time span; witness Bennett et al.'s (2007) argument that the news media largely passed along President George W. Bush's frames in the "war on terror" with little questioning alongside Kuypers et al.'s (2012) contention that the press blatantly challenged the president's post-9/11 frames in conveying them to the public. Counter to pessimistic views of presidential influence, the concept of presidential framing resilience I outline in more detail in the chapters that follow demonstrates how the president's frames show up across a range of media outlets, and reverberate throughout the media system. Even where they are ultimately altered or challenged, the communications are still repeated and conveyed; a key element of how the president drives public conversations and news coverage.

A substantial mass of research suggests the president increasingly faces an inhospitable environment for his messages in the press. Following Watergate and the Vietnam War, many argue media outlets took up a hyperadversarial relationship with political figures, challenging their messages confrontationally as a matter of everyday journalistic practice (Patterson 1994, 2003; Jamieson and Waldman 2004). Boydstun (2013) finds the explosive, skewed nature of agenda-setting in the media makes it unlikely any political actor can sustain influence over news. The technological modernization of the mass media has also dramatically altered the president's prospects for interpreting issues for the media. Innovative formats like political blogs and prime-time cable news talk shows prominently feature analysis by partisan commentators motivated to echo or undercut politicians' accounts of events (Jamieson and Cappella 2010; Iyengar 2011; Belt et al. 2012; Feldman et al. 2012; Levendusky 2013). A hostile media and partisan polarization have altered forms of presidential communication, including shifting a president's claims of a mandate following Election Day in a more defensive direction, to help shore up legitimacy in an age of disillusionment and conflict (Azari 2014).

As Heith (2013, 2) illustrates, since the 1990s the news media upon which the president has long relied to deliver his messages to a national audience has "multiplied and fragmented," making presidential prospects of reaching Americans more uncertain. Chadwick (2013) traces the development of our complex contemporary hybrid media system, marked by conflict, cooperation, and interdependence between older and newer media settings and logics, a system political actors have learned to navigate with varying levels of success. Cohen (2008) suggests this fragmented media environment offers less overall coverage of presidents and smaller audiences for presidential communications than earlier decades.

Still, an adept White House communications operation might capitalize on information sources such as 24-hour news networks and social media, as they continually offer new opportunities to inject into coverage the president's preferred reading of ongoing events (Kumar 2007; Hendricks and Schill 2015). One of the ways the presidency has adapted to the challenges of the contemporary media moment is by using new media to avoid the scrutiny and commentary of journalists (Laurence 2003; Owen and Davis 2008; Stuckey 2010). Rottinghaus (2010) argues that because the media filter presidential messages in a way that obstructs the president's ability to lead the public, the Administration is better served by trying to reach citizens directly. The Obama Administration has often preferred to position the president's message within the "cloud" of information and ideas on the Internet (Heith 2012). The 2008 and 2012 Obama campaigns used new media strategies to personalize campaign appeals (Bimber 2014), dedicated an unprecedented amount of resources to digital campaigning (Hendricks 2014), and used social media far more extensively than their opponents (Pew Research Center 2012b).

Yet there are clear limitations to these tactics. Edwards (2012, Kindle Location 677) concludes the White House e-mailing supporters is "preaching to the converted" and can only take a president so far. Stromer-Galley (2014) identifies how candidates use social media to encourage their backers to spread their messages, but the nature of the medium means that they cannot fully control how that message is disseminated, and ways it can be altered or undermined by others. That account and others (Farrar-Myers and Vaughn 2015; Hendricks and Schill 2015) illuminate how these trends unfold in campaigns and elections, but not necessarily in a policy context. Given the acknowledged constraints of communicating directly with supporters, we need to explore the wider implications of the president's digital communications strategies: in short, what else might he or she get out of it? When presidents and their surrogates email, tweet, or post on their websites the messages may be addressed to supporters, but the content is in the public domain. Yet little has been said about the impact of such presidential communications on coverage provided by traditional news outlets, whose coverage affects how the broader public thinks about politics (McCombs 2014). Thus, in the cases that follow I chart the process of presidential frame refraction and presidential framing side effects, tracing the ways presidential frames can evolve or change news coverage as they appear in the media, sometimes in ways that help the Administration's political efforts and, at other times, in ways that hurt. The how and why of each process is explained in more detail in subsequent chapters.

Presidential Framing, Framing Contests, and the News

To explore how President Obama and his opponents vied for control over how various facets of health-care reform would appear and be discussed in public discourse, I make use of the concept of framing. Framing as it will be used in this study entails selecting central organizing themes in order to focus attention on some elements of an issue or event and de-emphasize others, promoting a particular interpretation of a story (Altheide 1976; Entman 2004; Lakoff 2004; Bennett 2005; Callaghan and Schnell 2005). The framing process makes some aspects of our reality more noticeable than others and helps to set terms of debate (Reese et al. 2001; Kuypers 2009; Kuypers and D'Angelo 2010). Previous studies have also examined presidential communications by identifying how the president has employed framing and strategic rhetoric to depict events, issues, and controversies more favorably for the media and the public (Windt and Ingold 1987; Stuckey 1997; Busby 2001; Denton and Holloway 2003; Farnsworth and Lichter 2006; Kuypers 2006; Entman 2012; Hopper 2013). Presidents engage in framing efforts to situate issues within particular narratives that engender greater support for their political goals, and then aim to have those interpretations appear in the news, to reach a wider audience of citizens.

Yet presidents rarely frame issues without interference from opponents. Efforts to frame high-stakes issues for the public can produce competition among elites or "framing contests," with two sides that compete to interpret events successfully for the news media and the public (Wolfsfeld 1997; Entman 2004; Jamieson and Waldman 2004; Wolfsfeld and Sheafer 2006; Chong and Druckman 2007a, b; Schaffner and Atkinson 2010). These contests now play out in the dramatically altered communications environment outlined earlier, requiring additional studies of how presidents advantage or hinder themselves in disseminating their messages.

At the center of each chapter of this book is an analysis of key political actors' public statements regarding a specific facet of the ACA, and then subsequent news coverage of that topic, to study the extent to which the president and his detractors were each able to shape news narratives across a variety of outlets over time. I first identify several of the most prominent themes in the public statements of the president, his surrogates/defenders, and his opponents through qualitative inductive analysis, and then focus on frequently appearing words, phrases, references, and concepts that can be considered framing devices (see also Jamieson and Cappella 1998; Entman 2004; Kuypers 2006; Kuypers et al. 2012). These devices illustrate how both sides sought to have those initial themes framed, or interpreted and understood, by audiences. I then turn to an analysis of important and representative news media coverage for each case; in total, over a dozen different media outlets are analyzed in the book, including print, television, and online news providers. The news analysis then assesses the extent to which the Administration's framing was present in the coverage and the extent to which the political opposition's framing, with an alternative interpretation of events, was apparent. I review each framing contest for more than one time period as it plays out in the news because, as Reese et al. (2001, 15) point out, "unless frames endure over time they have relatively little importance for analysis." Entman et al. (2009, 177) also argue that frames are about future application, as "exposure during a given time period is presumed to increase probabilities of particular responses during a future period, while diminishing the probability of thinking about other potentially relevant objects or traits." Specifics regarding coding procedures, units of analyses, and intercoder reliability are discussed in the Appendix to the book. Finally, each chapter includes a discussion of public opinion polls that incorporated elements of key frames to offer some indication of the broader political impact of the framing contests as they played out in the news media.

Plan of the Book

In the following chapters, I explore key cases of the Obama Administration's efforts to frame health-care reform, vying with its political opponents in endeavoring to ensure its messages carried the day in media settings old and new.

I begin in Chapter 2 by delving further into the story that began this introduction regarding perhaps the most basic and fundamental focus for a framing contest surrounding policy: what a program would be commonly called. The chapter charts the beginnings of an Obama Administration effort to co-opt the nickname "Obamacare" for the ACA, an attempt to shift its meaning away from its pejorative invention and usage by opponents of health-care reform. Through an analysis of major print and television news sources, I demonstrate this communications campaign did affect coverage of "Obamacare" and shifted it toward a somewhat more positive portrayal of the policy itself, while also producing unexpected results for what "objective" news coverage of the law would now entail.

Beyond its name, a key element of building support for a policy reform entails framing how we understand a program's basic stipulations. Chapter 3 looks at media coverage describing the ACA's individual mandate requirement that all Americans maintain health insurance coverage before and after the Supreme Court's highly scrutinized 2012 ruling on the constitutionality of that provision. This chapter chronicles President Obama's depiction of the repercussions of failing to acquire insurance as resulting in offenders having to pay a "penalty" or "fine" vs. Chief Justice John Roberts' majority opinion describing the policy mechanism as only surviving constitutional muster as a "tax." Widely construed as a victory for President Obama, I explore how the ruling actually demonstrates the ways that even the entry of a political actor such as the Supreme Court, not well-suited to shape public debates, can complicate the ways the president's preferred frames appear in the news. In the long term, however, presidential framing advantages resurfaced, suggesting challengers may only effectively hijack the president's message in the media for so long.

Over the course of President Obama's time in office, the ACA went from a rough proposal to formal legislation to a comprehensive health-care reform program that needed to be put into practice. Chapter 4 charts presidential framing as the ACA's provisions were implemented, as I contrast the Obama Administration's effort to cast the problems surrounding the launch of the HealthCare.gov website as merely "glitches" against opponents' framing of the problems as indicative of the fundamental failure of the ACA amounting to "Obama's Katrina." This chapter illustrates how early coverage of the website problems reveals presidential framing resilience, even under the difficult circumstances of policy implementation flops. However, as the substance of the frames disseminated by the White House proved deficient as time passed, news coverage across many outlets became far more problematic for the president.

Other aspects of health-care reform's implementation were seemingly not planned for at all by the White House. Chapter 5 reviews the framing contest that emerged when President Obama's long-standing and oft-repeated pledge that Americans could keep insurance coverage they liked under the ACA was called into question by the cancellation of some plans as the law was implemented in October 2013. The president's opponents worked to turn these events into a major political controversy, framing it as a broken promise by a dishonest president. While the president was able to gain significant space for his preferred framing of events despite the challenging conditions, inconsistent messaging tempered the *Administration's* ability to secure overall favorable coverage, even in friendly partisan outlets.

Having explored the power and limits of presidential framing in all of these cases, my focus then turns to how Obama's framing effectiveness on health care, in this very particular media moment, measures up to that of some of his predecessors. I employ a comparative historical lens in Chapter 6, expanding my inquiry to evaluate the Obama Administration's effort to publically debunk opponents' frames that the ACA entailed "socialism" and "death panels" against how previous Democratic presidents John F. Kennedy and Lyndon B. Johnson sought to dispel accusations that health-care reform they championed amounted to "socialized medicine" in the news media of the 1960s. The evidence in this chapter suggests we revisit some of our common assumptions about the president's ability to shape the news in the mid-20th century in comparison to today, and about the relative ability of the media across these periods to impart accurate policy information to their audiences.

Finally, in the concluding chapter, I return to my argument about presidential framing advantages, although the complexities of the media landscape may mean the Administration cannot always predict precisely how its impact will manifest itself. I then consider the ramifications of these findings for the U.S. presidency, the news media, and the American political system.

Note

1 Pew Research Center polls show that from 2009 to 2012, the American public became warier of the Government's role in health-care reform (Pew Research Center 2012a). Tracking polls from the Kaiser Family Foundation demonstrated that negative views of the Affordable Care Act were more prevalent among Americans than favorable ones after the policy was signed into law (Kaiser Family Foundation 2013b). A March 2013 tracking poll from the organization found large percentages of the public unaware of several of the law's stipulations, such as prohibiting insurance companies from denying coverage because of preexisting conditions, and closing the Medicare prescription drug coverage gap, as well as holding misconceptions about the law, including that the ACA creates a government-run health plan (57%), provides government subsidies to illegal immigrants to purchase insurance (47%), and allows a government panel to make decisions about end-of-life care for Medicare recipients (40%) (Kaiser Family Foundation 2013a).

References

Altheide, David L. 1976. *Creating Reality: How TV News Distorts Events*. Beverly Hills: Sage.

Azari, Julia R. 2014. *Delivering the People's Message: The Changing Politics of the Presidential Mandate*. Ithaca, NY: Cornell University Press.

Belt, Todd L., Marion R. Just, and Ann N. Crigler. 2012. "The 2008 Media Primary: Handicapping the Candidates in Newspapers, on TV, Cable, and the Internet." *The International Journal of Press/Politics* 17: 341–369.

Bennett, W. Lance. 2005. *News: The Politics of Illusion*, 6th edition. New York: Pearson Longman.
Bennett, W. Lance, Regina G. Lawrence, and Steven Livingston. 2007. *When the Press Fails: Political Power and the News Media from Iraq to Katrina*. Chicago: University of Chicago Press.
Bimber, Bruce. 2014. "Digital Media in the Obama Campaigns of 2008 and 2012: Adaptation to the Personalized Political Communication Environment." *Journal of Information Technology & Politics* 11: 130–150.
Boerma, Lindsey. 2012. "Obama Reflects on His Biggest Mistake as President." *CBS News*, July 12. Accessed July 16, 2016. http://www.cbsnews.com/news/obama-reflects-on-his-biggest-mistake-as-president/.
Boydstun, Amber E. 2013. *Making the News: Politics, the Media, & Agenda Setting*. Chicago: University of Chicago Press.
Busby, Robert. 2001. *Defending the American Presidency: Clinton and the Lewinsky Scandal*. New York: Palgrave.
Callaghan, Karen and Frauke Schnell. 2005. *Framing American Politics*. Pittsburgh: University of Pittsburgh Press.
Chadwick, Andrew. 2013. *The Hybrid Media System: Politics and Power*. New York: Oxford University Press.
Chong, Dennis and James N. Druckman. 2007a. "Framing Theory." *Annual Review of Political Science* 10: 103–126.
Chong, Dennis and James N. Druckman. 2007b. "A Theory of Framing and Opinion Formation in Competitive Elite Environments." *Journal of Communication* 57 (1): 99–118.
Cohen, Jeffrey E. 1995. "Presidential Rhetoric and the Public Agenda." *American Journal of Political Science* 2: 87–107.
Cohen, Jeffrey E. 2008. *The Presidency in the Era of 24-Hour News*. Princeton: Princeton University Press.
Cohen, Jeffrey E. 2009. *Going Local: Presidential Leadership in the Post-Broadcast Age*. New York: Cambridge University Press.
Denton, Robert E. and Rachel L. Holloway, eds. 2003. *Images, Scandal, and Communication Strategies of the Clinton Presidency*. Westport: Greenwood.
Edwards III, George C. 2012. *Overreach: Leadership in the Obama Presidency*. Princeton: Princeton University Press.
Entman, Robert M. 2004. *Projections of Power: Framing News, Public Opinion, and U.S. Foreign Policy*. Chicago: University of Chicago Press.
Entman, Robert M. 2012. *Scandal and Silence: Media Responses to Presidential Misconduct*. Cambridge: Polity Press.
Entman, Robert E., Jörg Matthes, and Lynn Pellicano. 2009. "Nature, Sources, and Effects of News Framing." In *The Handbook of Journalism Studies*, eds Karin Wahl-Jorgensen and Thomas Hanitzsch, 175–190. New York: Routledge.
Eshbaugh-Soha, Matthew and Jeffrey Peake. 2011. *Breaking through the Noise: Presidential Leadership, Public Opinion, and the News Media*. California: Stanford University Press.
Farnsworth, Stephen J. 2009. *Spinner in Chief: How Presidents Sell Their Policies and Themselves*. Boulder. CO: Paradigm.
Farnsworth, Stephen J. and S. Robert Lichter. 2006. *The Mediated Presidency: Television News and Presidential Governance*. Lanham: Rowman & Littlefield.
Farrar-Myers, Victoria A. and Justin S. Vaughn. 2015. *Controlling the Message: New Media in American Political Campaigns*. New York: New York Univeristy Press.

Feldman, Lauren, Edward W. Maibach, Connie Roser-Renouf, and Anthony Leiserowitz. 2012. "Climate on Cable: The Nature and Impact of Global Warming Coverage on Fox News, CNN, and MSNBC." *The International Journal of Press/Politics* 17: 3–31.

Finnegan, Lisa. 2007. *No Questions Asked: News Coverage Since 9/11*. Westport: Praeger.

Fuller, Jaime. 2014. "Why the Major Networks Didn't Give President Obama Primetime Real Estate for His Immigration Speech." *The Washington Post*, November 21. Accessed July 16, 2016. https://www.washingtonpost.com/news/the-fix/wp/2014/11/20/why-the-networks-arent-giving-president-obama-primetime-real-estate-for-his-immigration-speech/.

Gamm, Gerald and Renee M. Smith. 1998. "Presidents, Parties, and the Public: Evolving Patterns of Interaction, 1877–1929." In *Speaking to the People: The Rhetorical Presidency in Historical Perspective*, ed. Richard J. Ellis, 87–111. Amherst: University of Massachusetts Press.

Hallin, Daniel C. 1986. *The "Uncensored War": The Media and Vietnam*. New York: Oxford University Press.

Heith, Diane J. 2012. "Obama and the Public Presidency: What Got You Here Won't Get You There." In *The Obama Presidency: Appraisals and Prospects*, eds Bert A. Rockman, Andrew Rudalevige, and Colin Campbell, 123–148. Washington, DC: CQ Press.

Heith, Diane J. 2013. *The Presidential Road Show: Public Leadership in an Era of Party Polarization and Media Fragmentation*. Boulder: Paradigm.

Hendricks, John Allen. 2014. "The New-Media Campaign of 2012." In *The 2012 Presidential Campaign: A Communication Perspective*, ed. Robert E. Denton, Jr., 133–156. Lanham: Rowman & Littlefield.

Hendricks, John Allen and Dan Schill. 2015. *Presidential Campaigning and Social Media*. New York: Oxford University Press.

Hopper, Jennifer Rose. 2013. "Pardoning the President: President Clinton, the Lewinsky Scandal, and the Politics of Presidential Redemption." *White House Studies* 13 (2): 159–186.

Iyengar, Shanto. 2011. *Media Politics: A Citizen's Guide*. New York: W.W. Norton.

Jacobs, Larry R. and Robert Y. Shapiro. 2000. *Politicians Don't Pander: Political Manipulation and the Loss of Democratic Responsiveness*. Chicago: University of Chicago Press.

Jacobson, Gary C. 2011. "Legislative Success and Political Failure: The Public's Reaction to Barack Obama's Early Presidency." *Presidential Studies Quarterly* 41: 220–244.

Jamieson, Kathleen Hall and Joseph Cappella. 1998. *"The Role of the Press in the Health Care Reform Debate of 1993–1994."* In *The Politics of News, the News of Politics*, eds Doris Graber, Denis McQuall, and Pippa Norris, 110–131. Washington, DC: CQ Press.

Jamieson, Kathleen Hall and Joseph N. Cappella. 2010. *Echo Chamber: Rush Limbaugh and the Conservative Media Establishment*. New York: Oxford University Press.

Jamieson, Kathleen Hall and Paul Waldman. 2004. *The Press Effect: Politicians, Journalists and the Stories that Shape the Political World*. New York: Oxford University Press.

Kaiser Family Foundation. 2013a. "Kaiser Health Tracking Poll: March 2013." March 20. Accessed July 15, 2016. http://kff.org/health-reform/poll-finding/march-2013-tracking-poll/.

Kaiser Family Foundation. 2013b. "Kaiser Health Tracking Poll: June 2013." June 19. Accessed July 15, 2016. http://kff.org/health-reform/poll-finding/kaiser-health-tracking-poll-june-2013/.

Kernell, Samuel. 1993. *Going Public: New Strategies of Presidential Leadership*. Washington, DC: CQ Press.

Kumar, Martha Joynt. 2007. *Managing the President's Message: The White House Communications Operation*. Baltimore: The Johns Hopkins University Press.

Kuypers, Jim A. 2006. *Bush's War: Media Bias and Justifications for War in a Terrorist Age*. Lanham: Rowman & Littlefield.

Kuypers, Jim A., ed. 2009. *Rhetorical Criticism: Perspectives in Action*. Lanham: Lexington Books.

Kuypers, Jim A. and Paul D'Angelo, eds. 2010. *Doing News Framing Analysis: Empirical and Theoretical Perspectives*. New York: Routledge.

Kuypers, Jim A., Stephen D. Cooper, and Matthew T. Althouse. 2012. "George W. Bush, the American Press, and the Initial Framing of the War on Terror after 9/11." In *The George W. Bush Presidency: A Rhetorical Perspective*, ed. Robert E. Denton, Jr., 89–112. Lanham: Lexington Books.

Lakoff, George. 2004. *Don't Think of an Elephant! Know Your Values and Frame the Debate*. Vermont: Chelsea Green.

Laurence, Jonathan. 2003. "Ross Perot's Outsider Challenge: New and Old Media in American Presidential Campaigns." In *The Media and Neo-Populism: A Contemporary Comparative Analysis*, eds Gianpietro Mazzoleni, Stewart Julianne, and Bruce Horsfield, 175–193. Westport: Praeger.

Lee, Han Soo. 2014. "Analyzing the Multidirectional Relationships between the President, News Media, and the Public: Who Affects Whom?" *Political Communication* 31: 259–281.

Levendusky, Matthew. 2013. *How Partisan Media Polarize America*. Chicago: The University of Chicago Press.

Livingston, Steven and W. Lance Bennett. 2003. "Gatekeeping, Indexing, and Live-Event News: Is Technology Altering the Construction of News?" *Political Communication* 20: 363–380.

Major, Mark. 2014. *The Unilateral Presidency and the News Media: The Politics of Framing Executive Power*. New York: Palgrave Macmillan.

McCombs, Maxwell. 2014. *Setting the Agenda: The Mass Media and Public Opinion*, 2nd edition. Cambridge: Polity.

Miles, Matthew R. 2014. "The Bully Pulpit and Media Coverage: Power without Persuasion." *The International Journal of Press/Politics* 19: 66–84.

Owen, Diana and Richard Davis. 2008. "Presidential Communication in the Internet Era." *Presidential Studies Quarterly* 38: 658–673.

Patterson, Thomas. 1994. *Out of Order*. New York: Vintage.

Patterson, Thomas. 2003. *The Vanishing Voter: Public Involvement in an Age of Uncertainty*. New York: Vintage.

Pew Research Center. 2012a. "Obama Health Care Law: Where Does the Public Stand?" June 15. Accessed July 15, 2016. http://www.people press.org/2012/06/15/obama-health-care-law-where-does-the-public-stand/.

Pew Research Center. 2012b. "How Presidential Candidates Use the Web and Social Media." August 15. Accessed July 16, 2016. http://www.journalism.org/2012/08/15/how-presidential-candidates-use-web-and-social-media/.

Pew Research Center Journalism Project. 2010. "Six Things to Know about Health Care Coverage." June 21. Accessed July 16, 2016. http://www.journalism.org/2010/06/21/six-things-know-about-health-care-coverage/.

Reese, Stephen D., Oscar H. Gandy, Jr., and August E. Grant. 2001. *Framing Public Life: Perspectives on Media and Our Understanding of the Social World*. New Jersey: Lawrence Erlbaum.

Rottinghaus, Brandon. 2010. *The Provisional Pulpit: Modern Presidential Leadership of Public Opinion*. Texas: Texas A&M University Press.

Schaffner, Brian F. and Mary Layton Atkinson. 2010. "Taxing Death or Estates? When Frames Influence Citizens' Issue Beliefs." In *Winning with Words: The Origins and Impact of Political Framing*, eds Brian F. Schaffner and Patrick Sellers, 121–135. New York: Routledge.

Stromer-Galley, Jennifer. 2014. *Presidential Campaigning in the Internet Age*. New York: Oxford University Press.

Stuckey, Mary E. 1997. *Strategic Failures in the Modern Presidency*. Cresskill: Hampton Press.

Stuckey, Mary E. 2010. "Rethinking the Rhetorical Presidency and Presidential Rhetoric." *The Review of Communication* 10: 38–52.

Tulis, Jeffrey. 1987. *The Rhetorical Presidency*. Princeton: Princeton University Press.

White House, The. 2014. "Remarks by the President on the Economy—Northwestern University." October 2. Accessed July 16, 2016. https://www.whitehouse.gov/the-press-office/2014/10/02/remarks-president-economy-northwestern-university.

Windt, Theodore and Beth Ingold, eds. 1987. *Essays in Presidential Rhetoric*, 2nd edition. Dubuque: Kendall/Hunt.

Wolfsfeld, Gadi. 1997. *Media and Political Conflict: News from the Middle East*. Cambridge: Cambridge University Press.

Wolfsfeld, Gadi and Tamir Sheafer. 2006. "Competing Actors and the Construction of Political News: The Contest over Waves in Israel." *Political Communication* 23: 333–354.

2

WHAT'S IN A NAME?

Taking Back "Obamacare"

Researchers interested in how people respond to a particular word or phrase might carefully construct an experimental study to measure participants' reactions. This could entail weighing the pros and cons of conducting the research in a more naturalistic or controlled lab setting, randomly assigning people to experiment and control groups exposed to different content, and assessing respondents' views before and after that exposure. Jimmy Kimmel is no social scientist. But in October 2013, his ABC talk show *Jimmy Kimmel Live* performed its own quasi-experiment, in a series of person-on-the-street interviews asking people walking on Hollywood Boulevard if they preferred: "the Affordable Care Act or Obamacare."[1] The resulting video clip does not give us any reliable, scientific evidence about how Americans might psychologically process those two names differently. However, the comedy piece does reveal that firstly, a number of people they spoke with clearly did not realize that these names referred to the same law, even years after its passage, and secondly, those individuals would quickly and emphatically say they liked the Affordable Care Act much better.

Watching those citizens come up with, on camera in the moment that the question is asked, all the things they find objectionable about Obamacare and yet what they like about the Affordable Care Act may not tell us much we can generalize to broader public opinion, but it does raise questions of what connotations the names carry in the average person's mind. "Just the name says it all," one man offers as an explanation for why the ACA is better than Obamacare, to the laughter of Kimmel's audience. To be fair, "Obamacare" is a nickname for the law created by its opponents, origins that help explain those latent negative connotations. As President Obama told an audience in the fall of 2013, he believed that in the future, when the ACA proved as popular as Medicare and

Social Security—"once it's working really well"—he predicted of his critics, "I guarantee you they will not call it Obamacare" (White House 2013).

In this same speech that the president anticipated "Obamacare" would eventually fall out of favor, he used it like it was going out of style, calling the ACA by that name 12 times as he touted its benefits for the public. Thus far, "Obamacare" has only become more omnipresent in U.S. public discourse over time, in part because of Obama himself making use of the name. This chapter explores how the president, his surrogates and supporters, and the news media have contributed collectively to the term's proliferation, and identifies changes in how it has been presented in media coverage. I find the Obama team promoted a more favorable framing of "Obamacare" via traditional and digital communications channels, encouraging supporters to do the same. Subsequently, news coverage in mainstream outlets, reaching a larger and more diverse audience than the president's base, tilted in a somewhat more positive direction for health-care reform where "Obamacare" was mentioned. I identify this as indicative of presidential framing resilience as outlined in Chapter 1, demonstrating the influence of presidential communication even under trying conditions, while also being realistic about its limits. Given the preponderance of negative news coverage featuring "Obamacare," this minimal impact might still be important, as is the increase of neutral depictions of the ACA alongside "Obamacare" in the media. Additionally, the case offers a look at a consequential presidential framing side effect, as the Obama communications effort altered acceptable mainstream journalistic standards.

Inventing "Obamacare"

Opponents to Democratic health-care reform plans get credit for adding "Obamacare" to the American political lexicon. Though he did not originate the nickname, which was first coined by a lobbyist in an obscure industry journal, presidential candidate Mitt Romney was the first prominent Republican politician to use the term in a critical, derogatory way.[2] Initially, the word was not applied specifically to the policy that would ultimately become the ACA. In May 2007, commenting on the health-care proposals of his Democratic rivals for the presidency, Romney told a crowd in Des Moines, Iowa, "The path of Europe is not the way to go. Socialized medicine, Hillary-care, Obama-care, they don't get it" (Reeve 2011). Even this form of rhetorical attack was not entirely new. It picked up on language used during the early 1990s debate on health-care reform, when critics frequently derided the Clinton Administration's plan as "Hillarycare" (Serafini 2007).

With President Obama in the White House actively pushing for and ultimately winning health-care reform's passage,[3] the use of "Obamacare" by conservatives greatly intensified. In 2010, Republican representatives used the word dozens of times on the floor of Congress, and by 2011, it was uttered hundreds of times in the national legislature (Cox et al. 2012). In August of 2011, President Obama briefly addressed the issue, telling a Cannon Falls, Minnesota, crowd, "I have no problem with people saying Obama cares. I do care. If the other side wants to be the folks that don't care? That's fine with me" (Madison 2011). This fell well short, however, of a concerted and lasting effort to reframe the term. As evidence of how partisan and contentious the phrase was at this point, in October 2011 some Democrats objected to the use of "Obamacare" in franked mailings, which are prohibited from being used for partisan purposes (Dumain 2012). As the 2012 Republican presidential nomination race heated up, Romney's opponents quickly adopted "Obamacare" in speeches attacking the president. Romney, in turn, was chastised by his rivals for the "Romneycare" health-care program he had supported as Governor of Massachusetts, with some using the unwieldy mouthful "Obamneycare" to link Romney to a president quite unpopular with Republican primary voters.

Reappropriating "Obamacare"

March 2012 brought a fresh approach by the president's team to the issue; his staff launched a primarily web-based campaign to reframe the term, sending an email from David Axelrod to supporters with the attention-grabbing subject line, "Hell yeah, I like Obamacare," and promoting a page on the campaign's website where backers could add their names to a list of those publicly declaring "I Like Obamacare," an act with vaguely subversive undertones given how closely associated the name was with the president's fiercest critics. The Obama campaign encouraged its Twitter followers to tweet the specific aspects of "Obamacare" they liked best and sold "I Like Obamacare" t-shirts and bumper stickers. On March 23, the campaign tweeted "Happy birthday to Obamacare," and at a fundraiser a week earlier, Obama himself reiterated, "You want to call it Obamacare—that's okay, because I do care. That's why we passed it" (Dwyer 2012).

If the name was originally employed by opponents to frame the ACA as excessive government involvement in Americans' health care in a frightening, totalitarian way, the president's team sought to shift that understanding to one in which Obama took prideful ownership of the law, as part of a compassionate government interested only in citizens' well-being. Obama's campaign spokeswoman Stephanie Cutter related, "On Obamacare, Republicans spent hundreds of millions branding Obamacare as a negative, and we believe we can turn that to our advantage. The term is incredibly popular with the president's supporters, who will fight to the end to defend the law after 70 years of work to pass health reform" (Cillizza and Blake 2012). A senior 2012 campaign staff member notes the reelection effort was focused single-mindedly on touting the president's accomplishments, particularly the ACA. "Obamacare," the staffer asserts, had become "so ubiquitous at that point (used by supporters and opponents alike) that it felt almost ridiculous not to use the term—at a certain point you have to accept reality." The campaign "wanted to 'own' the term by embracing it, rather than allowing it to continue to appear as if quasi-verboten . . . prior to the shift, 'Obamacare' was seen almost as a slur . . . and/but it was also the commonly accepted word for the law. So there was no good way even for supporters to talk about it except by seeming to slur it. So we believed that giving our supporters permission, as it were, to use the term and use it lovingly, would eliminate a lot of the awkwardness around the broader political dynamics of the law" (Personal communication, interview granted on the condition of anonymity, December 17, 2014). Many supporters indeed went on to embrace "Obamacare" as a positive term, making it their own, in ways that were then highlighted by the campaign.[4]

The reframing of "Obamacare," as the senior staffer relayed, "was first and foremost an effort to make supporters feel good about the law so that they would spread the word, etc., or at a minimum not think of it as The Accomplishment Which Shall Not Be Named" (Personal communication, December 17, 2014). How effective then were the Obama team and its backers at "spreading the word," or recasting the tenor of "Obamacare" in mainstream media outlets reaching larger, more diverse audiences than the campaign's email list and Twitter feed?

An Uphill Battle for Presidential Framing

The 21st century media environment already presents presidents with formidable challenges in attempting to frame policies and shape political debates. In this instance, Obama and his team embarked on what might be considered an even more daunting project: working to co-opt and reframe the established language of the president's opponents. Yet the importance of naming one's signature policies cannot be overstated. As Zarefsky (2005, 8) tells us in studying the discourse of President Lyndon B. Johnson's "war on poverty," presidents strategically influence how people think about a policy problem and its ideal resolution, and "definition is the president's greatest asset . . . to name an object or idea is to influence attitudes about it."

From the very start then, the Obama Administration faced interference from opponents, and in choosing to fight for control of the meaning of "Obamacare," the president launched a framing contest with those who devised the name precisely to convey what they disliked about the policy. There are scholarly studies (unlike Jimmy Kimmel's "experiment") that provide evidence on how consequential the outcome of such contests over naming policies can be for public opinion. For instance, in the debate over inheritance tax in the U.S., the Republican-backed "death tax" frame vs. the Democratic-preferred "estate tax" successfully caused survey respondents to believe the policy applied more widely than it actually did, thus increasing expressed opposition (Schaffner and Atkinson 2010). Health-care policy in the not so distant past was the site of momentous communications battles, as when opponents of prior Democratic Administrations' health-care reform efforts were framed as destructive "big government" and "socialism" (Jacobs and Shapiro 2000, 137), charges implied by the "Obamacare" moniker (Chapter 6 provides a more detailed historical comparison on this point).

By early 2012, the Obama team had seemingly lost the initial battle over what the ACA would commonly be called. The president and his staff then employed framing rhetoric highlighting the potentially positive connotations of the term "Obamacare," emphasizing "care" and that the president himself "cares" about Americans' well-being. The president thus engaged in "frame shifting," or promoting a new frame of reference contrasting with how a subject was previously perceived (Zarefsky 2004, 613), a power some of his predecessors had successfully wielded. Franklin Delano Roosevelt helped transform the meaning of "liberal" and labeled his foreign policy opponents "isolationists," contested terms that many have nevertheless subsequently adopted (Green 1987). After Jimmy Carter established wide support for "human rights" in American politics, the ambiguity of the phrase allowed later presidents to imbue it with their own set of meanings in service of their political goals, sometimes far removed from what Carter intended (Stuckey 2008). Potentially, for presidents to have their names rhetorically attached to policies could mean claiming credit for their perceived accomplishments—"Reaganomics," for instance, was often used by Reagan's detractors, but eventually embraced by the president's supporters.[5] President Clinton successfully focused the media's attention on his preferred framing of crime policy, stressing prevention over punishment, helping him "steal" the traditionally Republican-owned issue (Holian 2004). Presidents are not the only figures so motivated—the clear connection of language, framing, and power has led some members of oppressed groups toward linguistic reclamation projects, using and thus redefining sexist, racist, or heteronormative slurs (Godrej 2003).

Others are skeptical, however, about the ability to alter deeply ingrained meanings of words. Cognitive linguist George Lakoff (2004, xv) argues language activates frames that shape the brain's perception of events, and thus new language is needed for new frames, or "thinking differently requires speaking differently." Whereas the Obama Administration might have an incentive to challenge the framing of "Obamacare," it is unclear how wise it was to adopt opponents' rhetoric, and whether media coverage would treat its alternative narrative favorably. As initial frames have great staying power, and culturally congruent frames are most influential (Entman 2004), the Obama team problematically sought to dislodge widely held negative impressions of "Obamacare."

Furthermore, this formidable communications project took place in the contemporary media landscape, laden with minefields of hyper-adversarial political journalists and pundits, some among the latter group predisposed to challenge any messages emanating from a White House controlled by the opposition party. Given these dual challenges of 1) displacing conventional interpretations around "Obamacare," and 2) doing so within a frequently uncooperative news setting, the Obama team sought to use the innovations of new media to its advantage. The president and team had demonstrated tremendous prowess in the 2008 and 2012 campaigns in innovating digital strategies to reach, mobilize, and retain supporters, and made unprecedented efforts to integrate the web into everyday governance, even creating a White House Office of Digital Strategy. As the president's own staff members recounted above, a driving force behind co-opting "Obamacare" was to reach their supporters with this "redefinition" of the term. Of course, core Obama backers would likely not need convincing of the virtues of the president's health-care policy, regardless of what it was called. So what were the advantages of getting the Obama faithful to begin using this name in a positive way?

The answer lies in one of the lessons of the "Obamacare" case, that even in the 21st century media environment, the president can achieve framing resilience, but he cannot do it alone. The fragmented plethora of sources from which citizens today pick up pieces of information about politics mean the president must rely on those who work for him, prominent members of his political party, and supporters in the general public to help disseminate his preferred framings of issues and events. President Obama's own words recasting the idea of "Obamacare," combined with a concerted effort to sanction its use by other high-profile Democrats, left-leaning media commentators, and sympathetic ordinary Americans, created a path to effective presidential framing across popular mainstream news media sources.

Thinking about how "new" media influences "old" media in this novel communications context includes acknowledging how citizens and presidential surrogates now participate directly in popularizing framing rhetoric. Mary Stuckey (2010) has asserted that today we all produce and alter presidential messages, democratizing presidential communication. Susan Herbst (2007, 337) went so far as to declare presidential speech as "dying, and possibly even dead" when the media obfuscate the president's messages, and surrogates and citizens alike rewrite and transform presidential texts. Rather than a "death," I instead identify this as an evolution, as presidential communication successfully adapts to the innovative ways we now transmit and share information. Presidential "preaching to the choir" via the Internet might afford the president opportunities to reach the "unconverted" masses with his frames, creating new possibilities for public leadership through strategies tailored to this distinctive media milieu. The "Obamacare" case reflects a 21st century style of presidential communication comparable to what Jenkins et al. (2013) identify (largely in the private sector) as "spreadable" marketing—the Administration constructs its messages to be spread by the president's staff, sympathetic pundits, and ordinary citizens connected to the president through web-based channels, all of whom might adapt or remix the content to suit their own interests and purposes.[6]

To be sure, there are hazards to this strategy: allowing for this level of popular participation in a communication project can contribute to presidential framing side effects and presidential frame refraction that may deviate from intended results, sometimes beneficial to the president, sometimes not, as charted in the cases explored throughout this book. But although this course of action entails the president's team relinquishing some control, surrogates and supporters, energized by their ownership over the process, could carry the altered framing of "Obamacare" much further in a fragmented media landscape than the president alone. Still, we cannot neglect that the involvement of the president remains central—supporters would be unlikely to circulate "Obamacare" without first gaining the president's endorsement, given the term's history.

To sum up, a look at the news coverage in the "Obamacare" case in the next section points to presidential framing resilience. It reflects the influence of the president's digital communications strategies on frames in popular news outlets, some of which we would expect to be inherently resistant to adopting presidential narratives, and others explicitly hostile to this Administration. These new opportunities, however, take place in an admittedly unpredictable media environment where the Obama team's messaging also fundamentally altered conventional news norms used by journalists on health care in ways they had not likely envisioned beforehand.

"Obamacare" in the News before and after the "I Like Obamacare" Campaign

I analyze news coverage containing "Obamacare" three months before and after March 23, 2012, to determine whether the efforts of the president and his team had any impact on how the term was used. This time period was an important one in the health-care policy discussion, though it was already formally passed into law. Health-care reform had become a major issue in the 2012 presidential election, and was frequently discussed on the campaign trail by those seeking the Republican nomination. Further, this time period coincides with the oral arguments before the Supreme Court in *National Federation of Independent Business v. Sebelius*, a case with major consequences for both the policy's future and the president's political prospects (a topic discussed more in Chapter 3). The legislation's two-year anniversary also occurred during this time, and there was a high-profile public debate over whether religious organizations would have to pay for birth control coverage under the law's stipulations. These six months were a pivotal period for the president to build legitimacy for, and shape popular discourse on this key legislative accomplishment of his first term, as the electorate's determination of whether he would receive a second term loomed in the fall.

I selected four media outlets for the first part of the analysis: *The New York Times*, *The New York Post*, CNN, and Fox News.[7] They encompass traditional print and 24-hour news network outlets, alleged liberal and conservative leanings, and hard and soft news. We can therefore assess the impact, if any, of a primarily online presidential communications strategy on news coverage that reaches a much larger segment of the public, including outlets catering to the president's political opposition. Given the diversity of the 21st century news media that I outlined in the introduction, there are certainly limits to what we can assume about coverage more generally from just these four outlets. However, we might expect President Obama's attempt to shift the meaning of Obamacare to face its greatest challenges in conservative-leaning news outlets unreceptive to a Democratic president, and in prestige press outlets more likely to question domestic policy messages from any political actor. If we can identify the impact of presidential framing in such venues, represented in the selected outlets, it follows that the president might influence news content in a wide variety of other print, broadcast, and online outlets.

The analysis counts every instance that "Obamacare" was written or spoken in the coverage, identifies who was using the term, and assesses with the aid of an independent coder whether (in the immediate sentence or paragraph that the term was being used) the ACA as a policy was depicted in positive, negative, or neutral terms. My focus then is first, whether "Obamacare" was a phrase typically associated with negative depictions of the ACA, as it had originated, and second, whether that shifted in a more positive or neutral direction after the Obama Administration and reelection campaign sought to reframe the term. I also classify the speaker/writer of "Obamacare," because media consumers are likely to be discerning regarding which elite sources they identify as credible, based on partisanship and preexisting political beliefs (Zaller 1992; Druckman 2001; Rowling et al. 2013). It might come across very differently to audiences, for instance, if the person saying "Obamacare" is an "objective" journalist or a Republican candidate for president. Additionally, this allows us to see if the Administration's reframing effort affected the words chosen by supporters and media actors to describe the law in the news.

For the print outlets, I also assess how the term was visually presented: was it used as a seemingly neutral name for the policy, as though this was the law's actual title, without any indication it might come with particular connotations? Was it instead placed within quotation marks, indicating this was not the official name? Did "Obamacare" appear in the coverage as a result of directly quoting someone? For cable news, I evaluate whether the individual using "Obamacare" communicated in some way that this was not a neutral term, such as saying, "what they dubbed Obamacare" or "critics call it Obamacare." These distinctions are important because if early on, for instance, journalists used "Obamacare" as an ostensibly objective replacement for the ACA, they adopted the rhetoric of the opposition in talking about the policy to their audience. This also relates to the importance of analyzing two time periods—after Obama stated it was "okay" to call the law "Obamacare," would this cause some journalists who had previously avoided the term to presume it was now in line with standards of "fair" coverage?

December 2011 to March 2012: Differences in Usage, but Alike in Negativity

Figure 2.1 reveals a major difference between *The New York Times*, part of the "prestige press," and *The New York Post*, a tabloid newspaper in this first time period. Republican politicians were the most frequent users of "Obamacare" in the *Times*, and journalists most likely to use it in the *Post*. Three-quarters of "Obamacare" appearances in the *Post* presented the term as though it were merely the name of the policy, with no indication of its pejorative origins. By contrast, the vast majority of times that "Obamacare" appeared in the *Times* it was placed in quotation marks, appeared within a quote, or both. This last circumstance, the paper essentially doubling down on indicating this was a loaded term, could be found in examples such as the following, in an article quoting Mitt Romney: "We should be able to choose the insurance company of our choice. We should not have to have one foisted upon us by the president and 'Obamacare'" (Shear 2012). The *Times* had no consistent editorial policy on this, however; in some instances, additional quotation marks within a quote were used and at other times they were not.

All of the pieces in which the term was used as a purportedly neutral one in the *Times* were by the paper's columnists and opinion column (op-ed) writers—Paul Krugman, Ross Douthat, David Brooks, and Thomas Friedman—all employed "Obamacare" as such. The *Times* had nearly double the number of appearances of "Obamacare" in its pages compared to the *Post*, due to its far greater volume of news articles dealing with the dynamics of American politics and public policy. Ever concise, the *Post* sometimes even just referred to "O'Care" in its headlines.

Yet the coverage including "Obamacare" in this initial period is also a story of similarity across the papers—a large majority of appearances of the phrase accompanied negative sentiments about the policy (see Figure 2.2). This demonstrates how effectively Republican presidential candidates expressed their disdain for the ACA during the height of the primary season. Additionally, the results show that the editorially conservative *Post* allowed the language of the law's opponents to dominate even its more "objective" news coverage. Potentially, it was the *Post*'s soft news, tabloid style that made the informal "Obamacare" a more attractive way of describing the policy, but this does not diminish the name's connection to the president's detractors.

Turning to cable news and Figure 2.3, CNN's coverage involving "Obamacare" mirrored that of the *Times* in that Republican politicians were responsible for the largest percentage of its appearances. CNN's penchant for broadcasting interviews and lengthy portions of Republican presidential candidates' speeches meant that Michele Bachmann, Newt Gingrich, Rick Santorum, and Romney had plenty of opportunities to relay how they planned to repeal "Obamacare" as president. The network, for instance, showed Bachmann's speech when she suspended her candidacy, and told her supporters, "What

	Used by	Percentage of total uses	# of times used	"Objective"/ neutral use of term	Placed in quotation marks, or appeared in a quote or context given
The New York Times	Republican politician	45	37	0	37
	Journalist	16	13	0	13
	Editorial/Op-ed writer	30	25	13	12
	Commentator/Activist	7	6	0	6
	Citizen	2	2	0	2
	Total		83	13	70
				16%	84%

	Used by	Percentage of total uses	# of times used (% of whole)	"Objective"/ neutral use of term	Placed in quotation marks, or appeared in a quote or context given
The New York Post	Journalist	57	24	24	0
	Editorial/Op-ed writer	19	8	8	0
	Citizen	14	6	0	6
	Republican politician	10	4	0	4
	Total		42	32	10
				76%	24%

FIGURE 2.1 "Obamacare" in *The New York Times* and *The New York Post*, December 23, 2011–March 22, 2012

New York Times

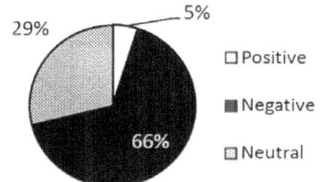

Used by	Positive %	Negative %	Neutral %
Republican politician		92	8
Journalist	16	12	72
Editorial/Op-ed writer		97	3
Commentator/Activist		67	33
Citizen			100
Overall	5	66	29

New York Post

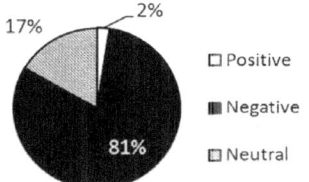

Used by	Positive %	Negative %	Neutral %
Journalist	4	88	8
Editorial/Op-ed writer		63	38
Citizen		75	25
Republican politician		83	17
Overall	2	81	17

FIGURE 2.2 "Obamacare" and Policy Depictions in *The New York Times* and *The New York Post*, December 23, 2011–March 22, 2012

President Obama had done in passing Obamacare endangered the very survival of the United States of America, our republic . . . I knew that it was my obligation to ensure that President Obama's program of socialized medicine was stopped before it became fully implemented" (*Michele Bachmann Suspends Candidacy*, January 4, 2012). As presented in Figure 2.3, on Fox News, commentators and hosts were most likely to use "Obamacare," reflecting the substantial presence of analysis and opinion in the 24-hour news network format.

When "Obamacare" appeared on cable news it was also usually in the context of framing the policy negatively. However, it was even rarer on both networks for the term to be used in conjunction with a favorable assessment of the policy than in print. In one glaring instance of such dominant negativity, on February 10, Fox News personality Eric Bolling told his audience, "You know how I feel about President Obama's socialist agenda. He shredded the Constitution with Obamacare" (*The Five*, February 10, 2012).

It was also unusual for those using "Obamacare" on cable to indicate it was not an objective name for the policy, as the final column of Figure 2.3 indicates, though this was even more infrequent on Fox News than CNN. This makes sense given the vast majority of those uttering the word were Republican politicians and pundits/program hosts, who would not feel compelled to provide such context, and who were most likely openly and unequivocally condemning the policy it referred to. However, some journalists also used the term freely without qualifiers. Fox News anchor Chris Wallace stated on February 12, "I think it's fair to say this is precisely why so many people . . . are opposed to

CNN

Used by	Percentage of total uses	Times Used	Positive	Negative	Neutral	Indication not an objective term
Republican politician/Surrogate	70	219	0	209	10	2
Pundit/Contributor/Host	18	56	7	27	22	7
Journalist	8	24	0	16	8	15
Citizen	2	6	0	4	2	0
Other	3	10	0	6	4	0
Total		315	7	262	46	24 (8%)
			2%	83%	15%	

Fox News

Used by	Percentage of total uses	Times Used	Positive	Negative	Neutral	Indication not an objective term
Pundit/Contributor/Host	57	160	1	108	51	2
Republican politician/Surrogate	34	96	1	91	4	1
Journalist	5	13	0	8	5	0
Democratic politician	1	2	1	0	1	1
Citizen	0	1	0	1	0	0
Other	3	9	0	7	2	0
Total		281	3	215	63	4 (1%)
			1%	77%	22%	

FIGURE 2.3 "Obamacare" and Policy Depictions on CNN and Fox News, December 23, 2011–March 22, 2012

Obamacare, because they are concerned with the idea that the government can mandate what people have to do, what private businesses have to do, what even religious institutions have to do" (*Fox News Sunday*, February 12, 2012). The prevalence of "Obamacare" and its negative association for the ACA a majority of times in each of the four outlets during this first time period helps lay bare the Obama team's incentive to embark on its reframing project.

March to June 2012: Less Negative, More Objective?

Moving to the second time period of analysis, Democratic Party-affiliated political actors now made a few appearances in the news using the term, as shown in Figure 2.4. Supporters were now spreading the revised framing of the nickname. One marker of the reframing campaign's effectiveness is that appearances of "Obamacare" in which the policy was discussed in a positive light more than doubled as a percentage of overall occurrences in both papers. Still, this represented only about 11% of the times the phrase appeared in the newspapers. In the *Times*, as outlined in Figure 2.5, negative portrayals of "Obamacare" continued to dominate. Interestingly in the *Post*, neutral depictions surged, a major shift from the previous three months, which can be seen in comparing Figure 2.5 to Figure 2.2. Negative portrayals were still a plurality, however, and sometimes jarring: the *Post*'s March 28th "Letters to the Editor" section was entitled, "Beware ObamaCare: It Might've Killed Cheney."

Compared to the months before the "I Like Obamacare" White House campaign, the percentage of the time that the name was presented as a seemingly objective term increased in both newspapers. By embracing the name, the president and his surrogates unleashed a presidential framing side effect, and they also gave news outlets a license to use the term as an objective one as opposed to treating it as partisan, subjective rhetoric. The importance of such a side effect is twofold. First, it indicates presidential influence on news content—without the Administration-driven campaign to co-opt "Obamacare," coverage would have looked different on this point. Second, it situates that influence in the unpredictability of anticipated reactions in the 21st century media landscape, as the purpose of the reframing campaign was to replace the derogatory connotations of the nickname with positive ones. Incidental to that intent, the Obama team affected the decisions of those constructing the news, regarding whether and in what context they *should* use "Obamacare" at all.

On cable news in the second time period, Administration officials made their first appearances using the term, contributing to the uptick in Democrats saying "Obamacare" that we can see in Figure 2.6. David Plouffe, for instance, was on CNN asserting, "I think by the end of this decade, if this law is fully implemented, we're going to be very glad they called it Obamacare, because the reality of what is happening here is so different than what the opponents claim. You're going to see more people covered, you're going to see savings in the

The New York Times

Used by	Share of total uses (%)	# of times used	"Objective"/ neutral use of term	Placed in quotation marks, or appeared in a quote or context given
Republican politician	40	59	2	57
Editorial/Op-ed writer	25	37	29	8
Commentator/Activist	17	25	2	23
Journalist	11	17	0	17
Democratic politician/Surrogate	5	7	0	7
Citizen	3	4	0	4
Total		149	33	116
			22%	**78%**

The New York Post

Used by	Share of total uses (%)	# of times used	"Objective"/ neutral use of term	Placed in quotation marks, or appeared in a quote or context given
Journalist	56	39	38	1
Editorial/Op-ed writer	27	19	16	3
Citizen	10	7	6	1
Republican politician	6	4	0	4
Democratic politician/Surrogate	1	1	0	1
Total		70	60	10
			86%	**14%**

FIGURE 2.4 "Obamacare" in *The New York Times* and *The New York Post*, March 23, 2012–June 23, 2012

What's in a Name? Taking Back "Obamacare" 31

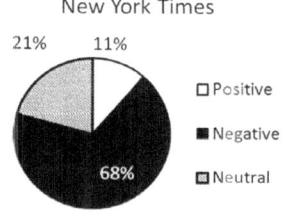

New York Times Used by	Positive %	Negative %	Neutral %
Republican politician	24	35	41
Editorial/Op-ed writer	11	57	32
Commentator/Activist	0	90	10
Journalist	4	76	20
Democratic politician/Surrogate	86	0	14
Citizen	50	50	0
Overall	11	68	21

New York Post Used By	Positive %	Negative %	Neutral %
Journalist	10	33	56
Editorial/Op-ed writer	5	58	37
Citizen	0	71	29
Republican politician	0	100	0
Democratic politician/Surrogate	100	0	0
Overall	9	47	44

FIGURE 2.5 "Obamacare" and Policy Depictions in *The New York Times* and *The New York Post*, March 23, 2012–June 23, 2012

health care system, you're going to see free preventive care for people, you're going to see women treated equally in the health care system" (*State of the Union with Candy Crowley*, March 25, 2012).

CNN's reporters also covered the effort to alter the framing of the term, while recognizing "Obamacare" had previously been the rhetoric of the opposition. This "inside baseball" account of presidential communication is a familiar feature of the contemporary media's more critical and often speculative approach to reporting on the actions and underlying motivations of political actors. Correspondent Jessica Yellin told Wolf Blitzer the Obama campaign had "been doing the messaging on this with a new effort to reframe Obamacare as a positive with these t-shirts that say 'Obama cares,' etc." (*The Situation Room*, March 27, 2012). Anchor Carol Costello previewed an upcoming news segment by saying, "Obamacare isn't a dirty word anymore. Just ask the Obama campaign" (*CNN Newsroom*, March 26, 2012). Costello, interestingly, began to use "Obamacare" as an objective description of the policy in March after the president embraced the term, whereas previously she had always indicated that it was not a neutral term. For instance, on January 26, she stated on air, "Romney suggests funding a larger military by defunding what he calls Obamacare," but on March 27 reported, "Today, the court will look at significant questions about the power of government. Can Obamacare really force most Americans to buy health insurance?" Overall however, CNN's coverage was more likely to indicate "Obamacare" was not a neutral term than in the first time period. The presidential effort to reframe

CNN

Used by	Percentage of total uses	Times Used	Positive	Negative	Neutral	Indication not an objective term
Republican politician/Surrogate	39	132	0	121	11	0
Pundit/Contributor/Host	28	96	10	41	45	5
Journalist	21	71	5	22	44	34
Citizen	3	9	4	1	4	0
Democratic politician/Surrogate	1	5	4	0	1	2
Other	8	26	2	10	14	2
Total		339	25 / 7%	195 / 58%	119 / 35%	43 / 13%

Fox News

Used by	Percentage of total uses	Times Used	Positive	Negative	Neutral	Indication not an objective term
Pundit/Contributor/Host	54	268	10	126	132	1
Republican politician/Surrogate	19	96	0	90	6	1
Journalist	10	50	2	20	28	3
Citizen	4	21	3	8	10	0
Democratic politician/Surrogate	2	8	8	0	0	1
Other	11	54	0	41	13	2
Total		497	23 / 5%	285 / 57%	189 / 38%	8 / 2%

FIGURE 2.6 "Obamacare" and Policy Depictions on CNN and Fox News, March 23, 2012–June 23, 2012

"Obamacare" drew attention to the fact that Obama had not, up until that point, controlled its meaning. This might cause many at CNN committed to balanced coverage to be more transparent in describing the term's origins.

On both networks, "Obamacare" was linked to negative depictions of the policy a majority of the time (see Figure 2.6), but this was a smaller overall percentage than in the previous time period. There was an increase in positive depictions of the policy alongside "Obamacare," as was the case in print. In one instance, Fox News' Chris Wallace asked a guest, "And let me ask you about the problems Republicans have, because there's a lot of Obamacare that people like. They like the idea that people can't be excluded from coverage because of . . . preexisting conditions, or that kids can stay on their parent's policy until they are twenty-six" (*Fox News Sunday*, April 1, 2012).

While CNN's coverage more frequently alluded to "Obamacare" not being an objective term than in the previous three months, there was little to no change in this regard on Fox News. Several Fox News journalists did not shy away from calling the policy "Obamacare," often in a negative context: Wallace on March 23 asked his guest, "Do you agree with the premise that the country, two years later has not rallied around Obamacare?" (*Fox News All Stars*, March 23, 2012). Fox News also covered the Administration's attempted reappropriation of "Obamacare," although usually in terms the Administration would likely not prefer. Following the president's "approval" of the term, Dana Perino, co-host of *The Five*, remarked sarcastically on March 26, "72 percent of the people polled in the CBS/New York Times poll today said they don't want the president's health-care bill, which thankfully we can now call Obamacare." Perino also mocked this turn of events on the March 29 episode of *The Five*, when she noted about the policy, "which we can now call Obamacare, because President Obama blessed the nickname."

The ACA over Time: Increasingly Known as "Obamacare"?

Following this look at the more immediate "before" and "after" of the Obama team's frame shifting campaign, I now extend the study to a lengthier time period, assessing the prevalence and usage of "Obamacare" in four years' worth of transcripts of the three Sunday morning news programs on the major broadcast television networks—*This Week* on ABC, *Face the Nation* on CBS, and *Meet the Press* on NBC—from the law's passage on March 23, 2010 through March 24, 2014. The Sunday news shows are generally regarded as part of the "prestige press" in the U.S. news media, less likely to gravitate toward soft news/infotainment topics, featuring powerful political actors as guests, and setting the agenda for other traditional news outlets in the week to follow. Airing once a week, the programs can be seen as both providing an account of what was being discussed in American politics in the week prior and helping set the tone for the week ahead. The analysis allows us to see whether "Obamacare" has become more or less common in the political vocabulary of such programming, to identify whether the actors using it have changed or stayed the same over a longer period, and to determine whether it has been linked to positive, negative, or neutral portrayals of health-care reform over time. This will also serve to give us a better account of presidential framing resilience and the staying power of the reframing effort in the news.

Republican politicians were the main speakers of "Obamacare" on the Sunday news shows over the initial three years following the ACA's passage, and the most common users in looking at the four years of coverage in total, as seen in Figure 2.7. Democratic politicians *never* used the term on the programs without a qualifier indicating it was not a neutral term for the policy until after the Obama team's aforementioned March 2012 media blitz.[8] The Obama team's digitally-centered "I Like Obamacare" campaign thereby made the news coverage different from how it otherwise might have been by giving Democratic supporters the green light to make use of the term in the news. Figure 2.8 illustrates how "Obamacare" use progressed in those four years. Its prevalence increased first as the 2012 campaign heated up, and then reached new highs as major provisions of the policy were implemented in 2013 into 2014.

Even prior to the "I Like Obamacare" campaign, some journalists on the Sunday shows such as *Face the Nation*'s Norah O'Donnell and *This Week*'s George Stephanopoulos used "Obamacare" as a synonym for the ACA. By contrast, David Gregory of *Meet the Press* and Bob Schieffer of *Face the Nation* used the moniker as a seemingly objective name for the law for the first time on February 24, 2013 and March 17, 2013 respectively. As shown in Figure 2.9, in the final year of analysis, journalists were using "Obamacare" on the Sunday programs a plurality of the time, surpassing Republican politicians. In a marked change from earlier years, hosts now regularly used "Obamacare" when posing questions to guests about the health-reform policy, again indicating the Administration's embrace of the word changed their assessment of when this name could credibly be employed. On the July 7, 2013 edition of *Face the Nation*, correspondent Major Garrett made such considerations explicit, noting in using "Obamacare" that, "the president uses and embraces that terminology, no longer pejorative." In the time since, the Associated Press, National Public Radio, and *The Los Angeles Times* have all publically asserted that though they caution against overuse of "Obamacare," the president's use of the term is one reason why journalists may appropriately employ it.[9]

If *who* was using "Obamacare" changed over the years, was there also a change in *how* the name was being employed? Figure 2.10 indicates yes. If the "I Like Obamacare" campaign was designed to encourage the "spread" of a more favorable framing of "Obamacare," Democrats appeared to be doing just that, particularly in the third and fourth years of the law's existence. "Obamacare" was being used more often on the Sunday news shows and alongside less overwhelmingly negative depictions of the ACA. By the final year of this analysis,

Used by	Percent of overall coverage	Total uses	ABC's This Week	CBS' Face the Nation	NBC's Meet the Press	Indication not an objective term
Republican politician/Surrogate	38	465	143	144	178	2
Journalist	28	342	100	56	186	25
Pundit/Contributor	26	317	158	66	93	4
Democratic politician/Surrogate	6	74	17	21	36	9
Other	1	17	10	1	6	0
Total	100	1,215	428	288	499	40 (3%)

FIGURE 2.7 "Obamacare" on the Sunday News Shows, March 23, 2010–March 23, 2014

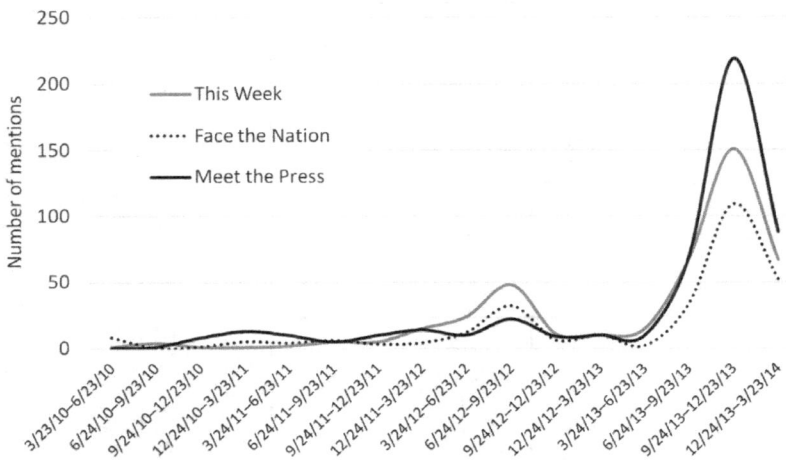

FIGURE 2.8 "Obamacare" Prevalence on Sunday News Programs, March 23, 2010–March 23, 2014

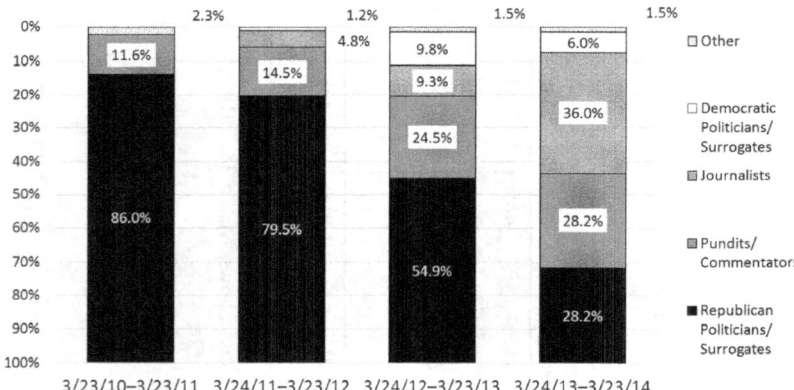

FIGURE 2.9 Changing Composition of "Obamacare" Users over Time on Sunday News Programs

a slight majority of the portrayals of the ACA involving "Obamacare" were neutral, which follows logically from the dramatic increase in journalists using the term on these programs. Increasingly, reporters were talking and asking about "Obamacare" as a synonym for the ACA, without overtly promoting or denigrating it, as their Democratic and Republican guests would be prone to.

Looking at more of the big picture then, over several years of Sunday news show coverage, presidential framing resilience is apparent. Even years after the concentrated effort to take back "Obamacare," that presidential reframing

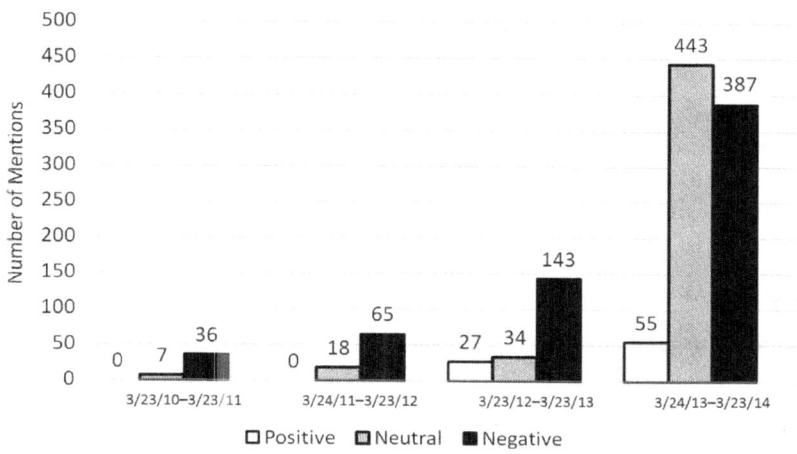

FIGURE 2.10 "Obamacare" Mentions and Policy Depictions on Sunday News Programs by Year

endeavor continued to have an influence on news content. Some of that impact was carefully calculated by the Obama team, such as associating "Obamacare" with more positive content about the ACA. Other aspects may be better classified as side effects, such as freeing up reporters to use the nickname. Ultimately though, this too aided the president's political goals by making the news surrounding "Obamacare" less overwhelmingly negative about health-care reform.

A Look at Public Opinion

At present, there is limited data available about the impact on public opinion of calling the ACA "Obamacare"—some surveys suggest respondents become more opinionated when the law is referred to as "Obamacare" as opposed to "health-reform law" in the question, with larger percentages of Americans expressing both favorable and unfavorable views. Democrats conveyed the largest change in favorability, with 73% in favor of "Obamacare" vs. 58% in favor of "the health-reform law" in mid-2013 (Kaiser Family Foundation Health Tracking Poll 2013). Democratic sources' positive use of the term in the news, and the presence of Obama's name likely help frame the term favorably for Democratic-identifying citizens. As for the broader public, in the fall of 2013, 46% opposed "Obamacare," compared to 37% who opposed the ACA, reflecting continued polarization depending on what the law is called (Liesman 2013). Further, in the same survey, Americans said they feel more familiar with "Obamacare" compared to the ACA, as 30% of the public reported they did not know enough about the ACA to judge it, in comparison to just 12%, who answered that about "Obamacare." This too speaks to the importance of the Obama Administration altering the framing of the term, so closely tied to the general public's perception of the policy. Future research might evaluate precisely what impressions "Obamacare" evokes in the minds of citizens, and the extent to which they are static or changeable. Potentially, "Obamacare" has become so pervasive and used by so many disparate actors in American politics that it is no longer bogged down by the detrimental connotations tied to its invention, just as the Obama team hoped would happen.

Conclusion

The immense amount of negative depictions of health-care reform that accompanied "Obamacare" in the news analysis of this chapter speaks to the effectiveness of the president's opponents at symbolically defining one of his key accomplishments. Early on, some journalists' use of "Obamacare," often with no indication of its negative origins, raises questions about their commitment to fair presentations of issues to their audiences. It is into this formidable communications setting that the Obama team launched their reframing campaign.

Despite these challenges, presidential influence is apparent in reviewing a sample of news coverage of both the six months around the "Obamacare" reframing effort and the first four years of the law's existence. That more reporters and news organizations identified "Obamacare" as an acceptable term in the years after the White House sought to re-appropriate it speaks to the tremendous impact the presidency has on affecting editorial standards of "objective" journalism, even with an inconsistent,[10] digitally centered communications campaign.

Further, the reframing effort was followed by a modest increase in positive news content across all four media outlets and (except in the *Times*) a substantial increase in neutral content. Over the four years of Sunday news shows, those supportive of the president (most Democratic politicians) and those who presumably are supposed to treat him fairly (journalists) started using "Obamacare" to a much greater extent. With the participation of such actors, then, the president and his team shifted the conversation surrounding the term in a more favorable direction for his signature health-care policy.

The Obama team's positive reframing of the nickname was simple, clear, and attention-grabbing at the time, from the words uttered by the president himself to the "I ♥ Obamacare" branding on the merchandise of the campaign and Democratic Party. That compelling message alongside encouraging supporters of both the political elite and ordinary citizen variety to carry it forward enhanced presidential framing resilience and the "spreadability" of the reframing. Democratic politicians, rather than continuing to seemingly rail against the tide in trying to compel others to return to the official name of the law, could easily endorse and repeat the presidential frame when appearing in the news. This stands in stark contrast to the framing contests surrounding HealthCare.gov and dropped health-care plans explored in Chapters 4 and 5, where the Administration disseminated highly problematic frames offering little political cover and few incentives for their fellow partisans or citizen supporters to spread the president's message.

The re-appropriation of "Obamacare" illustrates the porous nature of today's complex media landscape, as a reframing campaign carried out primarily via the web affected print and television news coverage. The involvement of the president himself in this effort was essential, bringing significant attention to his surprising, rebellious use of the term. But changing the conversation around "Obamacare" in the news relied on supporters to spread that message in a range of media venues, reflecting the myriad ways we encounter information in the 21st century. The escalating use of the term between 2010 and 2014 on Sunday news programs, as well as the increasing comfort of journalists and Democrats in employing it, suggest "Obamacare" has become a far more acceptable way of talking about the ACA for everyone. Given the amount of negative coverage of health-care reform found in this analysis compared to positive coverage, however, one wonders if critics of the law perhaps exclusively use "Obamacare," whereas supporters use it more intermittently. If that is the case, the president and his advisers' limited successes indicates perhaps more time, effort, and resources should have been put toward this reframing project, particularly given the side effects it engendered. Without a more sustained communications effort, the Obama team unintentionally gave media figures the freedom to use "Obamacare," without continuing to associate it consistently with the positive aspects of the health-care policy.

Having reviewed these clashes surrounding what health-care reform would be called, next we turn our attention to a framing contest over precisely what the Obamacare/Affordable Care Act policy required of American citizens. That communications conflict is the subject of Chapter 3.

Notes

1 The entire video can be seen here: https://www.youtube.com/watch?v=sx2scvIFGjE.
2 *The Atlantic Wire* pointed to this Romney usage and further explored the origination of "Obamacare" (Reeve 2011). The phrase was reportedly first used by the lobbyist Jeanne Schulte Scott in trade journal *Healthcare Financial Management* in March 2007. Like Romney, Scott was using the term alongside others like "McCain-care" and "Hillary-care" as opposed to commenting specifically on Obama's health-care proposals.
3 For a detailed account of how President Obama mounted a substantial public relations campaign in an effort to win passage of health-care reform, see Edwards 2012.
4 See some examples here, as featured originally on the 2012 campaign's website: http://www.journalism.org/2012/08/15/engagement-citizens/. Accessed July 14, 2016.
5 In his obituary, Chicago-based conservative-leaning radio broadcaster Paul Harvey was credited with originating the term "Reaganomics" (Holley 2009). The Reagan Presidential Library website states about the Republican president's economic policy that "Some skeptics derisively called his plan 'Reaganomics,'" but later in the same entry notes, "the success of Reaganomics was what it brought to the American people" (https://www.reaganfoundation.org/economic-policy.aspx), illustrating this dual usage.
6 See also Jones (2014) for a discussion of how "spreadability" applies to citizen-made communications parodying politicians that are shared widely on the Internet.

7   See Appendix A.2 for a more detailed discussion of how these articles and transcripts were accessed and analyzed.
8   Rep. Luis Gutierrez (D-IL) was the only Democrat to use the term on the three programs prior to David Plouffe's aforementioned appearance claiming the Administration would be "glad they called it Obamacare" but Gutierrez's statement was in the context of noting about Republicans, "They want to call it Obamacare." By contrast, after March 25, 2012, numerous prominent Democratic politicians, including Maryland Gov. Martin O'Malley, Sen. Dick Durbin (D-IL), Rep. Chris Van Hollen (D-MD), Newark's Democratic Mayor Cory Booker, and Sen. Harry Reid (D-NV), all used "Obamacare" on the Sunday talk shows without such qualifying remarks.
9   For instance, on the AP's official blog *The Definitive Source* on October 1, 2013, Tom Kent (Deputy Managing Editor and Standards Editor) wrote, "'Obamacare' was coined by opponents of the law and is still used by them in a derogatory manner. It's true that the White House, and even Obama himself, have used the term on occasion. But the Administration hasn't totally embraced 'Obamacare' and still uses the Affordable Care Act much of the time. We're sticking with our previous approach to 'Obamacare': AP writers should use it in quotes, or in formulations like 'the law, sometimes known as Obamacare, provides for . . . .' AP writers can use the term when necessary to refer to the law, but should do so sparingly." Stuart Seidel, NPR's managing editor for standards and practice, reported to NPR's ombudsman on September 6, 2013, "Republicans coined the term 'Obamacare' during the debate over the Affordable Care Act, seemingly as a means to generate opposition to the president's health-care initiative. During that time, NPR avoided using the term 'Obamacare.' Since passage of the legislation and its enactment into law, the president has said he rather likes the term 'Obamacare' and it has gradually come into the vernacular as a shorthand for referring to the Patient Protection and Affordable Care Act. I'm confident that NPR listeners and readers understand that whatever its origins, the term 'Obamacare' has lost its pedigree as a politically charged term" (Schumacher-Matos 2013). A Maynard Institute columnist noted that *The Los Angeles Times* had also reacted to the president's use of the term, with spokeswoman Nancy Sullivan relating that "*LA Times* reporters and editors may consider 'Obamacare' as an acceptable term for the Affordable Care Act. In recently revising our guidelines, senior editors responded to staff requests to allow the usage, in light of widespread public understanding of the term and the use of the term even by the White House and supporters of the act, not just opponents" (Richard Prince's Journalisms 2013).
10 Over a year after this reframing effort, it was still unclear how committed the Administration was to embracing "Obamacare." See for instance Epstein (2013) for an account of the White House and other prominent Democrats walking back some of their support for the name. The lack of clarity is apparent from a report in *The Hill* the exact same week, contending that the White House was actually not shying away from "Obamacare" as part of its official communications policy (Sink 2013). Certainly there were times when the president used the term liberally, as in the September 2013 speech cited at the beginning of this chapter.

References

Cillizza, Chris and Aaron Blake. 2012. "The Fix: President Obama Embraces 'Obamacare' Label. But Why?" *The Washington Post*, March 26. Accessed July 15, 2016. http://www.washingtonpost.com/blogs/the-fix/post/president-obama-embraces-obamacare-label-but-why/2012/03/25/gIQARJ5qaS_blog.html.

Cox, Amanda, Alicia Desantis, Alicia Parlapiano, and Jeremy White. 2012. "Fighting to Control the Meaning of 'Obamacare'." *The New York Times*, March 25. Accessed July

15, 2016. http://www.nytimes.com/interactive/2012/03/25/us/politics/fighting-to-control-the-meaning-of-obamacare.html.
Druckman, James N. 2001. "The Implications of Framing Effects for Citizen Competence." *Political Behavior* 23: 225–256.
Dumain, Emma. 2012. "Obamacare Now OK in Some Franked Mailings." *Roll Call*, July 12. Accessed July 15, 2016. http://www.rollcall.com/news/Obamacare-Now-OK-in-Some-Franked-Mailings-216067-1.html.
Dwyer, Devin. 2012. "@BarackObama: Happy Birthday 'Obamacare'." *ABC News*, March 23. Accessed July 15, 2016. http://abcnews.go.com/blogs/politics/2012/03/barackobama-happy-birthday-obamacare/.
Edwards III, George C. 2012. *Overreach: Leadership in the Obama Presidency*. Princeton, NJ: Princeton University Press.
Entman, Robert M. 2004. *Projections of Power: Framing News, Public Opinion, and U.S. Foreign Policy*. Chicago: University of Chicago Press.
Epstein, Reid J. 2013. "Taking 'Obama' Out of Health Care." *Politico*, November 19. Accessed July 15, 2016. http://www.politico.com/story/2013/11/barack-obama-obamacare-affordable-care-act-health-care-law-100034.html?hp=t1.
Godrej, Farah. 2003. "Spaces for Counter-Narratives: The Phenomenology of Reclamation." Presented at the Midwest Political Science Association Annual Meeting, Chicago.
Green, David. 1987. *The Language of Politics in America: Shaping Political Consciousness from McKinley to Reagan*. Ithaca: Cornell University Press.
Herbst, Susan. 2007. "The Rhetorical Presidency and the Contemporary Media Environment." *Critical Review* 19: 335–343.
Holian, David B. 2004. "He's Stealing My Issues! Clinton's Crime Rhetoric and the Dynamics of Issue Ownership." *Political Behavior* 26: 95–124.
Holley, Joe. 2009. "Beloved Radio Broadcaster Paul Harvey Dies at 90." *The Washington Post*, March 1. Accessed July 15, 2016. http://www.washingtonpost.com/wp-dyn/content/article/2009/02/28/AR2009022802096.html.
Jacobs, Larry R. and Robert Y. Shapiro. 2000. *Politicians Don't Pander: Political Manipulation and the Loss of Democratic Responsiveness*. Chicago: University of Chicago Press.
Jenkins, Henry, Sam Ford, and Joshua Green. 2013. *Spreadable Media: Creating Value and Meaning in a Networked Culture*. New York: New York University Press.
Jones, Jeffrey P. 2014. "The Convergence of Politics and Popular Culture in Election 2012." In *The 2012 Presidential Campaign: A Communication Perspective*, ed. Robert E. Denton, Jr., 115–132. Lanham: Rowman & Littlefield.
Kaiser Family Foundation Health Tracking Poll. 2013. Last modified June 19. Accessed July 15, 2016. http://kff.org/health-reform/poll-finding/kaiser-health-tracking-poll-june-2013/.
Lakoff, George. 2004. *Don't Think of an Elephant! Know Your Values and Frame the Debate*. Vermont: Chelsea Green.
Liesman, Steve. 2013. "What's in a name? Lots when it comes to Obamacare/ACA." *CNBC*, September 26. Accessed July 15, 2016. http://www.cnbc.com/id/101064954.
Madison, Lucy. 2011. "On Bus Tour, Obama Embraces 'Obamacare,' Says 'I Do Care'." *CBS News*, August 15. Accessed July 15, 2016. http://www.cbsnews.com/8301-503544_162-20092578-503544.html.
Reeve, Elspeth. 2011. "Who Coined 'Obamacare'?" *The Atlantic Monthly*, October 26. Accessed July 15, 2016. http://www.theatlanticwire.com/politics/2011/10/who-coined-obamacare/44183/.

Richard Prince's Journalisms. 2013. "AP, NPR Curb Use of 'Obamacare' Term." *Maynard Institute*, October 2. Accessed July 15, 2016. http://mije.org/richardprince/ap-npr-curb-use-obamacare-term#Affordable.

Rowling, Charles M. Penelope Sheets, and Timothy M. Jones. 2013. "Frame Contestation in the News: National Identity, Cultural Resonance, and U.S. Drone Policy." *International Journal of Communication* 7: 2231–2253.

Schaffner, Brian F. and Mary Layton Atkinson. 2010. "Taxing Death or Estates? When Frames Influence Citizens' Issue Beliefs." In *Winning with Words: The Origins and Impact of Political Framing*, eds Brian F. Schaffner and Patrick Sellers, 121–135. New York: Routledge.

Schumacher-Matos, Edward. 2013. "What We Hear When NPR Refers to 'Obamacare'." *NPR Ombudsman*, September 6. Accessed July 15, 2016. http://www.npr.org/sections/ombudsman/2013/09/06/219765368/what-we-hear-when-npr-refers-to-obamacare

Serafini, Marilyn Werber. 2007, May 5. "Beyond 'Hillarycare'." *National Journal* 39 (18): 24–30.

Shear, Michael D. 2012. "Romney Waves Away Opponents' Intensifying Attacks." *The New York Times*, January 9. Accessed July 15, 2016. http://www.nytimes.com/2012/01/10/us/politics/romneys-opponents-intensify-attacks-as-voting-nears.html?_r=0.

Sink, Justin. 2013. "WH Not Dropping 'Obamacare' Term." *The Hill*, November 21. Accessed July 15, 2016. http://thehill.com/blogs/blog-briefing-room/news/191134-white-house-not-dropping-obamacare-term.

Stuckey, Mary E. 2008. *Jimmy Carter, Human Rights, and the National Agenda*. College Station: Texas A&M University Press.

Stuckey, Mary E. 2010. "Rethinking the Rhetorical Presidency and Presidential Rhetoric." *The Review of Communication* 10: 38–52.

White House, The. 2013. "Remarks by the President on the Affordable Care Act." *The White House*, September 26. Accessed July 15, 2016. https://www.whitehouse.gov/the-press-office/2013/09/26/remarks-president-affordable-care-act.

Zaller, John R. 1992. *The Nature and Origins of Mass Opinion*. Cambridge: Cambridge University Press.

Zarefsky, David. 2004. "Presidential Rhetoric and the Power of Definition." *Presidential Studies Quarterly* 34: 607–619.

Zarefsky, David. 2005. *President Johnson's War on Poverty: Rhetoric and History*. Tuscaloosa: University of Alabama Press.

3

THE POLITICS OF FRAMING POLICY SUBSTANCE

Tax or Penalty?

In mid-September of 2009, a little over a week after his major public address to a joint session of Congress stumping for passage of health-care reform, President Obama sat down with George Stephanopoulos of ABC News for an interview in the Roosevelt Room of the White House. Stephanopoulos wasted no time in getting down to the politics of the individual mandate, or the proposed requirement that all Americans purchase health insurance. The inclusion of such a mandate was viewed by advocates as the necessary evil of a health-care overhaul plan that would also prevent insurance companies from rejecting applicants with preexisting conditions, and allow young people to stay on their parents' insurance until they were 26. The costs of these benefits would be offset, the law's backers argued, by the influx of more consumers into the insurance market, many of them young, healthy, and therefore less likely to purchase coverage without the government requiring it.

"Under this mandate," Stephanopoulos queried the president, "the government is forcing people to spend money, fining you if you don't. How is that not a tax?" Obama responded with an explanation of how all Americans with insurance were subject to higher premiums to pay for the risk-taking of those without coverage. As Stephanopoulos persisted, "That may be, but it's still a tax increase." The president replied, "No. That's not true, George . . . for us to say that you've got to take responsibility to get health insurance is absolutely not a tax increase." This back and forth continued, with the *This Week* host at one point producing the *Merriam Webster's Dictionary* definition of "tax" that he had written down in his notes, a move for which the president laughingly rebuked him, noting that looking up the word was proof "you're stretching a little bit right now." Finally, Stephanopoulos pressed one more time: "But you reject that it's a tax increase?" Obama responded emphatically: "I absolutely reject that notion" (*ABC News* 2009).

At one point in the above exchange, President Obama told his interviewer, "You can't just make up that language and decide that's called a tax increase." But in reality, political actors (including the president) have powerful incentives to strategically select even the most basic, seemingly innocuous words they employ in seeking to build or diminish support for public policies. For instance, did the requirement that Americans procure a minimum level of health insurance under the Affordable Care Act involve a "penalty" or a "tax" on citizens who failed to comply? Though common, everyday terms, these differing characterizations of how the individual mandate provision was enforced operate as framing devices as introduced in Chapter 1—an instantaneous means of promoting a particular interpretation of the policy. On the one hand, the "penalty" frame denotes that those subject to the policy have presumably done something to warrant punishment, and imposing such a "fine" thus appears more legitimate.[1] By contrast, a "tax" on this behavior attaches it to the negative connotations that many of the public ascribe to taxes generally, and risks the perception of a Democratic-controlled government forcing an unpopular "tax-and-spend" liberal agenda regarding health care on the nation.

In describing the mandate component of health-care reform to the American public, President Obama and his supporters predominantly used penalty/fine to describe the mechanism to enforce compliance. On June 28, 2012, when the Supreme Court issued its ruling in *National Federation of Independent Businesses v. Sebelius*, assessing the constitutionality of fundamental provisions of the ACA, Chief Justice John Roberts' majority opinion framed the mandate differently. Roberts' opinion declared Congress could not pass the individual mandate under the commerce or necessary and proper clauses, as this exceeded the legislature's authority. However, after identifying a judicial interest in "saving" the law as constitutional if possible, Roberts upheld the provision under Congress' power to tax. The Chief Justice thereby contradicted the Obama Administration's portrayal of the individual mandate in an unmistakably high-profile manner, asserting the provision could not survive if understood as anything but a tax—an "option" to buy insurance or pay the tax, and therefore, in a sense, not really a mandate at all.[2]

Broadly speaking, the ruling was perceived as a victory for the Obama Administration, largely upholding its signature legislative achievement,[3] and may have produced a small positive effect on public support for health-care reform immediately thereafter (Campbell and Persily 2013). In this chapter, I argue that this wide-angle evaluation of the case obscures the ways the specific reasoning of the ruling complicated the president's ability to frame the individual mandate, at least in the short term. The Supreme Court, a political institution hardly lauded for its ability to shape news coverage and public debates, was able to temporarily upend the framing contest in favor of depicting the mandate as a tax in several major media outlets. Over a longer period of time, however, as these news forums returned to primarily echoing the penalty frame, we can see the importance of presidential framing resilience.

This chapter centers then on the high-stakes communications contests of how the president and his opponents compete to frame the actual nuts and bolts provisions of policy reforms. Compliance with the stipulations of a law like the ACA, particularly a provision like the individual mandate, rests in part on whether citizens are aware of the policy and view it as legitimate.[4] As Jacobson (2011) notes, public opinion during the early years of health-care reform predictably followed conventional patterns, with majorities favoring benefits and opposing the costs required to pay for them. A 2013 survey revealed that only 12% of Americans supported the mandate and 41% felt citizens should not have to pay a tax/penalty if they failed to acquire insurance (Viebeck 2013). More recently, a Harris poll found that 64% of Americans would like to repeal the individual mandate provision (Thompson 2016). Yet as the Kaiser Family Foundation (KFF) found in 2014, although views of the mandate were generally unfavorable, people could be pushed toward more positive perceptions with more information about how it worked (DiJulio et al. 2014). Some of the mandate's critics charged that the national government might avoid public ire for raising taxes by casting the provision as a "penalty" for the public and yet conceding it was a tax in the courts, undermining democratic principles of political accountability.[5] Limited public information and malleability of opinions on the mandate encouraged both the president and his opponents to vigorously pursue their preferred framing and seek to have it echoed in news content.

Whether President Obama or the Supreme Court ruling in *NFIB v. Sebelius* would prevail in framing the individual mandate at key moments in the health-care reform debate, and over a long period of time, is a test of the chief executive's ability to achieve framing success amid a major challenge from the judiciary and the opposition party.

In this case, the actual words employed by the president and his opponents did not necessarily involve mutually exclusive categories[6]—the penalty could operate as a tax, or be termed a "tax penalty"—but the importance rests in the perceptions attached to the different framings of the policy. As Murray Edelman (1985) outlined, language has important symbolic power in politics, often operating unconsciously in the mind, yet significantly shaping understanding and experience. Mary Stuckey (1997) affirmed rhetoric's strong symbolic import, identifying it as a key way the president or his opponents seek to gain control of public policy debates. As a cautionary tale for this particular president, in 2009 the Obama Administration seemed to lose control of the narrative on climate-change legislation when opponents cast a "cap and trade" policy as "cap and tax."[7] Even just a cursory look at President Obama's refusal to give an inch on the tax label in the Stephanopoulos interview that began this chapter makes plain how essential the Administration felt it was to control the language used surrounding the individual mandate.

There is limited and conflicting data available about how these framing devices might impact public opinion on the mandate. Although a July 2012

KFF poll found that a slightly higher percentage of Americans (66%) expressed unfavorable views of the requirement when labeled as a "fine," in comparison to when it was called a "tax" (61%), such a survey does not fully capture the political dangers for President Obama, particularly given promises he made during the 2008 campaign, of the mandate being labeled a new tax increase. Meanwhile, the nonpartisan, nonprofit Enroll America, found that calling the provision a "fine" in the subject line of its emails urging people to obtain insurance was more likely to result in the email being opened than calling it a "tax" or a "penalty" (Kliff 2015). This may indicate that the penalty or fine frame would also be useful to the Obama Administration early on in getting people to pay attention to the mandate and sign up for coverage if they did not have it already, another key goal of the ACA. Additionally, the July 2012 KFF survey also showed that twice as many individuals believed they would end up paying the fee when it was described as a "tax" (26%) vs. a "fine" (12%). The foundation found that roughly one in five Americans thought they would be subject to the tax/fine, but experts estimated it would be far fewer, closer to one in ten Americans. This too presented a communication issue for the Obama Administration, as the tax characterization seemed to exacerbate citizens' assumptions the policy change would end up personally costing them money.

The Supreme Court: Potential Challenger to Presidential Framing?

In Chapter 2, I discussed a framing contest between the président and the opposition party. To what extent might the Supreme Court as an institution be able to compete with the president, the most visible, heavily covered figure in the U.S. government, to frame policy? Traditionally, the Federal judiciary is conceived as insulated from popular pressures and unconcerned with shaping the public's views, because its members are unelected and enjoy lifetime tenure. More recently however, some scholars have explored the ways the Supreme Court is a representative body. Numerous works have shown the Court's rulings in the modern era are typically in line with public opinion (Marshall 2008). Casillas et al. (2010) argue that the influence of public opinion on Court decisions is greatest, unexpectedly, on nonsalient cases, as justices perceive a risk to institutional legitimacy by repeatedly issuing unpopular rulings that could then garner unwanted negative attention. Granted neither Congress' power over Federal funding nor the president's command over the military by the Constitution, the Court relies heavily on its own mystique and the perception that its rulings are legitimate and to be complied with. Though public approval ratings of the High Court have declined a bit in recent years, it remains a governmental institution held in higher esteem than, for instance, Congress.

Researchers have also identified the Court's members as turning toward more public leadership, taking account of news coverage and increasingly seeking to use the press for personal and institutional purposes (Davis 2011). Political scientists though have failed to muster substantial evidence that shows the Court can affect Americans' views of political issues. Some have claimed the Court might help legitimize policy changes undertaken by the other branches (Dahl 1957; Black 1960), but careful systematic studies have concluded rulings do not typically shape public opinion, nor produce the social change desired by many bringing cases to their attention (Marshall 1989, 2008; Rosenberg 2008). In fact, scholars have found that Court decisions tend to mobilize opponents to the rulings (Rosenberg 2008). Further, the Court receives little press coverage (O'Brien 1986), and Americans are often not well-versed on the content of even its most high-profile decisions (Dost 2015). The Court is largely reliant on the media's autonomous evaluation of the importance of its rulings and what news providers believe warrants coverage, rather than being able to proactively influence such decisions (Sill et al. 2013). Here, we consider whether and how the Court's 2012 ruling altered the framing contest about the individual mandate in which the president and health-reform opponents had been engaged.

The Competing Frames

Obama's unequivocal assertions that the mandate was not a tax in his *ABC News* interview were not a spontaneous outburst. On September 29, 2009, the White House posted a list of talking points about health-care reform on its official website that included many of the arguments Obama had made, making the Administration's strategy abundantly clear. Included in the memo's bullet points were claims such as, "What President Obama is proposing is not a tax, but a requirement to comply with the law," and "What we're talking about is a penalty for the few people who will refuse to buy health insurance—even though they can afford it—and who expect the rest of us to pick up the tab for their care." The document also invited the comparison of the penalty to those enforced when people are caught speeding or without car insurance, asking rhetorically "Does anyone consider that a tax?" (White House 2009). These depictions of the penalty indicated that individuals subject to the fee were being legitimately fined for doing something wrong, taking unnecessary risks, and imposing costs on more responsible citizens. That interpretation was also hammered home by the law referring to the fee as a "shared responsibility payment." One claim used to endorse the individual mandate was that people with insurance had been paying a "hidden tax" in their premiums to cover the costs of care for those without insurance—one organization estimated this amounted to about $1,017 per family for a household and their employers in 2009 (Families USA 2009). In this most generous read of the individual mandate, it could be seen as a tax *cut* for many Americans.

There were other incentives for the Obama team to commit itself so firmly to the penalty frame. If the mandate was framed as a tax, Obama was vulnerable to claims he betrayed a campaign promise from 2008 not to increase taxes on the middle class. This desire to preclude the mandate from being seen as a tax increase was also evident in the wording of the statute itself, with Congress carefully avoiding referring to it as such in the final version of the law.[8] When Solicitor General Donald Verrilli defended the mandate before the Supreme Court on behalf of the Obama Administration, he did make the case it could survive as a tax, but only seemingly as a last-ditch effort, when his primary claim that the commerce clause empowered Congress to impose the requirement did not seem to be going over well with some of the justices (Fried 2013).[9] As of this writing, HealthCare.gov, the Federal government's official website for the ACA, informs citizens about the "fee" for not having insurance, noting, "The fee is sometimes called the 'penalty,' 'fine,' or 'individual mandate,'" but notably, the website does not report that it is sometimes called a tax.

Meanwhile, opponents of the health-care law sporadically brought the "tax" label into their public statements about the mandate, even prior to the Court's ruling (Weiner 2013: 88).[10] Immediately after the bill was signed into law, attorneys general from 13 states brought a lawsuit challenging the ACA using the "both" designation, arguing, "The Act represents an unprecedented encroachment on the liberty of individuals living in the Plaintiffs' respective states, by mandating that all citizens and legal residents of the United States have qualifying health-care coverage or pay a tax penalty."[11] When the Supreme Court ultimately weighed in on the constitutionality of the mandate in 2012, Chief Justice Roberts maintained that "although the statute called the payment a 'penalty,' the label did not control in the face of operational factors inconsistent with a punitive function," such as the amount and collection of the payment by the Internal Revenue Service (Weiner 2013).[12] The majority opinion declared, "it is reasonable to construe what Congress has done as increasing taxes on those who have a certain amount of income, but choose to go without health insurance," casting the provision as precisely the tax increase the White House had so strenuously denied implementing.

Not all conservative opponents to the ACA, however, were able to embrace the "tax" frame wholeheartedly. Several party leaders faced the dilemma of having previously supported an individual mandate in the not-so-distant past. The Heritage Foundation had promoted the policy in the late 1980s and early '90s, and prior backers such as Newt Gingrich now claimed they were "forced" at that time to support the mandate by the threat of "Hillarycare" under the Clinton Administration (Roy 2011). Republican members speaking on the floor of Congress would sometimes directly contradict each other, in quick succession, on whether the mandate entailed a penalty or a tax.[13] In particular, 2012 Republican presidential candidate Mitt Romney faced great difficulty in framing the mandate for the public, given his endorsement of a similar requirement for individuals to buy health insurance at the state level as governor of Massachusetts. This dilemma was apparent in the wake of the Court ruling in *NFIB v. Sebelius*—on July 2, 2012, senior Romney adviser Eric Fehrnstrom announced that Romney did not believe the mandate was a tax, falling in line with Justice Antonin Scalia's dissent in the case, but out of step with other Republicans using the ruling as a springboard for promoting Obama as disingenuously raising taxes (Shear 2012). The Romney campaign instead sought to depict the mandate as an "unconstitutional penalty" when implemented at the Federal level, as opposed to operating at the state level in Massachusetts. Just two days later, however, Romney stated publically that he did, in fact, believe the mandate was a tax, because the Supreme Court had spoken on the matter and declared it as such (Peters 2012). The president's opponents in this framing contest were often in a state of disarray. To what extent might the Court ruling help unify Republicans around the tax frame in the news, beyond this Romney reversal?

Framing the Individual Mandate in the News

This section presents my analysis of media coverage from what I identify as four critical time periods, to see how the mandate was described in the news in five different outlets—*The New York Times*, *The Washington Post*, *The New York Post*, CNN, and Fox News.[14] The selected time periods coincided with events that presented the greatest possibility that the mandate would be discussed specifically in the news and that framings of the policy might draw public attention. Popular news outlets in the contemporary era tend to focus on political conflict and the game-like aspects of politics, instead of providing in-depth reports on substantive public policy (Patterson 1994; Jamieson and Cappella 1998). We therefore need to review coverage from moments when media actors might be compelled by circumstances to cover the mandate more extensively than they normally would. I label the analyzed time periods as the following: (1) "Push for Reform," beginning on September 9, 2009, when President Obama gave a major prime-time address to a joint session of Congress urging them to overhaul health-care; (2) "Law's Passage," starting with the March 23, 2010 official signing of the ACA into law; (3) "Court Ruling," as the Supreme Court issued its decision in the *NFIB v. Sebelius* case on June 28, 2012; and lastly, (4) "Website Problems," beginning October 20, 2013, when continued difficulties with the HealthCare.gov portal led to concerns about the individual mandate deadlines, and ultimately, a decision by the White House on October 23 to push the deadline for Americans to purchase insurance or pay a tax/penalty back several weeks.[15] The three print outlets were analyzed for two weeks following each of the listed starting dates, and the cable news coverage was analyzed for three days of each period, a difference made necessary by the sheer volume of transcripts from the two news networks and the close examination required to identify the frames and their users.[16]

These four time periods and five news outlets allow us to explore the tax/penalty framing contest in several important ways. First, by counting the appearances of "tax," "penalty/fine," and various alternative methods of discussing the policy, we can get a sense of how often these frames were being repeated and by whom—elements which, as discussed in Chapter 2, may affect the credibility and persuasiveness of frames for citizens. Over four years separate the first analyzed time period from the last, permitting us to assess presidential framing resilience and its staying power in the news in comparison to the frames of the president's opponents. The time periods also allow us to explore the state of the framing contest before and after the Court weighed in on the mandate.

Second, variations in the selected news outlets help illuminate how framing contests on policy substance might play out in hard news vs. soft news, liberal- vs. conservative-leaning organizations, and "new" vs. "old" media. For more politically substantive, "prestige press" newspapers like *The New York Times* and *The Washington Post*, a strong commitment to educating their audience about policy matters might require a critical interrogation of the frames applied to provisions by political actors, so as not to pass them along unquestioningly to their audiences. Including a paper like *The New York Post* helps shed light on how tabloid news sources less beholden to that commitment and more interested in entertaining than informing readers about policy details, would deal with the mandate. On their face, "tax" and "penalty" are far less likely to appear as constructed, strategic frames in comparison to those explored in other cases in this book, such as those involving "death panels" or "Obamacare," complicating news providers' ability to expose the potential effect of those terms on perception of the policy. Yet we know that word choice mattered a great deal to the politicians involved here; as has been discussed, both sides of the debate sought to influence the language surrounding the mandate. Additionally, that some associate news sources like the *Times* and *The Washington Post* with liberal bias and outlets such as the *The New York Post* and Fox News with a conservative bent further fleshes out this inquiry; some organizations might be purposefully promoting framing devices such as "tax" and "penalty" to their readers/ viewers. This is another important reason for accounting for who was using each frame in the news. Finally, incorporating the transcripts of CNN and Fox News gives an indication of how this framing contest played out over time in the "newer" media format of cable news, allowing us to compare this with more traditional print sources.

The Rarity of Policy Substance Coverage

One takeaway from Figure 3.1 is how, even at these moments when we would expect the individual mandate to attract the most attention, it was explained to the public a relatively limited number of times, with the exception of the "Court Ruling" period. As Bennett (2005) argues, the contemporary news media rarely convey information about complex policy issues to their audiences. Even in the news outlets with a reputation for more substantive coverage, far more attention was given to the political maneuvering and conflict around health-care reform than its actual policy content. As seen in Figure 3.2, journalists and pundits/

	News Outlet	Push For Reform September 9th – September 23rd, 2009					Law's Passage March 23rd – April 6th, 2010					Court Ruling June 28th – July 12th, 2012					Website Problems October 20th – November 3rd, 2013					TOTAL
		Tax	Penalty	Not a tax	Both	Other	Tax	Penalty	Not a tax	Both	Other	Tax	Penalty	Not a tax	Both	Other	Tax	Penalty	Not a tax	Both	Other	
Cable	CNN		19				1	36		6		237	120	72	62	6	4	44		1		608
	Fox News		1				3	25				244	33	131	23		9	28		3		500
Print	Washington Post	2	14	3			1	3				59	35	8	24	2	4	34		2		187
	New York Times		11	1		2	3	3		1		59	25	16	21	4		14		8		168
	New York Post		7									31	13	18	5			5				79
	Total	2	52	4		2	8	67		7		630	226	245	135	12	13	125		14		1,542

FIGURE 3.1 Use of Framing Devices over Time in Print and on Cable News

	Push For Reform September 9th – September 23rd, 2009					Law's Passage March 23rd – April 6th, 2010					Court Ruling June 28th – July 12th, 2012					Website Problems October 20th – November 3rd, 2013					TOTAL
Used by	Tax	Penalty	Not tax	Both	Other	Tax	Penalty	Not tax	Both	Other	Tax	Penalty	Not tax	Both	Other	Tax	Penalty	Not tax	Both	Other	
Journalist		41	2		2	3	28		4		212	106	53	63	5	1	73		9		602
Editorial/Commentator/Pundit/Host	2	8				5	28		1		245	69	100	42	2	9	41		4		556
Republican politician/Surrogate							7		2		131	19	53	14	2	3	5		1		237
Democratic politician/Surrogate		3	2								3	24	28	4			5				69
Supreme Court/Justice											28	2	4	12	3						49
Citizen							4				11	6	7				1				29
Total	2	52	4	0	2	8	67	0	7	0	630	226	245	135	12	13	125	0	14	0	1,542

FIGURE 3.2 Actors Using Framing Devices over Time

commentators were most likely to use the framing devices in each of the four time periods.[17] Across all of the analyzed coverage, Republican politicians and surrogates were quoted directly or appeared on camera using one of the frames roughly 3.5 times more than Democratic politicians and surrogates. But did that mean the frames of health-reform opponents on the individual mandate were more prevalent than those of supporters?

"Push for Reform" and "Law's Passage": The Early Dominance of Penalty/Fine

The first two pie charts of Figure 3.3 tell a similar story about the framing of the individual mandate prior to the Supreme Court's 2012 ruling: "penalty" was overwhelmingly the most common way of talking about the repercussions of failing to acquire insurance across the five news organizations' coverage. For nearly every outlet during the "Push for Reform" and "Law's Passage" periods the penalty frame appeared a majority of the time. There were just two exceptions to this: *The New York Times* in the latter period, when "penalty" appeared the same number of times as "tax," and *The New York Post*, which had no mentions in that time. Regardless of whether a news source produced hard or soft news, was associated with liberal or conservative bias, or fell into the "old" or "new" media category, all privileged the president's framing of the insurance requirement. From an early period, we can identify presidential framing resilience—even where we might anticipate the Obama team's take on the mandate to perform poorly, such as in a tabloid or in conservative-leaning news, the Administration's ability to spread its frame is apparent. The president had a few key advantages in this regard. If initial frames are lasting and difficult to dislodge from people's minds (Entman 2004, 7), President Obama benefited from characterizing the mandate as a penalty/fine at a very early point, as the policy was first publically debated and passed into law. With the president the most prominent champion of health reform, the Administration was an important official source for news on the bill's provisions.

A second advantage was the failure of the president's opponents to consistently and prominently frame the mandate as a tax increase in these two periods. As political actors on both sides of the debate recognized the individual mandate was probably the most unpopular element of the reform policy, Obama's critics perhaps felt no great impetus to frame the punishment for failing to meet the mandate accordingly. Whether a penalty, a tax, or both, they might have reasoned, Americans were not going to like it any better. Fewer mentions of any of the frames in these first two time periods compared to the latter two also indicate that even the president and his team had little incentive to spend a lot of time talking about the widely disliked mandate in their early effort push to pass and promote the ACA, unless forced to by a media figure like George Stephanopoulos.

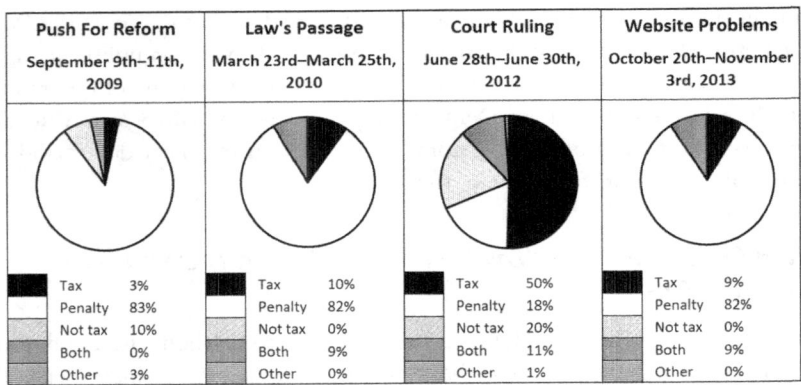

FIGURE 3.3 Proportional Use of Framing Devices over Time in Print and on Cable News

"Court Ruling" Time Period Coverage: Boost to the Tax Frame

In the days following the Supreme Court's ruling in *NFIB v. Sebelius*, the volatile 21st century news environment and its impact on presidential framing resiliency came into full view. In the "Court Ruling" period, "tax" became the most prevalent framing of the requirement across the five outlets, a plurality of the times it was labeled in each outlet, and the majority of the time on Fox News. Despite the Court's limitations in interacting with the press and public, in this instance, the majority opinion had a major impact on how the mandate was framed in the news. A ruling that was not only unexpected and dramatic in its content, but also required some in-depth explanation in the news, helped the Court to figure prominently in the framing contest around the mandate.

Within a justice's opinion, not merely the reasoning but also the tone and language used are highly significant, with more sensational stylistic choices likely to receive greater press and public attention (Davis 2011, 14). The way in which Chief Justice Roberts structured his opinion affected how this "breaking news" was covered by the media, and drew substantial interest toward the mandate as a tax frame.[18] Several news organizations, including CNN and Fox News, in their rush to tell viewers the ruling as quickly as possible, at first reported the decision incorrectly. Correspondents reporting live from the Court rushed to cameras with the lengthy opinion in hand, vying to "emerge from the chaos as today's grand champion of news-firstiness," as Jon Stewart joked that night on *The Daily Show*. The reporters and their producers quickly reviewed the beginning portion of the opinion, finding that the mandate unconstitutionally exceeded Congress' power under the commerce clause, which then caused some to assume and report the mandate had thus been struck down (*PBS News Hour* 2012). But as those journalists that had made this error walked back and corrected their reports over the next few minutes, heightened attention was given to the specifics of the reasoning that ultimately upheld the mandate and led to this confusion. Many media observers have pointed to increased competition and the frenetic pace of the news cycle as privileging speed over accuracy in the news. These outlets recklessly put their reputation in jeopardy by reporting such an attention-grabbing story incorrectly, not unlike some of the costly blunders, inaccuracies, and retractions outlets incurred when covering the close contest between Al Gore and George W. Bush on election night 2000 (Jamieson and Waldman 2004). There is little that the president can do about this kind of erratic behavior by contemporary news organizations that in turn might strengthen challenges to his preferred messages in their coverage.

In Chapter 1, I introduced the concept of presidential frame refraction, as presidential frames evolve with unfolding events to take on new meanings and applications, a process in this case triggered by the Court's ruling. The purpose of the penalty frame for the Administration was to cast a necessary but disliked provision in the most favorable way possible—better to treat an unpopular government-imposed cost on individuals as punishing bad behavior with a fine than as a tax increase. By employing the legal argument that the individual mandate could *only* survive as constitutional because it was a tax, Chief Justice Roberts altered the trajectory of the penalty frame. When the president and his surrogates emphasized their preferred frame, it could now be interacted with differently than before, when the penalty frame was largely either ignored or inconsistently challenged by opponents. Moreover, even *past* usage of "penalty" and "not a tax" could be cast in a new light. Roberts, with the legitimacy of the Supreme Court behind him,[19] and in a move heavily covered by the news media, tethered the Administration to a new "tax" and thereby opened the door to any protestation to the contrary coming across as deliberate obfuscation on their part.

And in fact, denial that the mandate was a tax continued to be precisely the Obama team's strategy in the immediate wake of the Court's ruling.[20] That the tax frame was so widespread in news content in this period was not due to a lack of effort by the Administration—immediately after the decision was handed down, the president and his surrogates sought every avenue to deflect attention from the "tax" framing and refused to validate it, sometimes going to great lengths to avoid doing so. In his remarks immediately after the opinion was made public, President Obama made no mention of the penalty or tax issue, choosing instead to stress the positive elements of the law and his view of the ruling as a victory for all Americans (White House 2012). In his briefing the next day, White House Press Secretary Jay Carney continued to talk about the policy as a penalty. When a reporter asked, "So you guys are still saying it's a penalty, not a tax?" Carney responded, "You can call it what you want," later adding, "It's a penalty because you have a choice. You don't have a choice to pay your taxes, right?" (American Presidency Project

2012). Obama's Chief of Staff Jack Lew appeared on *Fox News Sunday* on July 1, and in response to Chris Wallace asserting, "Mr. Lew, they called it a tax," stated, "No, actually, technically what they said is the Congress has many powers. There is the commerce clause, there's taxing powers, and it was constitutional. That's what they said. It doesn't matter what they call it." The president's campaign strategist David Axelrod said on the *Today Show*, "Whether you call it a mandate or tax, what it is is a penalty on the very few Americans who don't—can afford health care, don't pay for it, end up in our emergency rooms getting free care and then we all pay for it in the form of premiums" (Bruce 2012). Most Democratic politicians fell in line, illustrating the "spreadability" of the president's framing—across all four of the time periods, Democratic officials and surrogates were only featured in their own words in the selected news outlets referring to the mandate as a tax a mere three out of sixty-eight times they employed any of the frames. All three of those occasions were in the "Court Ruling" time span. Over all of the coverage reviewed in this chapter, Democrats in the news referred to the mandate as a penalty or *not* a tax nearly 90% of the time.

Meanwhile, many prominent Republicans took advantage of Roberts' boost to the tax frame and seized upon the publicity the surprise ruling had produced to add greater coherence to their communications around the mandate. Prior to this, during the "Push for Reform" and "Law's Passage" periods discussed earlier, Republican politicians and surrogates never appeared in any of the five outlets using solely the tax frame, instead referring largely to a "penalty," and in two instances, characterizing it as both a tax and a penalty. In the "Court Ruling" period, Republicans took Roberts' contribution to the framing contest, amplified his "tax" reasoning, and ran with the ways he had refracted the penalty frame. The majority opinion and Republican leaders thus helped shape the media narrative around the policy, at least in the short term, in the direction of the "tax." Senate Minority Leader Mitch McConnell was widely quoted in the news declaring, "Well, the Supreme Court has spoken. This law is a tax. The bill was sold to the American people on a deception" (Abdullah 2012). Reacting to the ruling, Senator Marco Rubio of Florida told CNN viewers that the Court's decision "reminds us that this is a broken promise. The president said he would not raise taxes on the middle class. This is a middle-class tax increase. And you know why we know it's a middle-class tax increase? Not because I'm saying it, because the Supreme Court has." Rubio thereby sought to wrap the tax frame in the authority of the High Court's pronouncements and remove it from the realm of partisan combat. Conservatives used the Roberts decision to reinforce a larger argument they were making against the ACA as a whole; that its various components amounted to a massive middle-class tax increase (Hicks 2012).

The above McConnell and Rubio quotes reflect how Obama's critics pushed Roberts' refraction of the president's frame a step further in its evolution. This challenge involved not merely refuting the penalty frame, but recasting the past, charging that the president had tried to hide a tax hike from the American people. In this "Court Ruling" span of coverage, *The New York Post* and Fox News had the highest percentage of appearances of the "not a tax" frame of all the outlets. With more right-leaning opinion content and more conservative sources than the other outlets, their coverage frequently featured Republicans emphatically reminding audiences that Obama had stated this wasn't a tax, going on to maintain the Court's ruling proved this was a conscious lie by the president. On numerous occasions on cable news, coverage juxtaposed analysis of the ruling with clips of President Obama employing the "not a tax" frame in the past, often including portions of the 2009 Stephanopoulos interview. Sandwiching that content between lengthy discussions of how the mandate had been declared a tax by the Court, however, seemed to cut into the persuasiveness of the president's prior claims. Some journalists also jumped on the bandwagon—CNN anchor Brooke Baldwin asked her guests on the day of the ruling whether they thought that "the Democrats were cowardly for not presenting this as a tax from the get-go?" The irony here was that because Roberts had been the decisive vote in upholding the ACA, counter to what Republicans would have wanted, his ruling operated as an independent verification of their framing from a neutral source. This bolstered the credibility of the party's effort to push that framing into damaging new directions for the president. Overall, the Chief Justice's legal argument worked to help reinforce and advance the policy framing of health-care reform's detractors.

There were limits, however, to the usefulness of the Roberts' opinion for Republicans in this framing contest. Romney, as recounted earlier, had difficulty reconciling the Court's ruling with his previous policy positions and statements. Others in the party, primarily outraged and feeling betrayed by the Chief Justice upholding the mandate, seemed dismissive toward Roberts' role in the framing fight. Republican National Committee chair Reince Preibus told Fox News' Greta Van Susteren on June 29, "Well, I mean, the Supreme Court says it's a tax. I mean, I personally don't agree, but it doesn't matter." Congresswoman Michele Bachmann (R-MN) called the tax portion of the ruling "the weakest argument" of all that had been deployed to save the individual mandate, when reacting to the decision on CNN.

Finally, the use of *both* "tax" and "penalty" to frame the mandate was most frequently found across the five outlets in the 2012 period. About a fifth of the references to the substance of the mandate in *The New York Times* and *The Washington Post*, the hard news-oriented outlets, framed the stipulation in this way. This suggests a changing editorial policy after the Court's ruling—presumably "tax penalty" was a more "balanced" way of discussing the mandate, incorporating both sides of the debate. For some news providers this was not merely a short-term adjustment, as is apparent by a look at the "Website Problems" period of coverage that I turn to next; the majority opinion combined with Republicans' promotion of the tax frame likely altered the *Times*' portrayal of the policy, even over a year later.

"Website Problems" Time Period Coverage: Back to "Normal"?

The last pie chart in Figure 3.3 shows a return to similar patterns of coverage as can be seen in the first two, and that stands in contrast to the pervasiveness of the tax frame in the third chart. Eventually, as the Court ruling faded from headlines, most outlets reverted back to the old, original "penalty" frame. If the idea of presidential framing resilience draws attention to the staying power of presidential frames in the news, here, although faced with a major challenge that diminished its effectiveness in the wake of the 2012 Court decision, Obama's preferred framing of the individual mandate rebounded. Across the five very different news sources I analyzed, the "penalty" frame appeared a majority of the time in every single one. There was not a single instance of framing the provision as solely a tax in all three of the analyzed newspapers. On cable news, 97.6% of journalists' use of one of the frames was that of "penalty." In fact, the only substantial presence of frames other than that of "penalty" could be found in the *Times*. The newspaper appeared so committed to what it believed to be an objective take on this matter that many *Times* contributors continued to adhere to the "tax penalty" framing it had taken up in the wake of the *NFIB v. Sebelius* ruling. At the same time, on Fox News, a few of the personalities most harshly and consistently critical of Obama persisted with the tax frame. Still, the overall coverage of the "Website Problems" time span shows that though a few of the conservative hosts of Fox News' round-table debate show *The Five* might continue to emphasize the mandate as a tax, the broader Republican Party and other health-care reform opponents were not as faithful in sticking to this framing strategy so long after the Court ruling.

Conclusion

The news media's propensity to shy away from covering policy substance and the Obama Administration's reluctance to draw a lot of attention to health-care reform's least popular component meant even across these four time periods, where events put a spotlight on the individual mandate, discussions of the policy mechanism were limited. Where framings of the mandate did appear, the Obama team, from a very early point, was able to effectively frame the mandate as a penalty and not a tax in the news. Despite some faltering along the way, the president's framing ultimately regained its influence at a later time period, as the ACA was being implemented in the fall of 2013. That the Administration's portrayal of the mandate rebounded across all five outlets looked at here, varying in type of news content, partisan leanings, and format, points to the resiliency of presidential frames. It was unlikely the White House could ever convince Americans to love the individual mandate, but it at least was able to prevent major news organizations from covering the policy predominantly as a campaign pledge-breaking tax hike in the long term.

That presidential framing resilience entails not uninterrupted dominance but the ability to bounce back from setbacks is apt in this case given the blow to the Obama Administration's framing efforts in the wake of the 2012 Court ruling. The fact that even the Supreme Court, with the aid of those Republicans who helped amplify the tax frame and push its implications further, could reshape the way the mandate was discussed in the news illustrates the difficulties the president encounters in trying to consistently frame key policy issues for the 21st century media over time. The combination of the Court, Republican messaging, and the spread of the tax frame by media actors resulted in presidential frame refraction—what was once championed by the White House as the least offensive way of talking about a very unpopular policy provision took on a new meaning, of the Administration deliberately misleading the public on health care and tricking Americans into a tax increase. While the president might often be assured of a prominent place for his frames in the news, it is unlikely such frames will remain uncorrupted in any one venue or over a long time period, as can be seen most dramatically in the "Court Ruling" coverage. Perhaps the Republican Party might have been better positioned to prolong this framing success if there had not been internal divisions and inconsistency in using Roberts' tax ruling as a springboard, particularly on the part of Mitt Romney, the party's standard-bearer in the 2012 election. Nevertheless, well after the *NFIB v. Sebelius* ruling, some news norms remained altered, such as *The New York Times*' propensity for splitting the difference between the competing frames and using the "tax penalty" designation.

The enduring impact of the president's frames is apparent in reviewing the restored dominance of the penalty frame in the analyzed coverage in the fall of 2013, as the health insurance exchange website's technical problems persisted. Heathcare.gov's flaws, however, presented a major challenge for presidential framing that proved far more difficult for the Obama team to engineer a comeback from, as we shall see in the next chapter.

Notes

1 To simplify this study, "penalty" and "fine" will be treated as the same way of framing the provision, because of the way they contrast directly with "tax." There may, of course, be nuances in the framing of the policy as a "penalty" vs. "fine" but they will not be explored here. For simplicity's sake, I will predominantly use "penalty" to describe this frame throughout the chapter.

2 Roberts' reasoning may have been unexpected to many political observers at the time, but the legal argument existed well before the ruling. Yale Constitutional Law Professor Jack M. Balkin, for instance, made this assessment several years before (*New York Times*, 2010) and it also came up during oral arguments for the case.

3 There was another portion of the law the Court did strike down, thereby altering the ACA's expansion of Medicaid to make it less coercive for State governments. However, this was a far more minor setback for the law than ruling the individual mandate unconstitutional would have been.

4   These concerns were particularly acute in the case of the ACA. A March 2013 Kaiser Health Tracking poll found that 57% of Americans felt they didn't have enough information about the ACA to know how it would affect them, and this was true of an even higher percentage of the uninsured (67%). This same survey showed that over a quarter of the public either thought the law did not include the individual mandate at all, or said that they didn't know if such a requirement was part of the ACA (Kaiser Health Tracking Poll 2013). A Gallup poll a year after the Court's 2012 ruling identified 43% of uninsured citizens as completely unaware that they needed to obtain insurance under the ACA (Jones 2013).
5   This charge has, for instance, been made by Randy E. Barnett, a law professor at Georgetown, who helped formulate the legal challenge that the individual mandate was unconstitutional.
6   For an opposing view on this point, see Justice Antonin Scalia's dissenting opinion in the case that argued they were mutually exclusive, at least from a constitutional perspective, claiming the mandate must be *either* a penalty *or* a tax, but that he could identify "no case where constitutionally the policy is both."
7   See for instance, "Who Pays for Cap and Trade?" *The Wall Street Journal*, March 9, 2009.
8   The issue of the wording of the law was raised by Justice Scalia in his dissenting opinion in the *NFIB v. Sebelius* case, as he challenged Roberts' reading of the mandate as a tax by stating, "The issue is not whether Congress had the *power* to frame the minimum-coverage provision as a tax, but whether it *did* so." Thus Scalia concluded the provision explicitly termed a penalty could not be identified as a tax because the Court "cannot rewrite the statute to be what it is not." Chief Justice Roberts addressed this in his majority opinion, claiming that to strike down the provision on this basis would mean that "even if the Constitution permits Congress to do exactly what we interpret this statute to do, the law must be struck down because Congress used the wrong labels." It also might be noted that despite the careful wording of the law's text, Senator Max Baucus (D-MN) did cite both Congress' commerce clause powers *and* its taxing and spending powers as making the individual mandate constitutionally permissible on the floor of the Senate (Congressional Record, Proceedings and Debates of the 111th Congress, First Session, Vol. 155, Tuesday, December 22, 2009, No. 198, S13721).
9   On the first day of oral arguments, the tax vs. penalty subject was raised as the Court questioned if the mandate was a tax, whether the Anti-Injunction Act of 1867 applied and thus prevented the mandate from being challenged in the judicial system before the "tax" was actually paid (which would have been years later, in 2015). At one point during that back and forth, Justice Stephen Breyer had to correct Verrilli for using "tax" to describe the "penalty," recognizing that it would weaken the Obama Administration's argument that the Anti-Injunction Act did not apply.
10 The Heritage Foundation also discussed the individual mandate as a tax (http://www.heritage.org/research/reports/2010/04/obamacare-impact-on-taxpayers).
11 The full text of the complaint can be found at http://myfloridalegal.com/webfiles.nsf/WF/MRAY-83TKWB/$file/HealthCareReformLawsuit.pdf.
12 As Metzger and Morrison (2013, 131) point out in the same volume, several lower courts had refused to even consider whether the individual mandate was constitutional based on Congress' tax power, because Congress had not demonstrated its intent to base the legislation on that power with enough clarity, instead using the "penalty" term and repeatedly emphasizing the law fell under the commerce power.
13 For instance, on the floor of the Senate on December 23, 2009, Senator John Ensign (R-NV) asserted, "Let's call this penalty what it really is—a tax," but moments later Senator Orrin Hatch (R-UT) countered, "the financial penalty enforcing the insurance mandate is just that, a penalty. It is not a tax, and therefore, it is constitutional

only if the insurance mandate it enforces is constitutional," which Hatch concluded it was not.
14 A more detailed description of the search terms used and how the articles/transcripts were analyzed can be found in Appendix A.3.
15 This last time period encompasses a few days prior to the White House's revision of the rules, to incorporate the prevalence of the tax/penalty frames in the coverage, both as pressure on the Administration intensified and then after the deadline change.
16 For each time period except the last one, CNN and Fox News transcripts were analyzed from the first three days of the two-week span. I analyzed the cable news transcripts for the "Website Problems" period beginning instead on October 23, as the White House announced its changes to the deadlines, making it more likely coverage would address the individual mandate in the three-day span. The more manageable volume of the print coverage allowed for beginning the analysis a few days earlier, on October 20, to incorporate how the mandate was covered in the build-up to these changes, as well as in their aftermath.
17 This analysis is an account of which actors stated/wrote the framing devices rather than who they were attributed to. So for instance, in a sentence such as: "President Obama's supporters insisted the law's penalty for people who do not buy health insurance is not a tax, but a penalty—as Mr. Obama has long maintained," the journalist is counted as technically "using" the framing device, but it is "attributed to" Obama's supporters and the president himself. Still, the frequency counts of who "used" the framing devices remain important, as they indicate both what frames media gatekeepers allow into the news (such as a reporter's decision to cite the views of the president, his Republican adversaries, or Supreme Court Justices in his or her article) and what quotes by various political actors are effective at gaining news attention.
18 Roberts' opinion also included the word penalty, but in the process of stressing that the provision was a tax, such as here: "The Affordable Care Act's requirement that certain individuals pay a financial penalty for not obtaining health insurance may reasonably be characterized as a tax."
19 To be sure, there are conflicting impressions of how secure the Supreme Court's legitimacy is in the contemporary era. Though the Court has sought to establish a nonpartisan identity at least as early as Chief Justice John Marshall's 1803 ruling in *Marbury v. Madison*, there has been continual debate about whether the justices are truly above the partisan fray, particularly in the wake of the controversial *Bush v. Gore* decision in 2000. Still, the Court retains at least some elements to its identity of being an impartial arbitrator in American politics, a perception actually bolstered by the conservative Chief Justice Roberts providing the decisive vote on the Court to uphold much of the ACA; a boost to President Obama, who had refused to vote for the Chief Justice's confirmation when in the Senate back in 2005. Some observers argued in the wake of the decision that Roberts' opinion in this case was shaped by precisely these considerations over institutional authority, and was in part an effort to detach the Court from perceptions it was part of the polarized party battles over health-care reform.
20 One exception to this was on July 24, 2012, on the campaign trail, Obama did call it a tax, saying, "By the way, if you've got health insurance, you're not getting hit by a tax." The president continued, "The only thing that's happening to you is that you now have more security because insurance companies can't drop you when you get sick." Conservative media outlets pounced on this moment as a presidential flip flop (see for instance: http://www.theblaze.com/stories/2012/07/14/obama-describes-individual-mandate-as-a-tax/). Obama and his team did not shift to consistently refer to the mandate as a tax from this point forward; this seemed to be an isolated incident.

References

ABC News. 2009. Transcript: President Barack Obama. September 20. Accessed July 14, 2016. http://abcnews.go.com/ThisWeek/Politics/transcript-president-barack-obama/story?id=8618937.

Abdullah, Halimah. 2012. "Ruling, tax fears play into campaign narrative for both sides." *CNN Politics*, June 28. Accessed July 14, 2016. http://www.cnn.com/2012/06/28/politics/ruling-campaign-impact/.

American Presidency Project, The. 2012. "Press Gaggle by Press Secretary Jay Carney." June 29. Accessed July 14, 2016. http://www.presidency.ucsb.edu/ws/index.php?pid=101084.

Bennett, W. Lance. 2005. *News: The Politics of Illusion*, 6th edition. New York: Pearson Longman.

Black Jr., Charles L. 1960. *The People and the Court*. New York: Macmillan.

Bruce, Mary. 2012. "White House Sticks to Individual Mandate as 'Penalty,' Not Tax." *ABC News*, June 29. Accessed July 14, 2016. http://abcnews.go.com/blogs/politics/2012/06/white-house-sticks-to-individual-mandate-as-penalty-not-tax/.

Campbell, Andrea Louise and Nathaniel Persily. 2013. "The Health Care Case in the Public Mind: Opinion on the Supreme Court and Health Reform in a Polarized Era." In *The Health Care Case: The Supreme Court's Decision and Its Implications*, eds Nathaniel Persily, Gillian E. Metzger, and Trevor W. Morrison, 245–273. New York: Oxford University Press.

Casillas, Christopher J., Peter K. Enns, Patrick C. Wohlfarth. 2010. "How Public Opinion Constrains the U.S. Supreme Court." *American Journal of Political Science* 55 (1): 74–88.

Congressional Record. 2009. Proceedings and Debates of the 111th Congress, First Session, Vol. 155, Tuesday, December 22. No. 198, S13721.

Dahl, Robert. 1957. "Decision-making in a Democracy: The Supreme Court as a National Policy-Maker." *Journal of Public Law* 6: 279–295.

Davis, Richard. 2011. *Justices and Journalists: The U.S. Supreme Court and the Media*. New York: Cambridge University Press.

DiJulio, Bianca, Jamie Firth, and Mollyann Brodie. 2014. "Kaiser Health Policy Tracking Poll: December 2014." *Kaiser Family Foundation*, December 18. Accessed July 14, 2016. http://kff.org/health-reform/poll-finding/kaiser-health-policy-tracking-poll-december-2014/.

Dost, Meredith. 2015. "Dim public awareness of Supreme Court as major rulings loom." *Pre Research Center*, May 14. Accessed July 14, 2016. http://www.pewresearch.org/fact-tank/2015/05/14/dim-public-awareness-of-supreme-court-as-major-rulings-loom/.

Edelman, Murray. 1985. *The Symbolic Uses of Politics*. Chicago: University of Illinois Press.

Entman, Robert M. 2004. *Projections of Power: Framing News, Public Opinion, and U.S. Foreign Policy*. Chicago: University of Chicago Press.

Families USA. 2009. "Hidden Health Tax: Americans Pay a Premium." May. Accessed July 14, 2016. http://familiesusa.org/product/hidden-health-tax-americans-pay-premium.

Fried, Charles. 2013. "The June Surprises: Balls, Strikes, and the Fog of War." In *The Health Care Case: The Supreme Court's Decision and Its Implications*, eds, Nathaniel Persily, Gillian E. Metzger, and Trevor W. Morrison, 51–68. New York: Oxford University Press.

Hicks, Josh. 2012. "Middle-class tax hikes or tax breaks: Which is greater under 'ObamaCare'?" *Washington Post*, July 6. Accessed July 14, 2016. https://www.washingtonpost.com/blogs/fact-checker/post/obamacare-tax-hikes-vs-tax-breaks-which-is-greater/2012/07/06/gJQAx6AyPW_blog.html.

Jacobson, Gary C. 2011. "Legislative Success and Political Failure: The Public's Reaction to Barack Obama's Early Presidency." *Presidential Studies Quarterly* 41: 220–243.

Jamieson, Kathleen Hall and Joseph Cappella. 1998. *"The Role of the Press in the Health Care Reform Debate of 1993–1994."* In *The Politics of News, the News of Politics*, eds, Doris Graber, Denis McQuall, and Pippa Norris, 110–131. Washington: CQ Press.

Jamieson, Kathleen Hall and Paul Waldman. 2004. *The Press Effect: Politicians, Journalists and the Stories that Shape the Political World*. New York: Oxford University Press.

Jones, Jeffrey M. 2013. "In U.S., 43% of Uninsured Unaware They Must Get Coverage." *Gallup*, June 28. Accessed July 14, 2016. http://www.gallup.com/poll/163280/uninsured- unaware-coverage.aspx.

Kaiser Health Tracking Poll. 2013. March 20. Accessed July 14, 2016. http://kff.org/health-reform/poll-finding/march-2013-tracking-poll/.

Kliff, Sarah. 2015. "Obamacare supporters don't like talking about it—but the individual mandate is working." *Vox*, December 29. Accessed July 14, 2016. http://www.vox.com/2015/12/29/10678384/individual-mandate-obamacare-enrollment.

Marshall, Thomas R. 1989. *Public Opinion and the Supreme Court*. Boston: Unwin Hyman.

Marshall, Thomas R. 2008. *Public Opinion and the Rehnquist Court*. Albany: State University of New York Press.

Metzger, Gillian E. and Trevor W. Morrison. 2013. "The Presumption of Constitutionality and the Individual Mandate." In *The Health Care Case: The Supreme Court's Decision and Its Implications*, eds, Nathaniel Persily, Gillian E. Metzger, and Trevor W. Morrison, 124–145. New York: Oxford University Press.

New York Times. 2010. "Room for Debate: Is the Health Care Law Unconstitutional?" March 28. Accessed July 14, 2016. http://roomfordebate.blogs.nytimes.com/2010/03/28/is-the- health-care-law-unconstitutional/.

O'Brien, David M. 1986. *Storm Center: The Supreme Court in American Politics*. New York: W.W. Norton.

Patterson, Thomas. 1994. *Out of Order*. New York: Vintage Books.

PBS News Hour. 2012. "News Outlets Don't All Get Ruling Right." June 28. Accessed June 14, 2016. http://www.pbs.org/newshour/rundown/news-outlets-dont-all-get-ruling-right/.

Peters, Jeremy W. 2012. "Romney Now Says Health Mandate By Obama is a Tax." *New York Times*, July 4. Accessed July 14, 2016. http://www.nytimes.com/2012/07/05/us/politics/romney-says-health-care-mandate-is-a- tax.html.

Rosenberg, Gerald. 2008. *The Hollow Hope: Can Courts Bring About Social Change?* Chicago: University of Chicago Press.

Roy, Avik. 2011. "How the Heritage Foundation, a Conservative Think Tank, Promoted the Individual Mandate." *Forbes*, October 20. Accessed July 14, 2016. http://www.forbes.com/sites/theapothecary/2011/10/20/how-a-conservative-think-tank- invented-the-individual-mandate/.

Shear, Michael D. 2012. "Romney Campaign and G.O.P. at Odds On Health Care 'Tax.'" *New York Times*, July 2. Accessed July 14, 2016. http://www.nytimes.com/2012/07/03/us/politics/romney-campaign-at-odds-with-gop-on- health-care-tax.html?_r=0.

Sill, Kaitlyn L., Emily T. Metzgar, and Stella M. Rouse. 2013. "Media Coverage of the U.S. Supreme Court: How Do Journalists Assess the Importance of Court Decisions?" *Political Communication* 30: 58–80.

Stuckey, Mary E. 1997. *Strategic Failures in the Modern Presidency*. New Jersey: Hampton Press.

Thompson, Dennis. 2016. "6 Years Later, Obamacare Still Divides America: Poll." *The Harris Poll*, May 5. Accessed July 14, 2016. http://www.theharrispoll.com/politics/Obamacare- Still-Divides-America.html.

Viebeck, Elise. 2013. "Poll: 12 percent back individual mandate taking effect in 2014." *The Hill*, July 9. Accessed July 14, 2016. http://thehill.com/policy/healthcare/309847-survey-four- in-10-want-individual-mandate-delayed.

Wall Street Journal. 2009. "Who Pays for Cap and Trade?" March 9.

Weiner, Robert N. 2013. "Much Ado: The Potential Impact of the Supreme Court Decision Upholding the Affordable Care Act." In *The Health Care Case: The Supreme Court's Decision and Its Implications*, eds, Nathaniel Persily, Gillian E. Metzger, and Trevor W. Morrison, 69–90. New York: Oxford University Press.

White House, The. 2009. "Word from the White House: Common Ground on Health Insurance Reform & the Real Health Care Tax." September 29. Accessed July 14, 2016. https://www.whitehouse.gov/blog/2009/09/29/word-white-house-common-ground-health-insurance-reform-real-health-care-tax.

White House, The. 2012. "Remarks by the President on Supreme Court Ruling on the Affordable Care Act." June 28. Accessed July 14, 2016. https://www.whitehouse.gov/the-press-office/2012/06/28/remarks-president-supreme-court-ruling-affordable-care-act.

4

BUMPY ROLLOUT, FAULTY FRAMING

HealthCare.gov's Debut

In mid-March of 2014, the website *Funny or Die* released a new episode of "Between Two Ferns with Zach Galifianakis," a satirical talk show web series that features the comedian of the title interviewing some surprisingly famous guests. This particular edition was no exception, as the person between those aforementioned two ferns was the sitting President of the United States. Although presidents and presidential candidates have long used entertainment programming to show a more human side to audiences who might not pay close attention to politics and news, Obama arguably took greater advantage than most of this format in all of its 21st century incarnations.[1] Such unprecedented appearances opened the president up to the criticism of some that it was beneath the dignity of the office to appear on a show like *Between Two Ferns,* perhaps best known for moments like Galkfianakis asking the singer Justin Beiber, "You've had three hairstyles. What's next for your career?" But as part of the Administration's publicity drive to get people to sign up for health insurance, especially younger, healthy Americans who might be opting to go without, President Obama and his team made a concerted effort to use communications channels like this one, already quite popular with those demographics.

Halfway through the webisode, with the president gamely playing along with the show's running joke of guests expressing general hostility to their interviewer, Galifianakis sighed in exasperation and asked, "Here we go, okay, let's get this out of the way, what did you come here to plug?" President Obama replied, "Well, first of all, I think it's fair to say that I wouldn't be with you here today if I didn't have something to plug. Have you heard of the Affordable Care Act?" Scratching his head, Galifianakis answered, "Oh yeah, I heard about that, that's the thing that doesn't work. Why would you get the guy that created the Zune to make your website?" "HealthCare.gov works great now," the president continued, "and millions of Americans have already gotten health insurance plans, and what we want is for people to know that you can get affordable health care. And most young Americans, right now they're not covered and the truth is they can get coverage all for what it costs to pay your cell phone bill." As the president made his pitch, Galifianakis checked his watch and wondered aloud, "Is this what they mean by drones?"[2]

How many young people successfully signed up for coverage because of the video is hard to say, but we do know that in the hours after it was posted, it became the number one driver of web traffic to HealthCare.gov (Daunt 2014). It was a huge hit on the web—as of this writing, it has over 34 million views on *Funny or Die* and more than 14 million on YouTube. And yet in this attention-grabbing appearance over six months after the launch of HealthCare.gov as the president worked to build awareness of the ACA, he was still confronted with a comedian mocking the inauspicious start for the website, including conflating the Affordable Care Act itself with something "that doesn't work."[3] The website's problems remained a very funny punchline for the show's deadpan host, perhaps made even more amusing by the fact the joke was made at the expense of the leader of the free world, right in front of him.

The rocky October 2013 debut of HealthCare.gov, the official Federal Government website setting up the health insurance markets vital to getting the ACA up and running,[4] did not, then, fade from public dialogue surrounding health-care reform, even long after many of its most dire technical problems had been ironed out. Further, the website's difficulties were still being discussed in ways the president would not prefer. From the start of this book, we have explored presidential framing resilience and the communications advantages the president enjoys, even in the kind of fragmented media landscape that requires the president appear on *Between Two Ferns* to reach certain segments of the population with his messages. In this chapter, we go back to the website's initial launch to investigate what led to such a lasting and damaging storyline around the ACA for the president. How did the Obama team frame HealthCare.gov's undeniable deficiencies in those early days, and what happened to those frames in the news?

Naturally, the president's opponents were eager participants in discussing the website's rollout. A major framing contest between the Administration and its critics emerged over this tumultuous period as the online exchanges to allow Americans to shop around for insurance options struggled to open for business. In its highly publicized launch, did HealthCare.gov exhibit some minor technical glitches due to overwhelming public demand for access to the website's health-care marketplace? Or were the website's initial problems part and parcel of a dangerously flawed underlying policy and a disastrous level of executive mismanagement of government, akin to the Bush Administration's infamous response to Hurricane Katrina? One way frames can define an issue is by promoting a particular interpretation of what the problem is, identifying who is at fault, and pointing to what solution is needed (Entman 2004; Lakoff 2004). In the first telling here, promoted by the president and his surrogates, the problems merely reflect the need for and popularity of the president's health-care policy, the only villain the failings of technology, and the ideal solution to plow ahead and fix the "glitches." In the second, championed by prominent Republican politicians, the framing suggests the trouble primarily rests with President Obama and his team, for a botched rollout of a health-care program ill-advised in the first place. The incompetence and misrepresentation suggested by this take on the Administration's actions presented a challenge to the legitimacy of the law and the credibility of the president himself. The solutions that follow logically from framing the website problems as such would be a repeal of the policy and a sharp political rebuke of the White House.

I find that, at first, the Obama Administration's framing of HealthCare.gov's struggles dominated media coverage across numerous outlets. Even in this difficult moment when an important, costly, and very public feature of the ACA's implementation appeared defective, we can detect presidential framing resilience and the president's ability to powerfully shape interpretations of events in the news. At the same time, this case lays bare the ways that presidential framing advantages are *conditional*, and can be frittered away depending on the strength of the Administration's communications choices. The White House's framing of HealthCare.gov's issues quickly proved flawed and insufficient, allowing the president's opponents to effectively frame the website problems as indicative of everything that was wrong with both the president himself and his health-care reform policy. Far more damaging media coverage for the Administration ensued, even in a relatively short time period.

Minimizing HealthCare.gov's difficulties as "just glitches" and later, spreading the view the president did not know how far the problems extended, also resulted in presidential frame refraction, or the diversion of those frames from their original path as they evolve over time in the news. The Administration's frames created a perception of Obama as detached and uninvolved in his signature domestic policy that might have served to make the president appear less responsible for the website's problems in the moment, but unintentionally helped to bolster a subsequent media narrative, encouraged by his critics, of the president as perilously out of touch. The president going before the public and framing the website problems in a way that would ultimately prove so unpersuasive, on an issue presumably of the utmost importance to him and his presidency, raised serious questions about his leadership, and not just among his harshest critics. We can identify how flawed initial presidential frames developed in harmful new directions for Obama over the weeks that followed, perhaps best exemplified by the Hurricane Katrina comparison that emerged in mainstream news sources.

Below, I outline the frames proffered by the White House and its detractors as the health-exchange website irrefutably failed to operate as it should have. I then turn to a sample of mainstream media coverage to see how these frames translated, or failed to translate, into the news.

Website Launches, Government Shuts Down

When HealthCare.gov opened for business on October 1, 2013, users immediately experienced significant problems. Many were unable to log in or register for the site, which crashed repeatedly or required excessively long wait times. On the provider end, insurance companies found the portal gave them incorrect information about some potential customers, and repeated or cancelled the enrollments of others. Few Americans were able to use the website to successfully shop for and purchase health insurance, which would now be required by law starting in 2014.[5] It was later revealed a mere six people were able to successfully sign up for coverage on HealthCare.gov that first day (Goldstein 2016). These complications, coming so soon after the launch and with great attention fixed on the ACA—over three years in the making at this point—finally being put into effect, were highly consequential for the perceived legitimacy of healthcare reform. Chapter 3 referenced one such offshoot, as the difficulty of insurance shopping online sparked a discussion about whether Americans should still be required to comply with the individual mandate, ultimately leading to the deadline being pushed back.

As President Obama and his advisers dealt with the HealthCare.gov fallout, they were greatly aided by another, though not entirely unrelated, set of events. On the exact same day of the website's launch, the Federal Government shut down as a result of an impasse over defunding and delaying the ACA's provisions, which a group of conservatives in Congress tied to continuing to fund the government as a whole. The shutdown proved extremely unpopular with the public, and particularly damaging for Republicans, who polls showed most Americans blamed (Balz and Clement 2013). On the one hand then, the news media undoubtedly accorded less attention to the website problems than they might have without the bigger, more sensational story of the first Federal Government shutdown in many years. On the other hand, HealthCare.gov's shortcomings meant the White House was not able to fully capitalize on the president's position of political advantage in the shutdown, and a fair amount of the time period's news content was still portraying the Administration and its actions negatively.

Spreading the President's Frames, with Some Revisions over Time

Just "Glitches"

In discussing the faulty launch of HealthCare.gov, the president and his surrogates made use of three central frames to limit the harm the situation might cause for the Administration and the policy's standing: in the first of these, they characterized the issues as minor technical problems and made liberal use of the term "glitches," commonly associated with problems that are predictable and temporary. In a statement on October 1, Obama noted, "Like every new law, every new product rollout, there are going to be some glitches in the sign-up process along the way that we will fix" (White House 2013c). The White House had set the stage for this glitches frame even before the website officially launched—President Obama told a crowd days before the exchanges came online:

> Like any law, like any big product launch, there are going to be some glitches as this thing unfolds . . . somewhere around the country, there's going to be a computer glitch and the website's not working quite the way it's supposed to, or something happens where there's some error made somewhere—that will happen. That happens whenever you roll out a new program. And I guarantee you, the opponents of the law, they'll have their cameras ready to document anything that doesn't go completely right, and they'll send it to the news folks and they'll say, look at this, this thing is not working. But most of the stories you'll hear about how Obamacare just can't work is just not based on facts. Every time they have predicted something not working, it's worked.
>
> *(White House 2013b)*

White House Press Secretary Jay Carney echoed this during his October 1 press briefing, saying, "I can't guarantee that there aren't glitches that are just technical in nature. And I'm sure there are, as we said there would be, as with any large-scale rollout of a policy like this" (White House 2013a). The Administration thus sought to cast the problems as normal and minor, as opposed to more fundamental issues resulting from poor planning. The president and his surrogates predicted and prepared everyone for the "glitches" ahead of time, emphasizing their own transparency and setting expectations for a launch with what they depicted as unavoidable hiccups.

Overwhelming Demand for Health Care Reform

The second frame employed by the Obama Administration was reading the website problems as a *positive* development with regard to the ACA, by claiming the site's issues were caused by exceptionally high traffic and demand. On Day 1, the president acknowledged the site was operating slowly and asserted, "the reason is because more than one million people visited HealthCare.gov before 7:00 in the morning. To put that in context, there were five times more users in the marketplace this morning than have ever been on Medicare.gov at one time. That gives you a sense of how important this is to millions of Americans around the country, and that's a good thing" (White House 2013c). Secretary of Health and Human Services Kathleen Sebelius appeared on CNN relating, "The volume related issues are ones that we welcome . . . it shows how many people are eager to get real information" (*CNN Newsroom*, October 1, 2013). In his press briefing that first day, Carney used a baseball analogy to liken the demand to:

> people trying to get tickets to the first Pirates home playoff game . . . I mean, you know when you go on the site and it's hard to load the page that it's because a lot of people like you want to find out if tickets are available, and the great news about this is it's not one game, it's not one night; the seats are unlimited and the availability will be there for every American family that wants affordable health insurance.
>
> *(White House 2013a)*

President Obama associated the interest in the health-care exchanges with the excitement surrounding a new Apple product's launch: "Consider that just a couple of weeks ago, Apple rolled out a new mobile operating system, and within days, they found a glitch, so they fixed it. I don't remember anybody suggesting Apple should stop selling iPhones or iPads or threatening to shut down the company if they didn't."[6] The president had also made this private sector product comparison before the exchanges came online, at a rally the week prior: "It's a website where you can compare and purchase affordable health insurance plans, side by side, the same way you shop for a plane ticket on Kayak—same way you shop for a TV on Amazon." The president went on to add, "If you've ever tried to buy insurance on your own, I promise you this is a lot easier. It's like booking a hotel or a plane ticket" (The White House 2013b). A week into the website's launch, Sebelius continued to make the online shopping experience analogy on *The Daily Show*, reporting to Jon Stewart, "I can tell you we've had not only lots of web hits, hundreds of thousands of accounts created . . . this is like a Kayak site, where you might check out what plane you want to get on."[7]

Some in the White House ignored the website problems altogether and stressed demand for the program by focusing attention on those who had successfully enrolled: Obama adviser Dan Pfeiffer tweeted to his followers, "Every person who signed up for health care today is someone the GOP must take health insurance away from to achieve their ultimate goal."[8] Casting the Administration's Republican foes as obstructionist and with mixed-up priorities was a popular motif in White House social media communications. On October 3, Organizing for Action's Twitter account @BarackObama tweeted, "Day three of the #BoehnerShutdown. Day three of the new @Obamacare marketplace providing health insurance options to millions." The Administration was able to reach its supporters directly—that particular message was retweeted over 1,300 times and "liked" by hundreds of people—and completely gloss over the difficulties of HealthCare.gov that were all over the news.

Assuring a Quick Remedy

Finally, applying a third frame to these events, the White House constructed the impression it was actively working to address the problems, and that they would soon be fixed. Like many politicians accused of doing something wrong, the president attacked his critics subtly and promised corrective action (Blaney and Benoit 2001; Busby 2001; Farnsworth and Lichter 2006). Following his contention that glitches in Apple products did not lead to calls for them to be taken off the market, President Obama argued this was because, "That's not how we do things in America. We don't actively root for failure. We get to work, we make things happen, we make them better, we keep going." He thus placed the creation and impending improvement of the website within a patriotic narrative of American ingenuity, optimism, and evolution, and suggested critics were unAmerican by contrast. Obama assured his audience the problems would be remedied, and that the Administration would "be speeding things up in the next few hours to handle all of this demand that exceeds anything that we had expected." This preliminary framing of the Obama Administration hard at work to address the "glitches" would later develop into the president's declaration of a "tech surge" to make HealthCare.gov fully functional.

The Republican Framing of HealthCare.gov

A poorly working government website does not in and of itself produce a major political crisis for the executive branch.[9] The presidential opponents side worked to elevate the problems as worthy of considerable controversy and warranting further investigation. As Robert Entman (2012) tells us, political scandals that can bedevil an Administration are often less about the actual circumstances surrounding a president's actions and more about the relative skill and effectiveness of political actors at promoting or deflecting the view that the events amount to malfeasance that warrants attention and scrutiny. One high-profile way Republican leaders sought to promote this view was by using their congressional oversight powers to open investigative hearings and force Administration officials to answer embarrassing, pointed questions about their mistakes in a bright, public spotlight (Haberkorn and Millman 2013; Kennedy and Camia 2013). Sometimes the party had to do little to shame presidential surrogates—even as Secretary Sebelius took her turn testifying before the House, some news outlets broadcast a split screen of HealthCare.gov showing the website was down once again (LoGiurato 2013). Congressional hearings were also a useful tool to generate further news about the website, providing journalists with new developments, fresh quotes, and novel video clips about the ongoing controversy to cover. Republicans in Congress gave the hearings titles such as "PPACA Implementation Failures: Didn't Know or Didn't Disclose," implying the problems could be attributable to either the Administration's negligence or its dishonesty, neither explanation good for the president (Ornstein 2013).

The president's opponents framed the problems with the website, from Day 1, as directly connected to flaws in the health-care policy itself. The Republican National Committee's website announced on October 1 that "Obamacare" was "not ready for primetime" and thus "Americans deserve to delay this trainwreck" (RNC Communications Blog 2013). Representative Tim Huelskamp (R-KS) tweeted a screenshot of error messages on the website with the caption "Obama on Mon. said, 'The ACA is moving forward . . . You can't shut it down.' Mr. President, you can't even get it started."[10] Over time, Republicans remained consistent in pushing this framing. Representative Fred Upton (R-MI) declared during congressional hearings, "This is more than a website problem, and, frankly, the website should have been the easy part. I'm also concerned about what happens next. Will enrollment glitches become provider payment glitches? Will patients show up at their doctor's office or hospital to be told that maybe they aren't covered or even in the system?" (Energy and Commerce Committee 2013a). Senator Marco Rubio (R-FL) introduced the "Delay Until Fully Functional Act," proposing to tie the onset of the individual mandate to the website working properly. Rubio's press release about the bill asserted that though what he really wanted was to repeal and replace the ACA, "until that becomes possible we must continue to focus on protecting Americans from the law's ongoing problems" (Rubio 2013).

The presidential frame that HealthCare.gov's problems were minor and easily fixable was immediately challenged by Republican politicians. "The president calls these glitches, a nice poll-tested, fairly benign-sounding word," Senator John Cornyn (R-TX) was quoted as saying in the first few days of the website controversy, "but these were systemic failures of the Obamacare exchanges—obviously, not ready for prime time" (Pear 2013). In the congressional hearings launched by Republicans, Representative Gregg Harper (R-MS) asked Henry Chao, an IT officer with the Centers for Medicare and Medicaid Services (CMS) and a key figure in the website's rollout, "Do you think *glitches* is the proper word to use to describe the rollout?" Chao responded, "I think there are problems. There are defects if you—you know, glitches is just a word that is commonly used right now." "Well, glitches doesn't seem to convey how serious the failure of the rollout has been, and so here we are," Harper retorted (Energy and Commerce Committee 2013c). The National Republican Congressional Committee's website sought to crowdsource the extent of the problems, to help add to their account of the "8 Obamacare Horror Stories about the Longest Wait Times for HealthCare.gov" urging people that "if you've had a difficult time logging onto Obamacare . . . share your story with us here, and we may add it in" (National Republican Congressional Committee 2013).

Obama's critics also seized on his comparisons of the website to tech products unveiled by the private sector. Representative Steve Scalise (R-LA) was on CNN arguing, "The president likes talking about Apple and Kayak and other websites that actually do work. This is a system that, you know, you go buy an iPad, even if it had a glitch, it still works. This is not a glitch. This is a national embarrassment" (*The Lead with Jake Tapper*, 22 October 2013). Rand Paul wrote an opinion piece for CNN.com recounting about HealthCare.gov, "Obama said that it was just like when Apple unveils a new product—there are bound to be glitches. I don't recall ever being forced by the government to buy Apple products. I don't recall Apple ever being tone deaf to the complaints of their customers either" (Paul 2013).

Recognizing that the website was unlikely to remain so dysfunctional indefinitely, Republicans soon shifted to emphasizing that while the executive branch could eventually fix HealthCare.gov, the policy flaws lingered on. Representative Todd Christopher Young (R-IN) noted during congressional hearings, "While the website can eventually be fixed, the widespread problems with Obamacare cannot" (House of Representatives Committee 2013). Representative Cathy McMorris-Rogers (R-WA) told Secretary Sebelius who was testifying before her committee, "I would just impress upon you, this is more than a broken website. This is a broken law" (Energy and Commerce Committee 2013a). While President Obama was trying to impart to Americans, "The Affordable Care Act is not just a website" (Dann 2013), his Republican opponents were calling their oversight hearings, "Obamacare Implementation Problems: More than Just a Broken Website."

Several Republican congressional members sought to extend a flawed HealthCare.gov's repercussions even further out, as not only bad health-care policy, but also a dangerous risk for Americans' privacy and cybersecurity. As Representative Tim Murphy (R-PA) articulated in his opening statement for a congressional inquiry into this concern, "Today's hearing is not just about the website. Websites can be fixed. What cannot be fixed is the damage that could be done to the American people if their personal data is compromised." Mocking the president's public pledge about health-care reform that is the subject of Chapter 5, Murphy told his audience, "Right now, HealthCare.gov screams to those who are trying to break into the system, if you like my health-care info, maybe you can steal it" (Energy and Commerce Committee 2013c).

Republicans also rebuked the Obama Administration for not requiring that navigators, individuals hired to help sign people up on the exchanges (made far more important by the website's shortcomings), were not required to go through a background check or fingerprinting (U.S. House of Representatives Committee 2013). White House officials and Democratic representatives sought to quell such concerns by maintaining people's personal medical information was not stored on HealthCare.gov, and that health-care opponents were just trying to scare Americans away from signing up. In the years since, however, the security of the site has been a continuing subject of investigation and controversy (U.S. Government Accountability Office 2016).

Presidential Frames Prove Lacking

In appearances in the news media, at public events, and via social media channels, the president and those who worked for him had endeavored to publicize their side of the framing contest, making HealthCare.gov's failings seem as minimal as possible, and even attributing them to perceived positive attributes of health-care reform. But the frames they had crafted proved unable to evolve credibly over time, as events continued to unfold, impairing the president's long-term framing advantages. Several initial presidential frames quickly lost their luster. Depicting the demand for affordable health care as responsible for the website's woes was undercut by the Administration's inability or refusal to make public how many individuals had signed up for insurance in those early days (Frates 2013). The president's aforementioned October 1 assertion that his team would be "speeding things up in next few hours" had indicated they had the capacity to remedy the issues almost immediately, which of course they did not. The more time that went by without a resolution, the greater the opportunity for Republicans to find new venues like congressional hearings to promote their side of the contest.

Cracks also began to appear in the "glitches" frame. As weeks passed and the website still failed to work properly, the minimization of HealthCare.gov's difficulties began to appear disingenuous and detached from reality. David Simas, a White House senior communications adviser, told CNN's Jake Tapper in an October 21 interview, "I think that the 8.6 million unique visitors in the first three days exceeded anybody's expectations and that level of volume triggered the initial problem with the HealthCare.gov website." By this point, that interpretation of events was not going over well with reporters. An indignant Tapper responded, "David, you're not still saying that it's just a volume question, right? I mean there are lots of individuals saying there are serious software issues, that the beta testing didn't happen, that there wasn't enough time to practice before the website launched . . . You're not actually still saying it's just a question of volume?" Simas drew Tapper's attention to the fact he had said *initial* problems with the site (*The Lead with Jake Tapper*, 21 October 2013).

But even two days after that exchange, the White House uploaded an official video to YouTube entitled "Get Covered," featuring ordinary Americans testifying as to how they were able to sort through what they depicted as trivial issues with the website to get access to affordable, comprehensive health coverage.[11] The video's message that HealthCare.gov's tech problems were no big deal met derision in the news (*CNN Politics* 2013). Some tech experts in the media and on the web were conducting their own independent investigation of the problems that revealed the website was built on faulty software and shaky programming foundations that went far beyond mere "glitches" (Auerbach 2013b; Weaver et al. 2013).

The limitations of the Obama team's frames became obvious as the president and his surrogates were eventually forced to contradict aspects of their preliminary portrayal of events. Secretary Sebelius on CNN on October 23 admitted about the website, "volume caused some problems but it also exposed some additional problems" (Botelho and Yan 2013). In a mid-November press conference, President Obama told reporters, "Buying health insurance is never going to be like buying a song on iTunes. You know, it's just a much more complicated transaction" (*Washington Post* 2013), precisely the opposite impression from what he had sought to convey about the ease of shopping for coverage just a short time earlier. Finally, a month into HealthCare.gov's uncertain start, there was a flurry of apologies and Administration officials accepting responsibility for what had occurred. Testifying before the House of Representatives, both Secretary Sebelius and Marilyn Tavenner, head of CMS, said they were sorry for HealthCare.gov's shortcomings (Pickert 2013). Vice President Joe Biden also apologized, calling the persistent issues "inexcusable" (McCalmont 2013). President Obama, meanwhile, publically acknowledged the Administration "had fumbled the rollout on this health care law" (Sink 2013), and when asked about the performance of those under him stressed that "ultimately, the buck stops with me" (Dennis 2013).

Impact of Presidential Framing Strategy on Fellow Democrats

The resiliency of presidential frames is, in part, dependent on their strength in providing political cover to the president's natural allies so that they will echo and spread them in the press. In Chapter 2, we looked at how the Administration's embrace of the term "Obamacare" was followed by Democrats and supporters using the name in a positive way. To be sure, in the face of HealthCare.gov's hardships, most prominent Democrats continued to support the law and to stress the benefits of the ACA. But another clear indicator of the shortcomings of the White House's communications strategy was the ensuing actions of many Democrats that indicated they were not endorsing the president's framing of events wholeheartedly.

Many Democratic public officials chose not to downplay HealthCare.gov's problems, even as they criticized their Republican counterparts for being obsessed with overturning the health law. During the congressional hearings called by Republicans to investigate the rollout, several Democrats employed the slogan "fix it, not nix it." Perhaps seeking to avoid the perception dogging the president and his advisers that they were incompetent, dishonest, or some combination thereof, Democratic representatives publically expressed their disappointment with how HealthCare.gov had been handled. Representative Anna Eshoo (D-CA) pressed a testifying Secretary Sebelius repeatedly on whether she had full confidence in the new deadline the Administration had set for the site to be fully functional, reminding her, "HHS did testify in September that they were 100 percent confident that the site would be launched and fully functional on time on October 1. That didn't work" (Energy and Commerce Committee 2013b). Congressman Al Green (D-TX) also posed tough questions to Sebelius, telling her, "I share your and the President's disappointment the website is not working as planned. November 30 is not soon enough. Many of my constituents have been waiting years to be able to purchase health insurance, and we owe it to them to get the marketplaces up and running." In early November, the embattled secretary also faced "friendly fire" from Democratic senators who had been integral to getting the ACA passed into law, including Max Baucus of Montana and Bill Nelson of Florida (Somashekhar 2013).

When the contractors responsible for creating the online exchanges came before Congress, Representative Diana DeGette (D-CO) pointed out that before the launch, these same individuals "said there was nothing wrong, and they expressed nothing but optimism. And so three weeks later, here we are. We're still hearing reports of significant problems . . . I want to stress for the Affordable Care Act to work, these problems need to be fixed, and these problems need to be fixed fast" (Energy and Commerce Committee 2013a). Although Democrats in Congress often lambasted Republicans for acting as though the website issues were indicative of a flawed policy, many did not treat the hearings as a total charade and instead asked real questions of the witnesses before them. Representative Henry Waxman (D-CA) pronounced before his committee that the people they represented "want this law to work. But they do want us to make sure that we hold everybody accountable and insist that the law and the promise of affordable health care become a reality for all Americans, and that means we've got to get this website fixed" (Energy and Commerce Committee 2013a).

Presidential framing of the website woes divorced the problems from the underlying health-care policy, whereas opposition frames invited a direct connection between the two. When some Democrats began to back policy changes because of HealthCare.gov's lapses, they bolstered the opposition's framing. Some of these officials, but not all, represented more conservative districts or faced tough reelection fights on the horizon. Senator Joe Manchin III (D-WV) proposed a one-year delay of the individual mandate (Lesniewski 2013a). Ten Democratic senators signed on to a letter crafted by Senator Jeanne Shaheen (D-NH) urging the Administration to extend open enrollment for the insurance exchanges, and argued "individuals should not be penalized for lack of coverage if they are unable to purchase health insurance due to technical problems" (Lesniewski 2013b). Such proposals would not logically follow from the White House's interpretation of what was happening. As the media and the public expressed skepticism of presidential frames, vulnerable Democrats began to jump ship, further endangering those frames. As Jamieson and Cappella (1998) point out, the novelty of intraparty conflict can generate outsized news attention in media coverage.

News Media Norms and the HealthCare.gov Controversy

Another shortcoming of the president's frames was that some did not fit well with established norms of contemporary news coverage. Unfortunately for the president, the news story of a slow and hard-to-use website was easy for journalists to cover and for viewers/readers to understand. Many networks had their reporters at computers and broadcast them trying, in real time, to log on to HealthCare.gov website. This typically made for compelling television, filling the screen with error messages and running clocks in the corner indicating how long these efforts, usually to no avail, were taking. Thirty-five minutes into an MSNBC correspondent's failed attempt to access the exchanges via the website and then over a phone helpline, she ended her piece declaring, "At this point, I'm going to hang up and call it a day. If I were signing up for myself, this is where my patience would be exhausted."[12] None of this comported with the idea the problems were minor and easily fixable.

Reporting on the shortcomings of HealthCare.gov was a story with both familiar and unique elements, well-suited for constructing the kind of commercially viable news product believed to attract larger audiences (Hamilton 2004). Given high levels of disillusionment and cynicism about government in the U.S., it would be unsurprising to most that a Federal Government website would be poorly constructed, making the news story accessible to even citizens with low levels of political information. At the same time that, despite years to plan for the rollout, the Obama Administration would botch such a central and visible component of a policy so closely associated with the president that it was widely known as "Obamacare" lent surprise and drama to the coverage. There was another unexpected, attention-grabbing twist to the HealthCare.gov tale: a president known for tech-savvy unprecedented use of the Internet in campaigning for office could not put together a group with the ability to properly construct a website.[13]

News coverage of the president's role in all this might also be particularly damaging as it fed into a preexisting media characterization of Obama as aloof and disengaged. As Larry Sabato (2000, 168) warns, "A wise politician is always acutely aware of the press' subtext about him and wary of taking actions that confirm the undesirable elements of it." Ronald Reagan, for instance, a president with a reputation for a detached leadership style and delegation of responsibilities (Ellis 1994, 33–34), suffered a deluge of negative news and a drop in approval ratings in the Iran-Contra scandal when it was discovered his subordinates had sold arms to Iran and illegally diverted the money to the Contras in Nicaragua (Cohen 2008). While established perceptions of Reagan's approach to the presidency aided his claim he was in the dark about much of the misconduct, polls showed more Americans thought it was worse if he had no knowledge of these actions than if he had authorized them himself (Ellis 1994, 94). Unlike President Reagan, characterizations of Obama's leadership style fluctuated over his presidency. NBC's Chuck Todd asked the president in an interview as HealthCare.gov floundered, "You've discussed the website issue. But there seems to be this growing perception, some of it is the press reporting, some of it's your staff, that you're not always on top of some things. Or this idea that you didn't know certain things." Secretary Sebelius, for instance, had revealed in late October that the president was unaware of the extent of HealthCare.gov's weaknesses early on (Botelho and Yan 2013). In response, the president first focused on assuring Todd that there was no question about his level of involvement in all things national security, and then went on to add, "You know, I think that my previous reputation was that I was this policy wonk digging into stuff all the time. And was immersed in the details. I think that stereotype is probably a little more true than the latest one" (Todd 2013).

Aside from that minor correction though, Obama found that the inadequacy of the frames he and his team had applied to HealthCare.gov required he play into this portrayal of a disinterested president. Presidential frames ultimately lost so much credibility that the president faced a choice in explaining why he had repeated them so unequivocally: had he misled the public or did he just not know what was really going on? These were precisely the limited interpretations his Republican opponents had endorsed. In mid-November, Obama told reporters:

> I was not informed directly that the website would not be working the way it was supposed to. Had I been informed, I wouldn't be going out saying, boy, this is going to be great. I'm accused of a lot of things, but I don't think I'm stupid enough to go around saying, this is going to be like shopping on Amazon or Travelocity a week before the website opens if I thought that it wasn't going to work. So clearly, we and I did not have enough awareness about the problems in the website. Even a week into it, the thinking was that these were some glitches that would be fixed with patches, as opposed to some broader systemic problems that took much longer to fix and we're still working on them.
>
> *(Washington Post 2013)*

Emphasizing his lack of prior knowledge also meant President Obama could take symbolic responsibility for the HealthCare.gov rollout even while casting the problems as stemming primarily from the actions of those below him, much as Reagan did in Iran-Contra. For HealthCare.gov failing, Obama relayed, "I take responsibility for that; my team takes responsibility of that. And we are working every single day, 24/7, to improve it. And it's better now than it was last week. And it's certainly a lot better than it was on Oct. 1 . . . You know, Kathleen Sebelius doesn't write code; yeah, she wasn't our I.T. person . . . ultimately, the buck stops with me. You know, I'm the president. This is my team. If it's not working, it's my job to get it fixed" (Frumin 2013). When the president defended his HHS Secretary by noting that she "doesn't write code," certainly it was brought to mind that, as Vice President Biden had put it a few weeks earlier, "Neither [the president] and I are technology geeks" (McCalmont 2013). Obama was unlikely to be held directly responsible for IT work in the executive branch.

Feeding into the media's picture of him as "President Passerby" (Milbank 2013; Wagstaff 2013) limited Obama's personal culpability for health care's rollout. But it came at a cost, opening up the president to politically debilitating new storylines in the media such as the comparison to President Bush's mishandling of Hurricane Katrina's aftermath, as we will see in the next section. This narrative dovetailed neatly with the Republican opposition's framing of HealthCare.gov as symptomatic of failed presidential leadership and a disastrous overhaul of America's health-care system.

HealthCare.gov News Coverage: A Damaging Story Becomes More So over Time

I now turn to the content of a sample of nightly news broadcasts, major newspapers, cable news programming, and online news content to assess how successful the frames of the president and his opponents were at taking hold in the news. I analyzed transcripts and articles from *ABC Evening News*, *CBS Evening News*, *NBC Evening News*, *The New York Times*, *The New York Post*, CNN, Fox News, CNN.com, and washingtonpost.com during the first week of HealthCare.gov's insurance marketplace launch, from October 1–7, 2013. Both myself and an independent coder reviewed the news content for appearances of presidential frames and opposition frames at the paragraph level; the results are found in Figure 4.1 below. A more detailed discussion of the coding protocol used is available in Appendix A.4.

During that critical first week in October, with all eyes turned to the launch of HealthCare.gov's online exchanges, the first few days of coverage in these outlets were kindest to the White House's framing of the scandal. Though the president's opponents were actively framing HealthCare.gov's problems as an indicator of fundamental policy flaws from Day 1, meaning that counterframe was available to the media, presidential frames were still dominant. News outlets very early on sometimes depicted the president's frames as fact: a *CBS Evening News* report by Wyatt Andrews on October 1 began, "As millions of people flooded the system, the government website for Obamacare HealthCare.gov temporarily broke under the strain." We can recognize presidential framing resilience in this substantial presence of the president's frames on October 1 and 2 across different types of news formats, from print to television to web-based. At least initially then, mainstream media coverage of the website's less than stellar debut was not as damaging as it could have been.

However, the Obama Administration gradually lost this framing advantage as the week went on, evident in a look across the week at the bottom of Figure 4.1. The deficiencies of the president and his surrogates' depiction of events resulted in opposition frames becoming more prevalent in the coverage by October 7. Extensive quotes in the news from the president and his team gave way to those from prominent Republicans, such as the Speaker of the House John Boehner

		Date							
		Oct. 1	Oct. 2	Oct. 3	Oct. 4	Oct. 5	Oct. 6	Oct. 7	Total
Print News Outlets									
NYT	Presidential Frames	12	3	9	1	2	5	0	32
	Opposition Frames	9	6	4	3	0	1	0	23
NYP	Presidential Frames	2	2	0	0	0	0	0	4
	Opposition Frames	3	1	0	0	0	0	0	4
Online News Outlets									
WashPo.com	Presidential Frames	5	11	5	6	9	2	0	38
	Opposition Frames	4	1	5	2	10	0	0	22
CNN.com	Presidential Frames	0	13	1	0	0	0	1	15
	Opposition Frames	0	3	1	0	0	0	4	8
Cable News Outlets									
CNN	Presidential Frames	20	18	4	8	0	4	4	58
	Opposition Frames	1	3	3	8	1	4	6	26
Fox News	Presidential Frames	21	9	8	4	0	9	9	60
	Opposition Frames	16	7	5	4	0	14	24	70
Broadcast Network News Outlets									
ABC/CBS/NBC	Presidential Frames	16	14	0	0	2	8	0	40
	Opposition Frames	4	4	0	0	0	11	0	19

		Oct. 1	Oct. 2	Oct. 3	Oct. 4	Oct. 5	Oct. 6	Oct. 7	Total
TOTALS	Presidential Frames	76	70	27	19	13	28	14	247
	Opposition Frames	37	25	18	17	11	30	34	172
		67%	74%	60%	53%	54%	48%	29%	
		33%	26%	40%	47%	46%	52%	71%	

☐ Presidential Frames
■ Opposition Frames

FIGURE 4.1 Appearance of Presidential and Opposition Frames in News Outlets over Time

(R-OH) calling "the decision to take the exchange offline for the weekend proof that its launch had been 'an unmitigated disaster.' 'What the Administration wanted to dismiss as simple glitches have turned out to be a system-wide failure,' he said in a statement. 'This announcement is more proof we need to delay the law and provide basic fairness, just as Republicans have called for'" (Sun 2013). Journalists also began to increasingly question Administration officials' framing of the causes of the problems—on the October 6 version of *Meet the Press*, Samantha Guthrie asked Secretary of the Treasury Jack Lew, "The White House says 8.6 million unique visitors came to the Web site this week trying to get health care but it cannot give a number on how many actually enrolled. There are more than glitches going on with this web site . . . it's been partially down all weekend. How do you justify that?"

Hostile partisan media sources are likely to turn against presidential frames the most quickly. Fox News and *The New York Post*, associated with taking editorial stances often disparaging of the president and his party, included opposition frames from an early point as a counter to the White House's version of events. For instance, on the day the website launched, conservative commentator Steve Hayes of *The Weekly Standard* appeared on *Fox Special Report with Bret Baier* wondering whether the glitches were "harbingers of very difficult times to come where your glitch isn't getting on and finding out what plans are available and how much they cost, and you get a system error when you log on to a computer site, but your glitch is you want a liver transplant or need a liver transplant and you can't get it because there's a bureaucratic problem or a computer problem." But even in the Fox News coverage, presidential frames had more appearances than opposition frames up until October 4. They were more likely to appear alongside opponents' frames than in several of the other selected outlets, but the concept of presidential framing resiliency points to the importance of these frames' inclusion as helping to shape the conversation in the news around issues, although there might be challenges or inconsistencies in how they are presented. By the same token, *The New York Times* coverage did not shift toward privileging the opposition's frames over the course of the week, perhaps indicative of its more favorable stance toward the Administration or its partiality toward relying on official sources and their versions of events (Bennett 2005).

This provides us with some sense of how the framing contest over HealthCare.gov played out over that first week, as the president gradually lost ground to opponents. How far did this trend toward more damaging coverage for the Obama Administration exacerbated by faulty framing extend? I analyzed the same group of media outlets[14] from November 11–25, 2013, when the analogy with Hurricane Katrina emerged in public debate. I evaluated with the aid of an independent coder how damaging media coverage was for the president by identifying whether or not this comparison was presented as a legitimate one in the news.

"Obama's Katrina"

Hurricane Katrina was a massive natural disaster in 2005 that led to the deaths of over 1,800 people and caused billions of dollars in property damage. President Bush's response to the hurricane became emblematic of incompetence, indifference, and ill-preparedness in the executive branch (Farnsworth 2009). Photos were taken of Bush flying over New Orleans in Air Force One looking out the window at the damage without stopping on his way from vacationing in Texas back to Washington, and he later stood before cameras telling his Federal Emergency Management Agency Director Michael Brown he was doing a "heck of a job" managing the disaster, which was hard to square with realities on the ground. These moments, widely circulated in the media, became lasting testaments to the inadequacy of the Bush Administration's response.

As seen in Figure 4.2, a plurality of the times that Katrina was brought up in the analyzed outlets during this two-week span, it was portrayed as a legitimate comparison. Republicans' framing of the health-care rollout difficulties, linking it to Obama's leadership and the ACA generally, indirectly invited this allusion to a symbol of devastating presidential mismanagement. But news organizations were not merely echoing Republican talking points in relating the two events to each other. Instead, the comparison appeared largely media-generated.

Take for example Michael D. Shear's highly influential *New York Times* article from November 14, "Health Law Rollout's Stumbles Draw Parallels to Bush's Hurricane Response." Many of the appearances of the Katrina analogy in the other analyzed news outlets made reference to the *Times* associating the two events, demonstrating the newspaper's enduring agenda-setting power even into the 21st century. Shear's article, while eventually referring to Republicans "readily" making the Katrina comparison and Obama aides "vehemently" rejecting it, began with the journalist autonomously connecting the two scenarios. The piece's second sentence reads, "The disastrous rollout of [Obama's] health care law not only threatens the rest of his agenda but also raises questions about his competence in the same way that the Bush Administration's botched response to Hurricane Katrina undermined any semblance of Republican efficiency." In a case of presidential frame refraction, the initial minimization of the rollout's shortcomings and the subsequent revisions to those presidential frames took on new meaning as the *Times* used them to sustain this "Obama's Katrina" parallel. It was not merely that the president had unveiled a website that wasn't working correctly, but that going around the country assuring people mere glitches plagued the website revealed a level of obliviousness to the severity of the problem that warranted a Katrina analogy. Further, as discussion of this comparison spread throughout the rest of the news media, it was given greater credibility and attention because it could not be dismissed as merely partisan rhetoric, as in "Republican leaders claim this is Obama's Katrina." This is similar to the legitimacy Justice Roberts' ruling afforded to the individual mandate as a tax in Chapter 3. Here the analogy came from an unexpected source, a paper generally accused of being sympathetic to Obama.

Outlet	Legitimate Comparison	Comparison Rejected	Mixed or Neutral
ABC/NBC/CBS News	9	4	6
CNN	17	11	6
CNN.com	4	4	2
Fox News	8	8	3
New York Times	3	2	0
Washingtonpost.com	4	5	4
Washington Times	6	4	0
Total	51	38	21

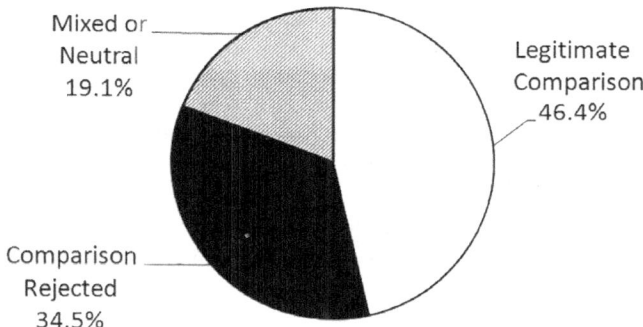

FIGURE 4.2 "Obama's Katrina" Analogy in the Analyzed Coverage, November 11–25, 2013

The president's frames were having a major impact on news narratives by this point, but far from the impact the White House would have preferred.

There were those Democratic supporters in the news media who emphatically rejected the analogy—strategist Paul Begala was on CNN on November 15 telling viewers, "The notion this is like Katrina, my pal and our colleague, Donna Brazile, she had family members who lost everything in Katrina. And she said that this is disgusting. Of course, it is, 1,833 people lost their lives in Katrina. This is bad, a political problem for the president. It's a technological problem. I do wish there had been more accountability here. I think HHS has screwed this up but you can't compare it to Hurricane Katrina." To be clear, many of the instances classified as legitimate comparisons in the news were not that the events of the website rollout and hurricane were the same, but that Obama's political circumstances mirrored Bush's at that time. For instance, on November 13, CNN's Wolf Blitzer posed the question, "If President Bush was remembered for the disastrous response to Hurricane Katrina, here's the question some are asking, including some Democrats: is this President Obama's political nightmare unfolding right now?" Still, arguably discussing a similarity in precipitous declines of political standing for the two presidents could imply that the catalyst for each was equally problematic. The fact that the analogy appeared over 100 times in just these analyzed outlets also shows the extent to which "Obama's Katrina" had become part of the public conversation about the Administration's handling of the website's defects, something we will also see in taking a brief look at social media in a moment. HealthCare.gov had become a story of systemic failure, and presidential frames were being reworked and advanced into politically damaging new directions not just by the opposition party, but by journalists.

A note about the cable news results—on a few occasions that the Katrina comparison was rejected, it was because news personalities were arguing the healthcare rollout was *worse* than Hurricane Katrina. For instance, on Fox News' *The Five* on November 15, co-host Greg Gutfeld brought up the Katrina analogy, but noted that there was a difference between these events, because "President Bush did not create Katrina." His colleague Eric Bolling agreed: "Right, right. One is a natural disaster. One is a self-inflicted mortal wound." Other pundits on CNN and Fox News rejected the notion that the two cases were comparable because Bush's mistakes were made in the midst of an unexpected crisis, while President Obama had years to plan for the law's rollout and had failed to do so sufficiently. Though there were only a handful of instances in which the Katrina analogy was rejected on cable news because the HealthCare.gov scandal was deemed "worse," those examples mean the coverage had an even more negative cast for the president than the quantitative evidence above might indicate.

The Twitterverse Reaction to "Obama's Katrina"

If "Obama's Katrina" was largely treated in the news as the logical outgrowth from the president's public stances on HealthCare.gov, how might this translate to social media as ordinary citizens evaluated that narrative? I searched Twitter for all tweets including "Obama" and "Katrina" on November 15, 2013. This date was selected because of its proximity to the aforementioned Shears article in the *Times*, which had generated a great deal more talk across the media about the persuasiveness of the analogy. Also, on the morning of November 15, George Stephanopoulos promoted that day's *Good Morning America* on ABC by tweeting "How can President Obama recover from his Katrina? GWB vet @matthewjdowd and I analyze today on @GMA."[15] My search yielded 854 tweets that involved the comparison, and 145 of them either mentioned or replied directly to this message from @GStephanopoulos.

While this sample does not tell us how the "Obama's Katrina" analogy fared generally on Twitter or in other social media forums, it does offer an indication of how the format offers citizens a chance to "talk back" to the news and critique media coverage. I applied the same method of analyzing the portrayals of "Obama's Katrina" here as in the news content above, with the unit of analysis as a single tweet.[16] Figure 4.3 shows the large majority of tweets that rejected this comparison. Users often did so angrily or sarcastically, driving home the point that no one had died because of a glitchy website. The news media itself became a frequent target

	Number of Tweets	%
Legitimate comparison	120	14
Comparison rejected	596	70
Mixed/neutral	138	16
Total	854	100

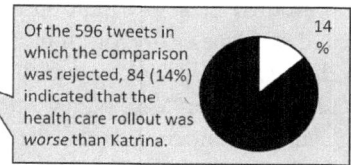

Of the 596 tweets in which the comparison was rejected, 84 (14%) indicated that the health care rollout was *worse* than Katrina.

FIGURE 4.3 Treatment of "Obama's Katrina" Analogy on Twitter, November 15, 2013

of derision—tweets declared the analogy offensive, racist because it trivialized the loss of black lives (several users asked why nothing was ever referred to as "Obama's 9/11"), evidence of the media's tendency toward hysteria and hyperbole, and irresponsible. Commenting on the news media from the outside, Twitter users argued that part of what made the analogy so absurd was how often the press seemed to apply it, referring to coverage that had given the Deepwater Horizon oil spill, swine flu, and Hurricane Sandy all the "Obama's Katrina" designation in the past.

The analogy transcended partisan politics in some ways; when David Gregory echoed the comparison on MSNBC that day, seemingly left-leaning Twitter users were vocal in their condemnation of the liberal news network. Furthermore, those rejecting "Obama's Katrina" on Twitter fell all along the ideological spectrum. As the callout in Figure 4.3 specifies, 84 of the 596 tweets deeming the comparison illegitimate claimed the Obama case was worse than Katrina. While this had been a feature of cable news in a very small number of instances, here such cases made up roughly 14% of the tweets rejecting the analogy. These messages fell along similar lines as the cable news commentary—that Katrina was a "natural disaster" but "Obamacare" was a "man-made disaster"—and that the analogy lacked merit because President Bush did not ask for nor had the ability to prevent Katrina, in contrast to Obama and health-care reform. Overall though in this very small sample, inferring from the "glitches" frame and its aftermath that the president had reached the "Katrina" point of his presidency was overwhelmingly rejected.

Public Opinion and the Framing Contest

The exposed weaknesses of the president's frames in the analyzed news coverage over time corresponds with damaging public perceptions of the president and his policies in this same period. A CBS News poll showed that only 12% of Americans thought the sign-up process was going well roughly three weeks following the website's launch (Dutton et al. 2013). Several surveys in November of 2013 showed that both the president's approval rating and support for the ACA declined as a result of the publicity surrounding HealthCare.gov's flaws. Sixty-three percent of the public expressed disapproval of President Obama's handling of the rollout (Balz and Craighill 2013).

The spread of opponents' frames as time dragged on were apparent in public opinion as well. An October 20 Washington Post-ABC News poll in which respondents were asked, "There have been problems with the website set up for uninsured people to sign up for health insurance. Do you think this is an isolated incident or do you think it's a sign of broader problems in implementing the health care law?" found that 56% agreed with the latter characterization (Washington Post-ABC News Poll 2013). Republican respondents were more likely than Democrats to associate the website issues with problems with the law itself. Problematically for the president, however, 55% of Independents also agreed with the "broader problems" response.

Polls also showed the political liabilities of the president emphasizing he had been in the dark about HealthCare.gov's flaws. A Fox News poll in mid-November of 2013 found that 45% of the public felt Obama was "good at taking personal responsibility for his statements and actions," whereas 51% believed he spent "too much time blaming others" (Fox News Poll 2013). The same survey asked respondents to gauge the president's level of awareness of the website and other controversies like IRS targeting of conservative groups and spying on foreign leaders, and 47% agreed with the statement Obama knew about these issues and was ducking responsibility, while 27% believed he was unaware but should have known. Only 18% felt the president was unaware but that this was understandable. Broken down by party affiliation, a plurality of Democrats (36%) preferred the "unaware but should have been" response and a large majority of Republicans (71%) believed Obama had advance knowledge.

As Entman (2012) discusses, major controversies can produce new kinds of polling questions, and reporting the results can help propel a political problem for the president forward in the news. The accusations made by House Republicans in their investigative hearings led to such polling in some outlets, like Fox News. The network's survey, conducted scientifically, found large majorities of the public were not confident that the personal information that they provided on HealthCare.gov would be kept confidential and private (Fox News Poll 2013). Again, the responses were tempered by party, with a majority of Democrats expressing confidence, and a majority of Republicans expressing a lack thereof. Whether this reflects general distrust in government or a lack of faith in the Obama Administration's management of the website specifically is hard to say, but publicizing such results helped intensify the political crisis for the president.

Conclusion

The initial coverage of HealthCare.gov's launch across a variety of mainstream news outlets suggests that the president has substantial advantages for shaping news narratives, as the concept of presidential framing resilience seeks to capture, even on a tough topic with opponents simultaneously advocating a very different interpretation of events. But the fast pace of the 21st century news cycle meant the news turned far less welcoming for President Obama's depiction of the problems even just a few days after the website went public. Presidential framing resilience is conditional, and the Obama team's initial frames quickly proved wanting. The president and his surrogates created the impression the website problems were minimal and would be solved quickly, promises that became less believable with each passing day. The gap between reality and their framing became so glaring they were forced to backpedal from some of their preliminary readings of events. Presidential framing of HealthCare.gov's launch did not match up well with established ways news organizations report on politics. They also offered little political protection for Democratic politicians and weak incentives to endorse and echo them in the media. By the end of only the first week of HealthCare.gov's shaky beginning, opposition frames were more pronounced in the analyzed coverage.

Even as the vulnerabilities of the Administration's frames were exposed, that President Obama had conveyed them so forcefully and his explanations for why that was the case exacerbated harmful news coverage. Without his clear backing of the glitches, overwhelming demand, and fixing the problem frames, the media might not have lent such prominence and credibility to the "Obama's Katrina" analogy by mid-November. That initial association with the glitches frame helped create a significant political crisis for the president as time progressed, and polls bear out how damaging such assessments were for public support and credibility for Obama and the ACA.

This chapter provides a preliminary foray into exploring the ways health-care's rollout and political actors' communications strategies were covered in the news. There are other factors that might also be integral to understanding the president's position and news coverage of the ACA's implementation around this same time. Just as Americans were facing the challenge of shopping the online exchanges, several insurance companies were cancelling some existing plans for being insufficient under the new ACA requirements. Critics then accused the president of "lying" for promising people could keep their health insurance plans if they liked them under health-care reform, prompting an Administration defense of Obama and a framing contest that is the subject of Chapter 5.

Notes

1 For instance, President Obama made appearances while in office on entertainment programming as far ranging as tooling around in a 1963 Corvette with Jerry Seinfeld on his *Comedians in Cars Getting Coffee* web series, to journeying to Marc Maron's Los Angeles garage to record an interview for the comedian's podcast. Not only did Obama have more appearances on NBC's *The Tonight Show* than any previous president, he was also the first sitting president to ever appear on the program (Sneed 2013).
2 The entire appearance can be viewed here: https://www.youtube.com/watch?v=UnW3xkHxIEQ
3 Obama himself (with a little help from Kathleen Sebelius) mocked the website's problems at the 2014 White House Correspondents Dinner, but the jokes focused more on the technological difficulties than implying any flaws in the policy itself, which might be considered "safer" territory than the joke Galifanakis made.
4 The decision of a majority of states not to create their own exchanges and websites made the Federal website even more integral to implementing the ACA (Desilver 2013). Health exchange websites run by some of the other states, such as Kentucky and Connecticut, were working much better at this early point (Kliff 2013).
5 Numerous explanations have since been offered for why the website failed to work properly. Some have pointed to the deficiencies of the companies cobbled together to create the site and their interaction with executive branch officials (Auerbach 2013a;

Lipton et al. 2013). Others have faulted Obama's management style and background and the lack of private sector experience among his top advisers (Alter 2014). One early autopsy of what happened blamed the White House's plans being shaped by trying not to provide any opening for Republicans in Congress to obstruct and defund the implementation process (Goldstein and Eilperin 2013). An internal government inquiry found that the Centers for Medicare and Medicaid Services, in charge of setting up the online insurance marketplace, was plagued by a lack of leadership and underestimated the complexity of the task before it (Goldstein 2016).

6 Secretary Sebelius also made this comparison to Apple products as the website debuted, see: http://abcnews.go.com/blogs/politics/2013/09/even-with-threat-of-shutdown-health-care-exchanges-ready-to-go/.
7 The entire interview, for which Sebelius was widely criticized for her weak performance in the face of Stewart's questions and criticisms, can be seen here: http://www.cc.com/video-clips/73au8e/the-daily-show-with-jon-stewart-kathleen-sebelius-pt—1.
8 The original tweet can be found here: https://twitter.com/pfeiffer44/status/385167196604755968.
9 One piece of supporting evidence for this is that when the Medicare Part D prescription drug plan championed by the Bush Administration was rolled out in 2005, its website too experienced technical difficulties and took a great deal of time to function properly, but this did not become a significant political headache for the president. In 2013, Democrats used this example to argue that back in 2005, they partnered with Republicans to fix the problems, an approach they maintained was lacking in the opposition party in this case. Politifact rated the comparison between the two rollout problems to be an accurate one (Contorno 2013).
10 See the original tweet here: https://twitter.com/CongHuelskamp/status/384903064966004736
11 The video can be seen here: https://www.youtube.com/watch?feature=player_embedded&v=AL2pySEg5p8.
12 This example, promoted by the Republican Party, can be seen here: https://www.youtube.com/watch?feature=player_embedded&v=6wCwXew9yGg.
13 As the president himself pointed out, however, Federal procurement rules and the process of awarding government contracts created far more restrictions and regulations in the process than a campaign would ever face (Todd 2013).
14 *The New York Post* during this time period did not have any articles involving the Katrina analogy, and so I replaced it for this time span with another conservative-leaning print outlet, *The Washington Times*.
15 See the original tweet here: https://twitter.com/gstephanopoulos/status/401315839019720704
16 See appendix A.4 for intercoder reliability statistics for this section.

References

Alter, Jonathan. 2014, March/April. "Failure to Launch; How Obama Fumbled HealthCare.gov." *Foreign Affairs* 93 (2): 39.

Auerbach, David. 2013a. "Debugging the HealthCare.gov Hearings." *Slate*, October 25. Accessed July 16, 2016. http://www.slate.com/articles/technology/bitwise/2013/10/healthcare_gov_problems_house_committee_hearing_is_a_spectacle_of_tech_illiteracy.html.

Auerbach, David. 2013b. "Err Engine Down." *Slate*, October 8. Accessed July 16, 2016. http://www.slate.com/articles/business/bitwise/2013/10/what_went_wrong_with_healthcare_gov_the_front_end_and_back_end_never_talked.html.

Balz, Dan and Scott Clement. 2013. "Poll: Major Damage to GOP after Shutdown, and Broad Dissatisfaction with Government." *The Washington Post*, October 22. Accessed

July 16, 2016. http://www.washingtonpost.com/politics/poll-major-damage-to-gop-after-shutdown-and-broad-dissatisfaction-with-government/2013/10/21/dae5c062-3a84-11e3-b7ba-503fb5822c3e_story.html.

Balz, Dan and Peyton M. Craighill. 2013. "Obama's Ratings Tumble after Health-Care Flaws." *The Washington Post*, November 19. Accessed July 16, 2016. http://www.washingtonpost.com/politics/obamas-ratings-tumble-after-health-care-flaws/2013/11/18/c9cdbc2c-507c-11e3-9fe0-fd2ca728e67c_story.html.

Bennett, W. Lance. 2005. *News: The Politics of Illusion*, 6th edition. New York: Pearson Longman.

Blaney, Joseph R. and William Benoit. 2001. *The Clinton Scandals and the Politics of Image Restoration*. Westport: Praeger.

Botelho, Greg and Holly Yan. 2013. "Sebelius: Obamacare Website Problems Blindsided the President." *CNN Politics*, October 23. Accessed July 16, 2016. http://www.cnn.com/2013/10/23/politics/obamacare-sebelius-interview/.

Busby, Robert. 2001. *Defending the American Presidency: Clinton and the Lewinsky Scandal*. New York: Palgrave.

CNN Politics. 2013. "WH Web Video Makes HealthCare.gov Issues Seem Simple." October 23. Accessed July 16, 2016. http://politicalticker.blogs.cnn.com/2013/10/23/wh-web-video-makes-healthcare-gov-issues-seem-simple/.

Cohen, Jeffrey E. 2008. *The Presidency in the Era of 24-Hour News*. Princeton: Princeton University Press.

Contorno, Steve. 2013. "Did Medicare Part D Have the Same Rollout Problems as the Obamacare Online Marketplaces?" *Politifact*, November 13. Accessed July 16, 2016. http://www.politifact.com/truth-o-meter/statements/2013/nov/13/steve-israel/medicare-part-d-and-obamacare-health-care-gov/.

Dann, Carrie. 2013. "Obama: 'The Affordable Care Act is Not Just a Website'." *NBC News*, October 21. Accessed on July 16, 2016. http://www.nbcnews.com/news/other/obama-affordable-care-act-not-just-website-f8C11431491.

Daunt, Tina. 2014. "ObamaCare Website Traffic Spikes after President's 'Funny or Die' Interview." *Hollywood Reporter*, March 11. Accessed July 16, 2016. http://www.hollywoodreporter.com/news/obamacare-website-traffic-spikes-presidents-687724.

Dennis, Steven T. 2013. "Obama Apologizes for People Losing Health Coverage." *Roll Call*, November 7. Accessed July 16, 2016. http://www.rollcall.com/news/policy/obama-apologizes-for-people-losing-health-coverage.

Desilver, Drew. 2013. "Most Uninsured Americans Live in States that Won't Run Their Own Obamacare Exchanges." *Pew Research Center*, September 19. Accessed July 16, 2016. http://www.pewresearch.org/fact-tank/2013/09/19/most-uninsured-americans-live-in-states-that-wont-run-their-own-obamacare-exchanges/.

Dutton, Sarah, Jennifer De Pinto, Anthony Salvanto, and Fred Backus. 2013. "Poll: Obamacare support, Obama approval sink to new lows." *CBS News*, November 20. Accessed on July 12, 2016. http://www.cbsnews.com/news/poll-obamacare-support-obama-approval-sink-to-new-lows/.

Ellis, Richard J. 1994. *Presidential Lightning Rods: The Politics of Blame Avoidance*. Lawrence: University Press of Kansas.

Energy and Commerce Committee, The. 2013a. "PPACA Failures: Didn't Know or Didn't Disclose?" October 24. Accessed July 16, 2016. https://energycommerce.house.gov/hearings-and-votes/hearings/ppaca-implementation-failures-didn-t-know-or-didn-t-disclose.

Energy and Commerce Committee, The. 2013b. "PPACA Implementation Failures: Answers from HHS." October 30. Accessed July 16, 2016. https://energycommerce.

house.gov/hearings-and-votes/hearings/ppaca-implementation-failures-answers-hhs#sthash.yzxKXIKi.dpuf.

Energy and Commerce Committee, The. 2013c. "Security of HealthCare.gov.", October 24. Accessed July 16, 2016. https://energycommerce.house.gov/hearings-and-votes/hearings/security-healthcaregov.

Entman, Robert M. 2004. *Projections of Power: Framing News, Public Opinion, and U.S. Foreign Policy.* Chicago: University of Chicago Press.

Entman, Robert M. 2012. *Scandal and Silence: Media Responses to Presidential Misconduct.* Cambridge: Polity Press.

Farnsworth, Stephen J. 2009. *Spinner in Chief: How Presidents Sell Their Policies and Themselves.* Boulder: Paradigm Publishers.

Farnsworth, Stephen J. and S. Robert Lichter. 2006. *The Mediated Presidency: Television News and Presidential Governance.* Lanham: Rowman & Littlefield.

Fox News Poll. 2013, November 10–12. Accessed July 16, 2016. http://www.foxnews.com/politics/interactive/2013/11/13/fox-news-polls-half-voters-think-president-lied-about-obamacare-majority-want/.

Frates, Chris. 2013. "How Many Have Signed Up for Health Care? Well, It Depends." *CNN Politics*, October 16. Accessed July 16, 2016. http://www.cnn.com/2013/10/15/politics/obamacare-insurance-signup/.

Frumin, Aliyah. 2013. "Obama on Health Plan Cancellations: 'I Am Sorry'." *MSNBC*, November 7. Accessed July 16, 2016. http://www.msnbc.com/hardball/potus-obamacare-cancellations-i-am-sorry.

Goldstein, Amy. 2016. "HHS Failed to Heed Many Warnings That HealthCare.gov Was in Trouble." *The Washington Post*, February 23. Accessed July 16, 2016. https://www.washingtonpost.com/national/health-science/hhs-failed-to-heed-many-warnings-that-healthcaregov-was-in-trouble/2016/02/22/dd344e7c-d67e-11e5-9823-02b905009f99_story.html.

Goldstein, Amy and Juliet Eilperin. 2013. "HealthCare.gov: How Political Fear Was Pitted against Technical Needs." *The Washington Post*, November 2. Accessed July 16, 2016. https://www.washingtonpost.com/politics/challenges-have-dogged-obamas-health-plan-since-2010/2013/11/02/453fba42-426b-11e3-a624-41d661b0bb78_story.html.

Haberkorn, Jennifer and Jason Millman, 2013. "Contractors Grilled on the Hill." *Politico*, October 25. Accessed July 16, 2016. http://www.politico.com/story/2013/10/obamacare-hearings-healthcare-glitches-098788.

Hamilton, James T. 2004. *All the News That's Fit to Sell: How the Market Transforms Information into News.* Princeton: Princeton University Press.

House of Representatives Committee on Ways and Means. 2013. "Hearing: Chairman Camp Announces Hearing on the Status of the Affordable Care Act Implementation." October 29. Accessed July 16, 2016. http://waysandmeans.house.gov/event/chairman-camp-announces-hearing-on-the-status-of-the-affordable-care-act-implementation-4/.

Jamieson, Kathleen Hall and Joseph Cappella. 1998. *"The Role of the Press in the Health Care Reform Debate of 1993–1994."* In *The Politics of News, the News of Politics*, eds Doris Graber, Denis McQuall, and Pippa Norris, 110–131. Washington, DC: CQ Press.

Kennedy, Kelly and Catalina Camia. 2013. "Health Chief Sebelius Apologizes for Botched Website." *USA Today*, October 30. Accessed July 16, 2016. http://www.usatoday.com/story/news/politics/2013/10/30/sebelius-health-care-house-hearing/3308771/.

Kliff, Sarah. 2013. "HealthCare.gov Is Busted. These Four State Exchanges Aren't." *The Washington Post*, October 25. Accessed July 16, 2016. https://www.

washingtonpost.com/news/wonk/wp/2013/10/25/healthcare-gov-is-busted-these-four-state-exchanges-arent/.

Lakoff, George. (2004). *Don't Think of an Elephant! Know Your Values and Frame the Debate*. Hartford: Chelsea Green.

Lesniewski, Niels. 2013a. "Manchin's Obamacare Mandate Delay Could Create Political Peril." *Roll Call*, October 25. Accessed July 16, 2016. http://www.rollcall.com/news/policy/manchins-obamacare-mandate-delay-could-create-political-peril.

Lesniewski, Niels. 2013b. "10 Senate Democrats Push to Extend Obamacare Enrollment Window." *Roll Call*, October 25. Accessed July 16, 2016. http://www.rollcall.com/wgdb/10-senate-democrats-push-extending-obamacare-enrollment-window/.

Lipton, Eric, Ian Austen, and Sharon LaFraniere. 2013. "Tension and Flaws before Health Website Crash." *The New York Times*, November 22. Accessed July 16, 2016. http://www.nytimes.com/2013/11/23/us/politics/tension-and-woes-before-health-website-crash.html?_r=0&pagewanted=all.

LoGiurato, Brett. 2013. "The Most Embarrassing Possible Split-Screen Happened While Kathleen Sebelius Testified on Obamacare." *Business Insider*, October 30. Accessed July 16, 2016. http://www.businessinsider.com/kathleen-sebelius-healthcare-gov-testimony-obamacare-website-2013-10.

McCalmont, Lucy. 2013. "Joe Biden: President Obama and I Not Tech 'Geeks'." *Politico*, October 31. Accessed July 16, 2016. http://www.politico.com/story/2013/10/obama-biden-obamacare-website-glitches-99159.html.

Milbank, Dana. 2013. "Obama, the Uninterested President." *The Washington Post*, May 14. Accessed July 16, 2016. https://www.washingtonpost.com/opinions/dana-milbank-obama-the-uninterested-president/2013/05/14/da1c982a-bcd7-11e2-9b09-1638acc3942e_story.html.

National Republican Congressional Committee, The. 2013. "Living Under Obamacare." October 28. Accessed July 16, 2016. https://www.nrcc.org/2013/10/28/8-obamacare-horror-stories-longest-wait-times-healthcare-gov/.

Ornstein, Charles. 2013. "A Cheat Sheet for the Obamacare Hearings." *Propublica*, November 25. Accessed July 16, 2016. https://www.propublica.org/article/a-cheat-sheet-for-the-obamacare-hearings.

Paul, Rand. 2013. "Rand Paul: Obamacare, Shutdown are Bad Ideas." *CNN Politics*, October 4. Accessed July 16, 2016. http://www.cnn.com/2013/10/04/opinion/paul-shutdown-obamacare/.

Pear, Robert. 2013. "Shutdown Din Obscures Health Exchange Flaws." *New York Times*, October 4. Accessed July 16, 2016. http://www.nytimes.com/news/affordable-care-act/2013/10/04/shutdown-din-obscures-health-exchange-flaws/.

Pickert, Kate. 2013. "Obama Official Apologizes for Broken Health Care Website." *Time*, October 29. Accessed July 16, 2016. http://swampland.time.com/2013/10/29/obama-administration-offers-official-apology-over-broken-obamacare-website/.

RNC Communications Blog. 2013. "Not Ready for Primetime." October 1. Accessed July 16, 2016. https://www.gop.com/not-ready-for-primetime/?

Rubio, Marco, U.S. Senator for Florida. 2013. "Sen. Rubio, Rep. Radel Introduce Legislation to Delay ObamaCare Mandate until Websites are Fully Functional." October 28. Accessed July 16, 2016. https://www.rubio.senate.gov/public/index.cfm/press-releases?ID=5EB20C17-C6B0-4BCD-9285-7B2D7D9B1435.

Sabato, Larry J. 2000. *Feeding Frenzy: Attack Journalism & American Politics*. New York: Lanahan Publishing.

Sink, Justin. 2013. "Obama: 'We Fumbled the Rollout'." *The Hill*, November 14. Accessed July 16, 2016. http://thehill.com/homenews/administration/190276-obama-we-fumbled-the-rollout.

Sneed, Tierney. 2013. "Presidents on Late Night Talk Shows in Charts." *U.S. News and World Report*, July 31. Accessed July 16, 2016. http://www.usnews.com/news/articles/2013/07/31/how-does-obamas-tonight-show-visit-stack-up-against-other-presidents.

Somashekhar, Sandhya. 2013. "Sebelius Team Working on 200 Fixes to Obamacare Web Site." *The Washington Post*, November 6. Accessed July 16, 2016. https://www.washingtonpost.com/news/post-politics/wp/2013/11/06/sebelius-team-working-on-200-fixes-to-obamacare-web-site/.

Sun, Lena H. 2013. "Md. Hit by Insurance Exchange Glitches." *Washingtonpost.com*, October 5.

Todd, Chuck. 2013. "Exclusive: Obama personally apologizes for Americans losing health coverage." *NBC News*, November 7. Accessed on September 23, 2016. http://www.nbcnews.com/video/nbc-news/53492840

U.S. Government Accountability Office. 2016. "HealthCare.Gov: Actions Needed to Enhance Information Security and Privacy Controls." March 23. Accessed July 16, 2016. http://www.gao.gov/products/GAO-16-265.

U.S. House of Representatives Committee on Oversight and Government Reform, Staff Report, 2013 "Risks of Fraud and Misinformation with Obamacare Outreach Campaign." September 18. Accessed July 16, 2016. http://oversight.house.gov/wp-content/uploads/2013/09/Republican-Staff-Report-on-Navigators.pdf.

Wagstaff, Keith. 2013. "The ObamaCare Debacle Marks the Return of 'President Passerby.'" *The Week*, October 23. Accessed July 16, 2016. http://theweek.com/articles/458260/obamacare-debacle-marks-return-president-passerby.

Washington Post, The. 2013. "Full Transcript: President Obama's Nov. 14 News Conference on the Affordable Care Act." November 14. Accessed July 16, 2016. https://www.washingtonpost.com/politics/transcript-president-obamas-nov-14-statement-on-health-care/2013/11/14/6233e352-4d48-11e3-ac54-aa84301ced81_story.html.

Washington Post-ABC News Poll. 2013, October 25. Accessed July 16, 2016. https://www.washingtonpost.com/page/2010-2019/WashingtonPost/2013/10/21/National-Politics/Polling/release_271.xml.

Weaver, Christopher, Shira Ovide, and Louise Radnofsky. 2013. "Software, Design Defects Cripple Health-Care Website." *Wall Street Journal*, October 6. Accessed July 16, 2016. http://online.wsj.com/news/articles/SB10001424052702304441404579119740283413018.

White House, The. 2013a. "Press Briefing by Press Secretary Jay Carney." October 1. Accessed July 16, 2016. https://www.whitehouse.gov/the-press-office/2013/10/01/press-briefing-press-secretary-jay-carney-1012013.

White House, The. 2013b. "Remarks by the President on the Affordable Care Act." September 26. Accessed July 16, 2016. https://www.whitehouse.gov/the-press-office/2013/09/26/remarks-president-affordable-care-act.

White House, The. 2013c. "Remarks by the President on the Affordable Care Act and the Government Shutdown." October 1. Accessed July 16, 2016. https://www.whitehouse.gov/the-press-office/2013/10/01/remarks-president-affordable-care-act-and-government-shutdown.

5
PORTRAYING PRESIDENTIAL PLEDGES AND DROPPED PLANS

In the fall of 2013, in the midst of a government shutdown precipitated by partisan conflict over the Affordable Care Act and the glitch-ridden rollout of the HealthCare.gov website recounted in the previous chapter, the Obama Administration faced yet another political crisis. This controversy emerged from the debate surrounding the ACA's passage several years prior, when President Obama promoting health-care reform stated:

> That means that no matter how we reform health care, we will keep this promise to the American people: If you like your doctor, you will be able to keep your doctor, period. If you like your health care plan, you'll be able to keep your health care plan, period. No one will take it away, no matter what.
> (New York Times *2009*)

This was not a single-time pledge, but one the president frequently repeated, including after the ACA became law, such as on April 1, 2010, when he said of the new legislation, "And if you like your insurance plan, you will keep it. No one will be able to take that away from you. It hasn't happened yet. It won't happen in the future" (White House 2010). In October 2013, these repeated assurances were called into question as some Americans began to receive letters from their insurance companies canceling their policies because they did not meet the minimum requirements for health insurance mandated by the ACA.[1]

Had the president lied to the public to ensure the passage of his signature legislative achievement, casting doubt on both his personal credibility and the legitimacy of the law? Or did such accusations of lying mischaracterize the nature of the circumstances and ignore that what the president had promised was technically true? Obama's opponents had strong incentives to frame the president's prior statements as unequivocal lies and a betrayal of public trust, and to encourage the news media to cover what was unfolding in accordance with the severity of those accusations. The president and his supporters, on the other hand, had good reason to defend their actions and counter the "lying" charge, working to ward off the media frenzy that can emerge from perceived broken presidential promises.

This chapter examines the framing contest between the Obama team and its opponents over the dropped plans issue, and then turns to a sample of news coverage to assess the extent to which those frames, promoting or quelling a controversy, were presented. I identify very different media reactions to these frames across different types of outlets, reflecting today's fragmented news landscape. Coverage on cable news networks associated with partisan leanings followed patterns of privileging the frames of the president or his opponents, in line with their ideological brands. The analysis suggests the important role hostile partisan news sources can play in promulgating a controversy surrounding the president, forcing politicians and mainstream objective news sources to react accordingly. It also identifies how friendly partisan outlets can facilitate presidential frame refraction in ways that benefit the White House, but also how the conditional nature of presidential framing resilience can result in limits to supportive coverage, even in these sympathetic news sources.

In the case of the dropped plans, presidential communication advantages were hampered by the disjointed, inconsistent frames the Obama team deployed to counter the accusations against him. Newspapers known for more politically substantive news and adhering more closely to tenets of objectivity than their cable news counterparts, were more likely to privilege opponents' "lying" frame than the Administration's frames. Additionally, the analyzed print coverage reflects the potential "dark side" of presidential communications influence and exposes a damaging presidential framing side effect: it was the White House responding to opponents' damaging frames that appeared to turn these events into a controversy "worthy" of news coverage in more hard news-oriented outlets.

The Causes and Liabilities of Presidential Policy Promises

President Obama's oft-repeated pledge that if Americans liked their health-care plan they could keep it under the proposed reform was grounded in the challenge the White House faced in overcoming public fears about policy change, and lessons learned from the defeat of the Clinton Administration's health-care reform effort in 1993–1994. A July 2009 *New York Times*/CBS News poll, for instance, showed 37% of the public "very concerned" and another 25% "somewhat concerned" that they would be forced to change doctors under the health-care reform plans being debated (Nagourney and Thee-Brenan 2009). The decision to include this assurance in the president's speeches stemmed undoubtedly from trying to ease some of these apprehensions, even though at that time some observers projected it was very unlikely this pledge could be upheld were the law to be enacted (Associated Press 2009; FactCheck.Org 2009).

Political realities and the demand for presidential public leadership, then, can incentivize presidents to use lofty language of certainty to help sell their policies, even at the risk of such statements later proving demonstrably false. Thomas Patterson (1994, 50f) argues the central role of the news media in American politics encourages this, producing attention-grabbing sound bites such as George H.W. Bush's infamous "Read my lips, no new taxes." Though such a promise sounds great on camera, it makes little sense as a governing principle and was eventually broken. Obama reassuring the public that they could keep their current plan under his health-care system overhaul was, similarly, a media-ready slogan easily relayed to the public but risky in its substance, making a guarantee he might have little control over.

When presidents in the past have employed such pledges to achieve short-term political goals, they have occasionally faced the possibility of endangering the credibility of both themselves and the policy they were promoting. David Zarefsky (2005, xii) demonstrates how this problem unfolded for President Johnson in the War on Poverty, as "the very choices of symbolism and argument which had aided the adoption of the program were instrumental in undermining its implementation and in weakening public support for its basic philosophy." Eric Alterman (2004, 5) asserts that what come to be viewed as presidential "lies" have a habit of "destroying the very policy that the lie had originally been told to support." He contends that as the Bush Administration built support for the Iraq War, some of the president's assertions that ultimately proved false resulted from honest mistakes and faulty intelligence, but that Bush and his surrogates "could easily have communicated the complexity of this judgment to the country had honesty been among [their] primary concerns. In fact, they purposely insisted on exactly the opposite: certainty of knowledge where none was possible" (Alterman 2004, 298). A similar assessment might be levied against the Obama Administration's unwillingness to be forthright with Americans about the inevitable uncertainties in making drastic changes to the U.S. health-care system. At its heart, the dropped plans issue was a rhetorical problem for the president, as PolitiFact.com (2013) pointed out in deeming Obama's pledge its "lie of the year," "Obama's ideas on health care were first offered as general outlines then grew into specific legislation over the course of his presidency. Yet Obama never adjusted his rhetoric to give people a more accurate sense of the law's real-world repercussions, even as fact-checkers flagged his statements as exaggerated at best."

News Media Norms and Presidential "Lying"

Conventions of contemporary journalism offer us a mixed picture on how we might expect the news media to cover a presidential pledge that appeared to fall short. Patterson (1994) recounts the media's cynical tendency to depict presidential hopefuls as routinely lying in the promises they make on the campaign trail, despite research showing that once in office, presidents tend to keep many of the pledges they make as candidates, or at least make a good-faith effort to do so (Fishel 1985; Bernstein 2012; Politifact 2015). On the one hand, this might mean that arguments casting the president as overpromising to sell a policy to the public might gain little traction in a news environment that favors novel, sensational content. But a broken promise, such as "Read my lips, no new taxes," can result in inordinate scrutiny and immense coverage in the press (Patterson 1994), as President George H.W. Bush learned the hard way. In the Iran-Contra scandal, charges that President Reagan had broken his vow never to negotiate with terrorists were particularly damaging as they came at a time the mainstream media were casting doubt about Reagan's foreign policy competency more broadly (Dickinson 1994, 159). In the Obama case, the dropped plans issue emerged just as the news cycle was devoting tremendous coverage to the shortcomings of the ACA's rollout and HealthCare.gov debacle, generally undermining faith in the president as an effective manager and in the viability of health-care reform itself.

It is also very unlikely the news media Obama was dealing with would give him a free pass on the discrepancy between what he had stated and the reality of what was unfolding. As outlined in the introduction to this book, over the past few decades partisan news sources and subjective analysis by pundits has proliferated, and those affiliated with the opposition party will eagerly exploit such missteps. Among more "objective" outlets, reporters began to place greater emphasis on their adversarial role toward politicians, ushering in what some have even depicted as an era of "attack dog" journalism (Nacos 1990; Patterson 1994, 2003; Jamieson and Waldman 2004). Although the mainstream news media might be predisposed to give "balanced" coverage to both sides of a framing contest, they also consider themselves committed to coverage exposing wrongdoing or deception in government. As President Obama was depicted by opponents as misleading Americans about a domestic policy issue, this might be far more likely to provoke the news media into taking up its self-proclaimed "watchdog" role, in contrast to presidents who might be accused of lying about their personal lives or foreign policy issues in the interest of national security. Presidential frames would have to be carefully constructed to prevent news content from turning in this damaging direction.

Presidential Opponents' Framing: Broken Promises, Broken Policies

For their part of the framing contest, the president's opponents sought to convince the public that Obama had broken his promise to the American people, and had only made that pledge in the first place to trick them into allowing a dangerous health-care reform law to go into place. Prominent Republican politicians publicized news of the canceled plans and worked to depict this development as both a major blow to the legitimacy of the ACA and evidence of the president's fundamental untrustworthiness. The Republican National Committee official blog entitled its October 31, 2013 post simply "Obama lied." The day before, Senator Ron Johnson (R-WI) introduced the "If You Like Your Health Care Plan You Can Keep It" Act, calling to mind the president's prior claims while also presenting a legislative "remedy" to the issue. Representative Fred Upton (R-MI), in one of the congressional hearings investigating HealthCare.gov's problems, declared "Sadly, it seems that the administration's assurances about being ready to launch were just as empty as the President's promises that this law would mean lower costs while allowing Americans to keep the coverage and doctors that they have and like" (Energy and Commerce Committee 2013a).

Immense attention fixed simultaneously upon the canceled plans and HealthCare.gov glitches neatly dovetailed with Republicans' "not ready for primetime" mantra about the ACA. Representative John Shimkus (R-IL) noted in congressional hearings, "The administration's promise, if you like your health-care plan, you can keep it. That is what he said. And that was a lie. It was not correct. It was deceptive to the American people, and you know, we are all receiving the letters of denied plans, and even from hardened Democrats" (Energy and Commerce Committee 2013b). These politicians thus sought to portray themselves as defenders of the public interest, not merely calculating partisans. In early November, Senator John Cornyn (R-TX) told reporters, "we know that lying to Congress is a crime, but unfortunately, lying to the American people is not" (Shear 2013). "Promise after promise from this Administration has turned out to be not true," according to Speaker of the House John Boehner (R-OH), who connected the current events to long-standing Republican calls to repeal the ACA: "So when it comes to this health care law, the White House doesn't have much credibility. Now, let's be clear. The only way to fully protect the American people is to scrap this law once and for all. There is no way to fix this" (*USA Today* 2013). Mitt Romney, doing a rare interview after his loss in the 2012 presidential election, went on *Meet the Press* and maintained that when Obama "told the American people that you could keep your health insurance if you wanted to keep it, period—he said that time and time again—he wasn't telling the truth. I think that fundamental dishonesty has really imperiled the whole foundation of his second term" (Pengelly 2013).

Despite the significant political backlash Republicans faced from some members of their party precipitating a government shutdown in this same period, the malfunctioning health-care website, and thus, the inability of people with canceled plans to easily access their new options, helped strengthen their framing of Obama's broken pledge as part of a systemic failure of both the ACA and his presidency.

Presidential Frames on Dropped Plans: Weathering a Political Storm

The framing efforts of the president and his surrogates included several alternative interpretations of these same events: they emphasized that people were not being dropped from plans but instead "transitioned" to new, better insurance; that insurance companies were to blame rather than the law or the president; and finally, that the president's promise technically held true and thus was never broken. This last framing device was supported by emphasizing that: (1) nothing in the law stated Americans could not keep their existing plans; (2) President Obama had only been talking about plans bought before the law was passed; and (3) that the plans under discussion could hardly be considered insurance, they fell so woefully short in protecting those holding them. In direct contrast to the consistency and uniformity in the Republicans' framing, the president and his defenders vacillated among the above interpretations during this period.

In mid-October, when news organizations first began to report on the plan cancelations, the White House initially pursued a strategy of denial of any broken promise. Valerie Jarrett, senior adviser to the president, tweeted on October 28, "FACT: Nothing in #Obamacare forces people out of their health plans," offering a quick and direct social media defense from opponents' attacks. In his October 29 press briefing, White House Press Secretary Jay Carney reacted to questions about the dropped plans by indicating the president's pledge had been upheld all along, because "if you had insurance coverage on the individual market when the Affordable Care Act was passed into law and you liked that plan and you wanted to stay on it, even though it didn't meet the minimum standards that the Affordable Care Act would bring into place on January 1, 2014, you can keep the coverage. You're grandfathered in" (White House 2013a). Nor were presidential defenses entirely confined to White House officials; House Minority Leader Nancy Pelosi (D-CA) chimed in on October 30, "If you were in a plan in 2010 when the president said, 'If you're in a plan and you like your plan, you can keep your plan,' you can [keep your plan]. If you've enrolled since then, you'll get a conversion letter" (Lillis 2013).

As time went on, some in the Administration focused on shifting blame for events to insurance companies. Carney contended in his November 5 briefing, "The provision in the law was the manifestation of the assurance that if you have a plan you want to keep, you can keep it. Insurance companies that chose to strip away benefits from existing plans in the interim, that canceled existing plans in the interim, they took away that grandfathering opportunity. And that's a reality" (White House 2013b). In an October 30 speech, President Obama pointed to "bad apple insurers," who sold consumers highly deficient coverage, noting, "But ever since the law was passed, if insurers decided to downgrade or cancel these substandard plans, what we said under the law is, you've got to replace them with quality, comprehensive coverage because that too was a central premise of the Affordable Care Act from the very beginning" (Lee 2013).

Even as the White House sought to use the insurance industry as a lightning rod, some insurance executives dutifully went forth into the news media to defend presidential frames. For instance, appearing on *Meet the Press* in late October, Florida Blue Cross Blue Shield Chief Executive, Patrick J. Geraghty, argued, "We're not cutting people—we're transitioning these people. What we've been doing is informing people that their plan doesn't meet the test of the essential health benefits. Therefore, they have a choice of many options we make available through the exchange, and in fact, with subsidy, many people will be getting better plans at a lesser cost" (*Meet the Press*, October 27, 2013).

In early November, President Obama recast his original statement, asserting, "Now, if you have or had one of these plans before the Affordable Care Act came into law, and you really liked that plan, what we said was you can keep it if it hasn't changed since the law passed" (Wolf 2013). Finally, in a November 7 interview with *NBC News*, President Obama apologized to Americans whose plans had been dropped, saying, "I am sorry that they are finding themselves in this situation based on assurances they got from me" (Todd 2013).

Presidential Frames and the Democratic Party

In Chapter 4, we explored the limits of support among many prominent Democrats for the Obama team's "glitches" frame, particularly as it proved increasingly unconvincing with the passage of time. In the case of the dropped plans, although there were some in the president's party who echoed his frames, like Nancy Pelosi, the failure of presidential frames to provide enough cover for many Democrats to spread them was even more obvious than in the HealthCare.gov case. By mid-November 2013, the weaknesses of presidential frames were made plain by the criticism received from some prominent Democrats. On November 12, former President Bill Clinton stated publically that the president should "honor the commitment the federal government made," and allow people to keep their dropped plans, even if it required changing the law. Democratic Senators Mary Landrieu (LA), Kay Hagan (NC), and Mark Udall (CO) indicated that Congress might need to act immediately to allow those affected to retain their existing plans. Senators Landrieu and Joe Manchin (WV) introduced the "Keeping the Affordable Care Act Promise" bill and it was even endorsed by a more liberal figure in the party, Senator Jeff Merkley (D-OR). Thirty-nine Democrats in the House joined Republicans to vote for the "If You Like Your Health Care Plan You Can Keep It" bill in mid-November (Parker and Pear 2013).

When a stalwart Obama supporter like Massachusetts Governor Deval Patrick was asked by *Meet the Press*' David Gregory whether the president's assertion "was a broken promise, or was that deception, or both?" Patrick opted for "Neither." The governor went on to qualify, "For 95% of the people in America that is the truth. For the small number of people who have a health care plan which in fact will not insure them when they get sick, it is not true" (*Meet the Press*, November 3, 2013). Patrick vocally praised what he saw as the virtues of the ACA, but he had still characterized the president's statement as "not true" for everyone rather than echoing some White House officials that the pledge was "technically true."

Congresswoman Martha Fudge (D-OH) told the press that the president "made a mistake, and he needs to fix it. I think it's appropriate for the White House to fix it, because he's the one that created the problem" (Huey-Burns 2013). In mid-November, "tensions flared" when House and Senate Democrats met with White House officials to express their displeasure with the dropped plans problem and to urge the Administration to act, lest they be forced to join on to one of the Republicans' legislative fixes to the problem (Parker and Shear 2013; Weigel 2013).

On November 14, the Obama Administration bowed to this building political pressure and announced that insurers could now extend for a year the healthcare plans they had canceled for failing to meet the ACA's minimum standards (*Washington Post* 2013).[2] The delay was not a decision driven by policy considerations (and, in fact, some experts argued it was damaging from a policy standpoint), but placated Democrats afraid the dual issues of HealthCare.gov and the dropped plans were causing them to suffer politically (Chait 2013; Klein 2013; Weigel 2013). It was also in part an acknowledgment that the White House had lost the messaging war over the canceled plans. Even if we assume that policy changes were necessary, making them helped substantiate opponents' frames that the ACA was riddled with flaws that needed to be addressed immediately.

News Media Coverage Analysis: Presidential Frames Largely Fall Short

To see how this framing contest was waged in the news and to what effect I analyzed four media outlets, including both print and cable news sources—*The New York Times*, *The Washington Post*, Fox News, and MSNBC—for a full month as the controversy unfolded, from October 20 to November 20, 2013. Matthew Levendusky (2013) has demonstrated how partisan media like Fox News and MSNBC, despite relatively small audiences, impact the parameters of American political debate and propel stories into mainstream media that might not have otherwise gained traction. This chapter covers one month's worth of coverage across the four outlets to assess when and where presidential and opposition frames first appeared, to evaluate how such frames spread, or fail to spread, in a diverse media environment.

To assess which side of the framing contest was more successful at gaining space for their frames in the various news outlets, this analysis classifies a paragraph in the coverage as including opposition framing of events, which I will refer to as "Obama as Lying," when it depicted the president as lying, not being truthful, or something with equivalent meaning when he stated Americans could keep their health plans. Any paragraph that mentioned the president breaking his promise/pledge, or discussed the circumstances as a threat to Obama's credibility were also coded as appearances of Obama as Lying. A paragraph was coded as including presidential framing—which I call "Defending

News Outlet	Total paragraphs in which a frame was used	Obama as Lying Frame		Defending Obama Frame		Mixed Frame	
		#	%	#	%	#	%
The New York Times	69	41	59.4%	19	27.5%	9	13.0%
The Washington Post	113	79	69.9%	27	23.9%	7	6.2%
Fox News	647	533	82.4%	97	15.0%	17	2.6%
MSNBC	174	39	22.4%	126	72.4%	9	5.2%

FIGURE 5.1 Overall Coverage of Frames across Analyzed Outlets, October 20, 2013–November 20, 2013

Obama"—when it referred to the dropped plans issue as being mischaracterized by critics and absolving the president of any wrongdoing. That could take the form of any of the Administration's aforementioned justifications for why people could not keep the insurance they liked, from the pledge as technically true, casting blame elsewhere, and clarifying what the president "really meant was . . ." The "Mixed" category encompassed any paragraph in the coverage that had elements of both the Obama as Lying and Defending Obama frames in it. A trained independent coder replicated the content analysis of the coverage; reliability statistics are discussed in Appendix A.5.

Even in *The New York Times* and *The Washington Post*, more committed to balanced coverage than the cable news networks and with reliably left-leaning editorial boards, framing the "dropped plans" as a shameful indictment of the ACA and President Obama was far more prevalent than alternative interpretations, as Figure 5.1 makes clear. These lopsided results speak to the conditional nature of presidential framing resilience and all of the ways the White House's communications strategy had fallen short. Rollicking back and forth between multiple strategies of denial, blame avoidance, revisions of past statements, and finally, apology, gave the appearance of no plausible explanation to square the president's prior statements with what was happening.

In some of the other chapters of this book we have seen *The New York Times* occasionally provide friendlier territory for presidential frames, slower to turn against the HealthCare.gov "glitches" frame than other outlets, for instance. Despite my finding here that its coverage over this month provided more space to the Obama as Lying framing of events, the *Times* faced accusations of sugarcoating some of the president's difficulties. The *Times'* public editor took the paper to task for being overly gentle in its coverage of the controversy, citing an editorial that said the president "clearly misspoke" when he made the pledge, and a news article that described the "incorrect promise," rather than more accurately, in her view, calling it a *false* promise (Sullivan 2013).

The stark contrast between the treatment of the frames of the president and his opponents on right-leaning Fox News and left-leaning MSNBC programming, as we might expect, falls in line with the ideological brands they have carved out for themselves. MSNBC's *The Ed Show* host Ed Schultz defended Obama from Bill Clinton's critiques and downplayed there was any kind of presidential promise to begin with. The former president, according to Schultz, "I think went off the rails and defended the junk insurance industry. The commitment the president made that the federal government was going to allow you to keep your insurance if you like it. I don't recall President Obama making a commitment. He made a passing comment that if you like your insurance, you can keep it" (*The Ed Show*, November 13, 2013). Dean Baker of the Center for Economic and Policy Research, appearing as a commentator on MSNBC, also ridiculed the controversy, saying Obama:

> also said you could keep your doctor. Does that mean he's going to keep doctors from retiring or dying? Presumably, what he meant was that the Affordable Care Act would not directly cancel plans that were in effect. And it doesn't cancel plans that were in effect. It grandfathers all the plans that were in effect at the time the bill was passed. So, if a lot of people are running around like chicken with their heads cut-off, my God, plans are being canceled. And you just go, well, plans that were put in place after the ACA was passed.
>
> (All In with Chris Hayes, *November 12, 2013*)

MSNBC's Presidential Frame Refraction: Vilifying Insurance Companies

Although weaknesses of the president's frames inhibited their ability to spread in mainstream news and among many of their Democratic supporters, a supportive outlet like MSNBC could not only stand apart by championing those frames, but also by using their coverage to make some more compelling and coherent. Thus far the instances of presidential framing refraction I have recounted involved the media or the president's opponents vesting his frames with new applications and meanings to his political detriment. By contrast, MSNBC took presidential frames indicating that if insurers were stripping away benefits or providing poor coverage with too many gaps, this was their fault and not the Administration's, and carried this mild form of responsibility-shifting into new terrain, imbuing it with a far more vigorous public shaming of the insurance industry. Presidential frame refraction here worked to the Obama team's benefit, as the progressive cable news network made insurance companies the real villains of the dropped plans story.

On 18 different occasions in the month of analyzed transcripts, MSNBC personalities referred to "junk insurance" policies that were being canceled, and bolstered the perception that rather than breaking a promise, the president and his health-care law were saving Americans from being preyed on by underhand insurance companies. Hosts and guests on the channel sharply rebuked insurance companies not merely for canceling plans, but for providing misleading information to customers in the process and high-pressure-selling Americans on pricey replacements.[3] On the November 4 edition of *All In with Chris Hayes*, the host told his viewers to carefully scrutinize a lot of the media reports they were seeing about dropped plans and cancelation letters (presumably on other channels), advising, "you should be asking, is the reporter taking the insurance company at face value?" Hayes and his guests then took an in-depth look at cancelation letters that tried to lock customers being dropped into new, more expensive plans with that company and omitting any information about the government's health insurance exchanges where they might be able to find cheaper, better options and gain access to government subsidies. Hayes asked his guest, "Are they cynically using the excuse of Obamacare in the letter to deflect blame so that they can kind of get away with what used to be called panic selling, folks?"

Congressman Jim McDermott of Washington, one of the few Democrats willing to back the president's frames, was on MSNBC on November 11 arguing Obama said people could keep their plans "if the insurance companies kept the program the same, but the insurance companies want to make more money. So they cancel the policies, raise the prices, give a few whistles and bells, and say this is what we now have. It is all fabricated to destroy the safety net" (*The Ed Show*, November 11, 2013). Criticisms of the insurance industry fit well with the liberal network's distrust of the private sector. Wendell Potter of the Center for Public Integrity talked about his old employer, Cigna Health Insurance, as a guest on *The Ed Show*'s October 29 episode, telling the audience, "one of the reasons why we had to have health-care reform in the first place because a lot of companies including those I used to work for had made a lot of money selling junk insurance, selling coverage to people that doesn't protect them and the reason is because those plans are very, very profitable. Insurance companies do not have to pay very much on claims." On MSNBC, insurance companies became multifaceted bad guys, not merely dropping people from plans but also duping consumers into quickly buying costlier plans while concealing from them the fact that they might find a better deal by shopping around.

Part of the value of presidential frame refraction to the president's communication project in this instance is that on their own, Obama and his team probably could not have attached this new meaning to the president's blame-shifting frame.[4] Support of the insurance industry was key for the Obama Administration in initially getting the ACA passed, and even during this month-long time period, the president was meeting with insurance executives to work on fixes to the dropped plans problem (Jackson and O'Donnell 2013). The Administration did not have the same freedom to be as harshly critical as left-leaning media personalities, although advancing the frame in this direction certainly bolstered the portrayal of insurance companies as the real culprits behind the canceled policies problem. MSNBC was clearly an outlier among the four outlets in its coverage, however. Notably, in this particular framing contest, the coverage in *The New York Times* and *The Washington Post* looked a lot closer to that of Fox News than MSNBC.

Presidential Lying on Fox News

Meanwhile, Fox News personalities faithfully propagated opposition frames regarding the dropped plans issue, indicating this was a significant transgression and symptomatic of the president's personal dishonesty. The Obama as Lying frame was a very large majority of the frames appearing on the network, and they had the smallest percentage of Defending Obama frame appearances of all four networks. On October 28, anchor Megyn Kelly announced, "Breaking tonight, Fox News has just confirmed that while the president was promising you could keep your health-care plan the White House has known for almost three years if not more that the promise wouldn't hold for millions of Americans. And we have evidence." Guest Marc Thiessen on the same broadcast declared, "When President Obama looked at the American people in the eye and said if you like your health insurance, you can keep your current plan, period, no matter what, that was a bald-faced lie. And he intended—in fact, I think that they intended for these people to lose their health insurance." On November 8, host Sean Hannity told viewers, "When the president after all those times saying if you like your plan, you can keep it, then he contradicted himself. But if you notice, he looks down and reads it. It was written, prepared, approved. This is a planned lie. Let's roll the tape." A few days later, on November 11, Hannity teased an upcoming segment by stating, "Now, coming up tonight, we examine the biggest lies in the history of American politics. That's coming up next. We'll ask if President Obama's broken promise measures up to the most historic tall tales of them all."

Cable News' Early Coverage of the Controversy

The timing of appearances of the frames across the four outlets suggests that partisan media outlets play an important role beyond defending their ideological interests that can complicate presidential framing capabilities by propelling damaging stories forward elsewhere in the media. Following the trajectory of what Levendusky (2013, 149) calls "frame diffusion," early discussion of the controversy on cable news was followed by the national newspapers incorporating framing of the president's actions as a "broken promise" in their coverage. Both the Obama as Lying and Defending Obama frames first appeared on the analyzed Fox News and MSNBC coverage on October 21, but it was not until October 28 that Obama as Lying showed up in *The New York Times* and *The Washington Post*. Defending Obama also made its first appearance on that same day of October 28 in the *Post*, and (to the president's detriment) even later, on October 30, in the *Times*.

Fox News was quite consistent in encouraging connections between the dropped plans and Obama's personal honesty in its coverage. The Obama as Lying frame appeared on the cable network at least twice each day between October 21 and 28, with the exception of October 26. MSNBC, by contrast, perhaps sought to quell the controversy by refusing to give it much airtime—after October 22, appearances of either frame did not resurface on the left-leaning network until

October 28. For a full week in the news cycle then, the *Times* and the *Post* gave no space to the framed communications of the president or his opponents on this issue, while Fox News hammered away at it on a daily basis (and even Defending Obama appeared on the right-leaning network at least twice each day during that week, with the exception of October 22 and 26).

As I have emphasized from the outset in this book, presidential communication influence in the contemporary news environment can be of a subtler variety and hard to discern. The *Times* and the *Post* first started to include the frames in their coverage on the same day as one of the earliest direct Obama Administration communications about this controversy; the aforementioned Valerie Jarrett tweet where she "fact-checked" the assertion that "Obamacare" was forcing people out of their plans. Two things are worth noting about that. First, by October 28, certain media outlets, such as Fox News, had framed the dropped plans in a damaging way loudly and emphatically enough that the Administration itself felt compelled to respond. This also speaks to the fragmentation of today's media, as prestige press outlets might largely ignore stories with tremendous traction on cable news. Second, in what I would classify as a presidential framing side effect, by countering the criticisms of Obama and the ACA on this point, the White House also generated more coverage of the dropped plans controversy in the mainstream media, including newspapers like the *Times* and the *Post*. It is possible that these outlets determined the story became a legitimate one that warranted their attention only after the Administration addressed it directly. This was not the intent of the Defending Obama frame, and on the whole this side effect was detrimental to the Administration's goals, broadening the coverage of a story they would prefer to minimize.

Few Daily Victories for Presidential Frames

As seen in Figure 5.2, throughout the month of analyzed coverage, Obama as Lying outnumbered appearances of the other two frames. Looking at the daily amount of coverage involving frames, how often did the president's critics "win" the day across the four selected outlets over this crucial month? Obama as Lying appearances outnumbered Defending Obama appearances on 25 of the 32 days, with the worst news days for the White House falling on October 29 (a difference between the two frames' appearances of 46); October 31 (difference of 33); November 4 (difference of 45); and November 15 (difference of 32). Meanwhile, Defending Obama appearances were greater than Obama as Lying appearances on just 2 of the 32 days analyzed, October 30 (by just a single appearance) and November 3 (by 2).

That means that the only two days in which the White House won the framing contest in the day's coverage across these four outlets were followed immediately by the most damaging daily coverage for the president. When presidential defenders such as Jarrett, Carney, and Pelosi launched a counterinterpretation of the dropped plans in late October, their framing of events

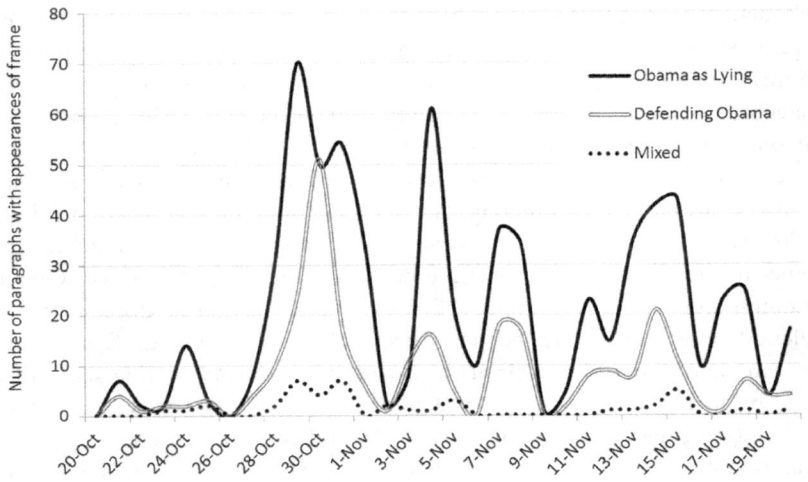

FIGURE 5.2 Daily Appearances of Frames in Analyzed Outlets, October 20, 2013–November 20, 2013

did garner coverage in the analyzed outlets, but news narratives quickly shifted toward privileging opponents' frames that Obama had deliberately misled the public. The decisiveness and speed of that swing uncovers yet again the provisional nature of presidential framing resilience in the contemporary news media. The weakness of the Administration's communications defense emboldened its critics, offered insufficient political cover to encourage supporters to publically align themselves with their frames, and failed to compel even neutral media actors to equitably balance their coverage of "presidential lies" with the White House's version of events.

President Obama did himself no favors when he publically apologized to those Americans with canceled plans, as Figure 5.3 shows. After that November 7 apology, in the three outlets other than Fox News, appearances of Obama as Lying increased, even in the friendly confines of MSNBC. On Fox News, the raw number of appearances of Obama as Lying decreased, highlighting the tremendous amount of attention given prior to that framing of events on the cable channel. However, even on Fox News, the ratio of appearances of the Obama as Lying frame to the Defending Obama frame went from 5:1 prior to the president's apology to 13:2 afterwards. Further, though the Defending Obama frame was still a clear majority among the frames apparent in MSNBC's coverage from November 7 to 20 (65.6% compared to 31.1% involving Obama as Lying, and 3.3% involving Mixed), the tone of the coverage was still less friendly to the Defending Obama frame than it had been prior to the president saying he was sorry (79.8% compared to 13.1% involving Obama as Lying, and 7.1% involving Mixed). This raises doubts about whether once the Administration's initial framing of the controversy proved wanting that an outright apology was the best course of action.

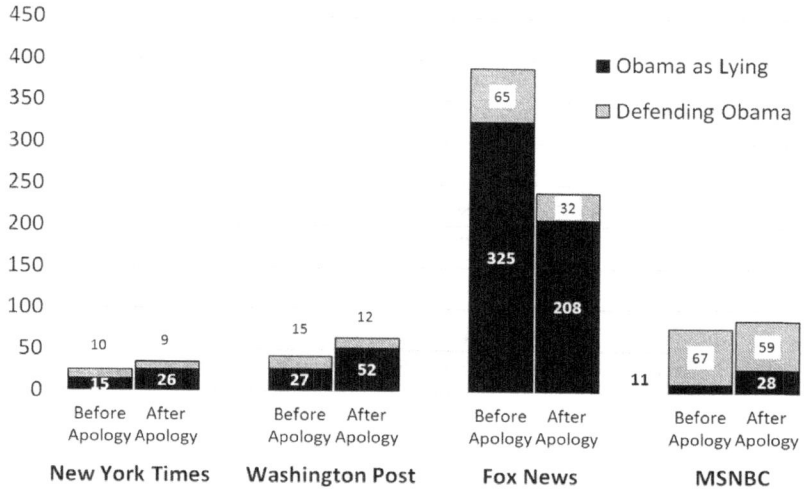

FIGURE 5.3 Appearances of "Obama as Lying" and "Defending Obama" Frames before and after November 7 Apology

Public Opinion

As in the HealthCare.gov case, the negative news and controversy surrounding the canceled plans led to new polling questions about the president's accused offense, in turn generating further polls and coverage (Entman 2012, 133). If the Obama team's frames had not fared well in the news I looked at here, they did not do much better with the public. A mid-November Fox News poll asked, "President Obama repeatedly told Americans that under the health-care law, 'If you like your health care plan, you can keep it. Period.' It turns out that isn't true. Which of the following best describes President Obama's actions?" A plurality of 50% chose that he had "knowingly lied to get the law passed," with 40% selecting "he did not know people would lose their insurance" (Fox News Poll 2013). President Obama's apology was viewed quite negatively by the public in the same survey, as only 38% believed he was sincere and 58% that he had apologized for political reasons.

In mid-November, Quinnipiac asked respondents, "Do you think President Obama knowingly deceived the public when he said that if people liked their health insurance plans they would be able to keep them under the 2010 health care law or don't you think so?" Forty-seven percent answered no and 46% "yes/deceived," with a margin of error of ±1.9% (Quinnipiac University Poll 2013). A clear partisan divide is apparent in the breakdown of the results, as 71% of Republicans, 17% of Democrats, and 51% of Independents believed the public had been deliberately deceived. Just as reliably partisan media outlets selectively emphasized framing the president as a liar or falsely accused depending on their ideological leanings, partisan citizens largely backed similarly divergent interpretations of events. Perhaps most damaging for the president's political prospects was the majority of independents who believed the public had been deceived, suggesting the prominence of the "Obama as lying" frame even in more objective media outlets may have influenced how Americans understood the events.

Opponents' frames encouraged viewing the dropped plans issue as exposing Obama's flaws as a leader. That association appeared in public opinion as well. November polls from both CNN and Quinnipiac showed for the first time in his presidency, a majority of Americans did not believe President Obama was honest and trustworthy (CNN Political Ticker 2013; Quinnipiac University Poll 2013). In the CNN survey, only 40% felt the president could manage the government effectively, down 12 percentage points from June 2013. Gallup polls showed a 5-point dip between September 2013 and November 2013 in the percentage of Americans who viewed Obama as honest and trustworthy and in those who felt he could manage the government effectively (Saad 2013). While President Clinton during the Lewinsky scandal took hits to his personal honesty and trustworthiness ratings but memorably retained high job approval numbers, the controversies over dropped plans and HealthCare.gov's faulty rollout damaged the public's evaluation of Obama's performance as president. A breakdown of one Washington Post-ABC News poll found that viewing President Obama as honest and trustworthy was a better predictor of whether respondents would approve of his job performance than several other qualities gauged by the survey (Cillizza and Sullivan 2013). *CBS News* on November 20, 2013 showed Obama at the lowest job approval rating of his presidency, with just 37% of the public expressing approval, compared to 46% in October—a considerable shift in a relatively short time period (Dutton et al. 2013).

Conclusion

A tremendous amount of news coverage was dedicated to the ACA's rollout in this time period, and Chapters 4 and 5 give us just a preliminary look at how some popular news outlets dealt with these events that proved so difficult for the Obama Administration to cast a favorable light upon. One lesson we might draw from this sketch of presidential communication and coverage however is that where controversies emerge from rhetoric and reality coming into conflict, a clear, focused, coherent presidential framing of events is vital to limiting the political damage. Where a president stands accused of obscuring the truth, a multitude of splintered, complicated narratives to explain away these discrepancies does little to rehabilitate the president's reputation.

The high stakes for the president in such a framing contest are apparent from the Obama experience. Even in more "objective" outlets, Republicans' framing promoting the dropped plans as a crisis for the ACA and the president's credibility was far more prevalent in much of the coverage than the frames defending Obama. An outlet such as MSNBC did prove far more hospitable for the president's frames, even modifying some through presidential frame refraction to make them more persuasive. Yet even this White House-friendly news source produced less hospitable coverage of the president's frames over time. Furthermore, not only did the Obama team's frames fail to produce uniform, vocal support among Democratic political elites, but several high-profile party figures, including a former president, publically contradicted those narratives. Accessing and maintaining the advantages of presidential framing resilience requires an Administration construct a communications strategy that will keep co-partisans in the fold, because it cannot assume their unquestioning support in the absence of a persuasive defense.

Consistently across all four outlets, President Obama's eventual apology did not appear to secure him more favorable coverage, and in all of the analyzed news sources, the presence of the opposition's frames increased relative to other frames. Having offered a laundry list of potential explanations for why Obama's pledge about keeping insurance one liked was not a broken promise, the president's late-arriving expression of regret only served to cast doubt on the sincerity of the framing of events the Administration had been proffering to that point. The direct, focused nature of the opposition's frames helped them gain a prominent footing even in unlikely media settings and forced the president, having seemingly lost the framing contest, to amend the actual substance of his signature policy in accordance with some of the demands of his harshest critics.

In the past two chapters, I have explored the limits of presidential framing in the modern-day news environment, both self-imposed and the product of outside constraints. But how do President Obama's framing opportunities stack up against those of his Democratic predecessors seeking to build and maintain support for health-care reform in earlier eras? That comparison is the subject of Chapter 6.

Notes

1 Such mandated essential benefits included things like hospitalization, maternity care, and prescription drugs.
2 The deadline was further delayed the following year, in what some observers believed was an effort to keep the cancelations from coming back to hurt Democrats in the 2014 midterm elections (Cowley 2014). This shows what a continuing political problem this issue presented for the president and his party.
3 The progressive cable news network was not the only liberal media outlet to participate in what I term presidential frame refraction. An *American Prospect* column warned this kind of predatory conduct by insurance companies could be afoot (Waldman 2013), and a few days later the blog *Talking Points Memo* (Scott 2013) published an investigative piece amassing evidence to support that claim.
4 In fact, in some cases the president seemed to undercut this idea, although the phrasing he used was somewhat unclear. At the end of October, Obama stated that "almost all the insurers are encouraging people to join better plans with the same carrier, and stronger benefits and stronger protections, while others will be able to get better plans with new carriers through the marketplace, and that many will get new help to pay for these better plans and make them actually cheaper" (Lee 2013). He certainly does not indicate that some companies might be purposefully hiding those better options in the marketplace from consumers.

References

All In with Chris Hayes. 2013. Transcript. *MSNBC*, November 12. Accessed on September 23, 2016. http://www.nbcnews.com/id/53542686/ns/msnbc-all_in_with_chris_hayes/

Alterman, Eric. 2004. *When Presidents Lie: A History of Official Deception and Its Consequences.* New York: Viking.

Associated Press. 2009. "Promises, Promises: Obama's Health Plan Guarantee." June 19. Accessed July 12, 2016. http://www.wbur.org/2009/06/19/obama-health-care-3.

Bernstein, Jonathan. 2012. "Campaign Promises: What They Say is How They'll Govern." *Washington Monthly*, January/February. Accessed July 12, 2016. http://www.washingtonmonthly.com/magazine/january_february_2012/features/campaign_promises034471.php?page=1

Chait, Jonathan. 2013. "Congressional Democrats Freak Out over Obamacare." *New York Magazine*, November 14. Accessed July 12, 2016. http://nymag.com/daily/intelligencer/2013/11/congressional-democrats-freak-out-over-obamacare.html.

Cillizza, Chris and Sean Sullivan. 2013. "The Fix: President Obama's Credibility Problem." *The Washington Post*, November 19. Accessed July 12, 2016. http://www.washingtonpost.com/blogs/the-fix/wp/2013/11/19/president-obamas-credibility-problem/.

CNN Political Ticker. 2013. "President's Marks as Manager Take Hit in New CNN/ORC Poll." November 25. Accessed July 12, 2016. http://politicalticker.blogs.cnn.com/2013/11/25/presidents-marks-as-manager-take-hit-in-new-cnnorc-poll/.

Cowley, Geoffrey. 2014. "Obama Gives Substandard Health Plans Another Reprieve." *MSNBC*, March 16. Accessed July 12, 2016. http://www.msnbc.com/msnbc/another-reprieve-substandard-health-plans.

Dickinson, Greg. 1994. "Creating His Own Constraint: Ronald Reagan and the Iran-Contra Crisis." In *The Modern Presidency and Crisis Rhetoric*, ed. Amos Kiewe, 155–178. Westport: Praeger.

Dutton, Sarah, Jennifer De Pinto, Anthony Salvanto, and Fred Backus. 2013. "Poll: Obamacare Support, Obama Approval Sink to New Llows." *CBS News*, November 20. Accessed July 12, 2016. http://www.cbsnews.com/news/poll-obamacare-support-obama-approval-sink-to-new-lows/.

Energy and Commerce Committee, The. 2013a. "PPACA Implementation Failures: What's Next?" 2013. Hearing Before the Subcommittee on Health. House of Representatives. 113th Congress, First Session. December 11, 2013b. Serial No. 113-108.

Energy and Commerce Committee, The. 2013. "Obamacare Implementation Problems: More than Just A Broken Website" Hearing before the Subcommittee on Health, November 14. House of Representatives. 113th Congress, First Session. Serial No. 113–95.

Entman, Robert M. 2012. *Scandal and Silence: Media Responses to Presidential Misconduct.* Cambridge, UK: Polity Press.

FactCheck.Org. 2009. "Keep Your Insurance? Not Everyone." August 18. http://www.factcheck.org/2013/10/reality-confronts-obamas-false-promise/.

Fishel, Jeff. 1985. *Presidents and Promises: From Campaign Pledge to Presidential Performance.* Washington, D.C.: CQ Press.

Fox News Poll. 2013. "Fox News Poll: Half of Voters Think President Lied about Obamacare, Majority Want Benghazi Probe to Continue." November 13. Accessed July 12, 2016. http://www.foxnews.com/politics/interactive/2013/11/13/fox-news-polls-half-voters-think-president-lied-about-obamacare-majority-want/.

Huey-Burns, Caitlin. 2013. "Senate Dems to Meet with WH Aides on Obamacare." *Real Clear Politics*, November 13. Accessed July 12, 2016. http://www.realclearpolitics.com/articles/2013/11/13/reid_confident_obamacare_can_be_fixed_120658.html.

Jackson, David and Jayne O'Donnell. 2013. "Obama Meets with Health Insurance CEOs." *USA Today*, November 15. Accessed July 12, 2016. http://www.usatoday.com/story/news/nation/2013/11/15/obama-obamacare-health-insurance-ceos/3581067/.

Jamieson, Kathleen Hall and Paul Waldman. 2004. *The Press Effect: Politicians, Journalists and the Stories that Shape the Political World*. New York: Oxford University Press.

Klein, Ezra. 2013. "Obamacare is in Much More Trouble than It Was One Week Ago." *The Washington Post*, November 13. Accessed July 12, 2016. https://www.washingtonpost.com/news/wonk/wp/2013/11/13/obamacare-is-in-much-more-trouble-than-it-was-one-week-ago/.

Lee, Jesse. 2013. "Fact-Check: Changes & Improvements in the Individual Market under the Affordable Care Act." *White House Blog*, October 30. https://www.whitehouse.gov/blog/2013/10/30/fact-check-changes-improvements-individual-market-under-affordable-care-act.

Levendusky, Matthew. 2013. *How Partisan Media Polarize America*. Chicago: The University of Chicago Press.

Lillis, Mike. 2013. "Pelosi Pushes Back Hard on Dropped Plans." *The Hill*, October 30. Accessed July 12, 2016. http://thehill.com/homenews/house/188697-pelosi-defends-obamacare-in-face-of-criticism-over-dropped-plans.

Nacos, Brigitte Lebens. 1990. *The Press, Presidents and Crises*. New York: Columbia University Press.

Nagourney, Adam and Megan Thee-Brenan. 2009. "New Poll Finds Growing Unease on Health Plan." *The New York Times*, July 29. Accessed July 12, 2016. http://www.nytimes.com/2009/07/30/us/politics/30poll.html.

New York Times, The. 2009. Obama's Speech on Health Care Reform. June 15. Accessed July 12, 2016. http://www.nytimes.com/2009/06/15/health/policy/15obama.text.html?pagewante d=4.

Parker, Ashley and Robert Pear. 2013. "House Approves Bill that Allows Policy Renewals." *The New York Times*, November 15. Accessed July 12, 2016. http://www.nytimes.com/2013/11/16/us/politics/obama-to-meet-with-insurance-executives.html?pagewanted=all.

Parker, Ashley and Michael D. Shear. 2013. "With Enrollment Slow, Some Democrats Back Change in Health Law." *The New York Times*, November 13. Accessed July 12, 2016. http://www.nytimes.com/2013/11/14/us/politics/democrats-threaten-to-abandon-obama-on-health-law-provision.html?ref=politics&_r=1.

Patterson, Thomas. 1994. *Out of Order*. New York: Vintage Books.

Patterson, Thomas E. 2003. *The Vanishing Voter: Public Involvement in an Age of Uncertainty*. New York: Vintage.

Pengelly, Martin. 2013. "Mitt Romney Criticizes Obama for Not 'Telling Truth' Over Healthcare." *The Guardian*, November 3. Accessed July 12, 2016. https://www.theguardian.com/world/2013/nov/03/mitt-romney-barack-obama-obamacare-republicans.

PolitiFact.com. 2013. "Lie of the Year: 'If You Like Your Health Care Plan, You Can Keep It." December 12. http://www.politifact.com/truth-o-meter/article/2013/dec/12/lie-year-if-you-like-your-health-care-plan-keep-it/.

PolitiFact.com. 2015. "The Obameter: Tracking Obama's Campaign Promises." Accessed July 12, 2016. http://www.politifact.com/truth-o-meter/promises/obameter/

Quinnipiac University Poll. 2013. "Obama Job Approval Drops to Lowest Point Ever, Quinnipiac University National Poll Finds; Health Care Act Won't Improve Health Care, Voters Say." November 12. Accessed July 12, 2016. http://www.quinnipiac.edu/news-and-events/quinnipiac-university-poll/national/release-detail?ReleaseID=1975.

Republican National Committee Official Blog. 2013. October 31. Accessed July 12, 2016. https://www.gop.com/obama-lied/?.

Saad, Lydia. 2013. "Obama's Image as 'Strong and Decisive Leader' Takes a Hit." *Gallup*, November 13. Accessed July 12, 2016. http://www.gallup.com/poll/165833/obama-image-strong-decisive-leader-takes-hit.aspx.

Scott, Dylan. 2013. "Special Investigation: How Insurers are Hiding Obamacare Benefits From Customers." *Talking Points Memo*, November 4. Accessed July 12, 2016. http://talkingpointsmemo.com/dc/insurance-companies-misleading-letters-obamacare.

Shear, Michael D. 2013. "Apologizing, Obama Yields to Criticism of Health Law." *The New York Times*, November 7. Accessed July 12, 2016. http://www.nytimes.com/2013/11/08/us/politics/obama-apologizes-to-americans-dropped-by-insurers.html.

Sullivan, Margaret. 2013. "Roundup: Staff Departures, an 'Incorrect Promise' and More." *The New York Times*, November 13. Accessed July 12, 2016. http://publiceditor.blogs.nytimes.com/2013/11/13/roundup-staff-departures-an-incorrect-promise-and-more/.

Todd, Chuck. 2013. "Obama Personally Apologizes for Americans Losing Health Care Coverage." *NBC News*, November 7. Accessed July 12, 2016. http://www.cnbc.com/id/101159465.

USA Today. 2013. "'Scrap This Law Once and For All': Other Views." November 14. http://www.usatoday.com/story/opinion/2013/11/14/obamacare-john-boehner-president-obama-editorials-debates/3550453/.

Waldman, Paul. 2013. "Time to Investigate Those Insurance Company Letters." *The American Prospect*, October 29. Accessed July 12, 2016. http://prospect.org/article/time-investigate-those-insurance-company-letters.

Washington Post, The. 2013. "Full Transcript: President Obama's Nov. 14 News Conference on the Affordable Care Act." November 14. Accessed July 16, 2016. https://www.washingtonpost.com/politics/transcript-president-obamas-nov-14-statement-on-health-care/2013/11/14/6233e352-4d48-11e3-ac54-aa84301ced81_story.html.

Weigel, David. 2013. "If You Like Your Panic, You Can Keep Your Panic." *Slate*, November 14. Accessed July 12, 2016. http://www.slate.com/articles/news_and_politics/politics/2013/11/democrats_and_ _affordable_care_act_fixes_the_party_has_no_choice_but_to_wait.html.

White House, The. 2010. "Remarks by the President on Health Insurance Reform in Portland, Maine. April 1. Accessed July 12, 2016. https://www.whitehouse.gov/the-press-office/remarks-president-health-insurance-reform-portland-maine.

White House, The. 2013a. "Press Briefing by Press Secretary Jay Carney." October 29. Accessed July 12, 2016. https://www.whitehouse.gov/the-press-office/2013/10/29/press-briefing-press-secretary-jay-carney-112913.

White House, The. 2013b. "Press Briefing by Press Secretary Jay Carney" November 5. Accessed July 12, 2016. https://www.whitehouse.gov/the-press-office/2013/11/05/press-briefing-press-secretary-jay-carney-11052013.

Wolf, Byron. 2013. "Obama Further Alters 'You Can Keep Your Plan' Pledge." *CNN Political Ticker*, November 5. http://politicalticker.blogs.cnn.com/2013/11/05/obama-further-refines-you-can-keep-your-plan-pledge/.

Zarefsky, David. 2005. *President Johnson's War on Poverty: Rhetoric and History*. Tuscaloosa: University of Alabama Press.

6

OF SOCIALIZED MEDICINE AND DEATH PANELS

Framing Contests over Health-Care Reform in Comparative Perspective

There were attacks levied against the Affordable Care Act that President Obama and his team appeared not to have anticipated, such as about the disastrous operation of HealthCare.gov, or accusing the president of deliberately lying to Americans about keeping their health insurance. However, there were other criticisms they could surely bank on. On the eve of the ACA's passage, speaking to an audience in Missouri, Obama said of Republicans who refused to back the law, "I get a sense with some of these folks, it's just never going to be the right time. But the truth is, we have debated health care in Washington not just this past year, we've been debating it for 70 years. You know who was pushing health-care reform? Harry Truman. Harry Truman was pushing health-care reform. And by the way, you know what they said? They said, he's pushing socialized medicine. Harry Truman" (White House 2009d.).

Not only was Truman's plan framed as "socialized medicine" by opponents, but he helped set the standard for the many health-reform-pushing Democratic presidents after him by quickly and categorically trying to prevent that framing of his proposal from taking hold. Just a few months after becoming president following Franklin D. Roosevelt's death, Truman sent Congress a message on November 19, 1945, concerning what many viewed as the unfinished business of the New Deal—his health plan called for building new hospitals, investing public money in medical research, disability protections, and national health insurance to cover every citizen. In the section advocating for this last provision, which Truman called "prepayment of medical costs," he asserted: "Everyone should have ready access to all necessary medical, hospital, and related services. I recommend solving the basic problem by distributing the costs through expansion of our existing compulsory social insurance system. This is not socialized medicine."[1] After recounting some of the specifics of how this would work, including patients remaining free to choose their own doctors and hospitals and physicians to participate or not, Truman wrote:

> None of this is really new. The American people are the most insurance-minded people in the world. They will not be frightened off from health insurance because some people have misnamed it "socialized medicine." I repeat—what I am recommending is not socialized medicine. Socialized medicine means that all doctors work as employees of government. The American people want no such system. No such system is here proposed.
> *(American Presidency Project 1945)*

Despite President Truman's attempt to dispel such fears, his plan failed to come to fruition. For decades after Democratic presidents pursued health-care reform, only to also see most of those efforts result in failure. That spotty record makes the passage of Medicare in 1965 and the Affordable Care Act in 2010 all the more noteworthy. There are numerous reasons why health-care reform efforts of the past fell short, among them a lack of clear public support. As several of the cases explored in this book attest to, health-care policy tends to be complex and laden with technical details. Those features can make reforms hard to explain effectively to the public, and allow policy opponents to exploit fear and low levels of knowledge among citizens. Like "Give 'Em Hell Harry," Truman's successors also worked to dismantle anxiety-inducing, destructive framings of their health-care plans lest they shift the political environment against reform.

I began this book by discussing the presidency media system in the 21st century moment and some of the ways it breaks notably from the past. In this chapter, I explore how those changes in the presidency and the media over time have affected the president's ability to frame his health-care proposals in the news. More specifically, I look at how Democratic presidents separated by over 40 years worked to overcome some of the most harshly critical framings opponents applied to their health-care plans and how the news media of their time covered those frames. During Presidents John F. Kennedy and Lyndon B. Johnson's push for Medicare in the early 1960s some opponents framed the proposal, just as in Truman's experience, as "socialized medicine," a charge that was raised again by critics of the ACA in 2009–2010, who also warned of the catastrophic consequences the law would usher in, such as "death panels" (see "The Affordable Care Act, 'Socialized Medicine' and 'Death Panels'" in this chapter).

This case is somewhat different from several of the other framing contests dealt with in the other chapters of this work. Rather than, for instance, the president and his critics constructing competing, complete frames depicting the individual mandate provision as either a "tax" or a "penalty," the Kennedy, Johnson, and Obama experiences here involve seeking to cast opponents' framing as fabricated and deceitful. These presidents offered a variety of reasons why the reforms they advocated could not credibly be classified as socialism, and, in the Obama case, why death panels were a lie.[2] Looking at opponents' frames in the news then, I identify how effective each president was at combating these damning narratives in popular media coverage of his time. How these efforts played out in two very different news media contexts, and the extent to which each president and his detractors could influence news narratives in each period can shed some light on how presidential framing advantages have ebbed and flowed over time. We can better flesh out presidential framing resilience and what effective presidential communication looks like today by considering how it compares to the past.

I find that President Obama, who undeniably had more sophisticated institutional and technological resources to quell the most extreme negative depictions of health reform than Kennedy and Johnson, surprisingly also benefited from a news media environment where his counter to opponents' framing was often independently substantiated. However, the fast pace of the 21st century news cycle and the ability of Americans to acquire political information from non-traditional sources meant the "socialized medicine" and "death panel" charges persisted over time, at least in some forums. Meanwhile, Kennedy and Johnson, although dealing with a narrower, manageable news media structure pre-Internet and cable television, had a much more difficult time getting news content to echo their challenges to the Medicare as socialized medicine frame. That difficulty, in part, appears attributable to the conventions of "objective" journalism of the time emphasizing presentation of "facts" of events as opposed to "balance" in reporting. Returning to the main argument of this book then, the comparison across these Administrations reveals how presidential framing resilience might be indicative of communications strengths available to 21st century presidents that their mid-20th century counterparts did not have. This is unexpected given the far more complex and fragmented news environment of today than decades earlier.

These three presidents pursued different strategies in seeking to fight the spread of their critics' frames, indicating not only how the office of the presidency and technologies have changed over time, but also how an individual president's communication style shapes how the White House will engage in such a contest. Within this story of difference and change, however, is also a thread of continuity: each president selected similar themes to counter opponents, and all three had some difficulty getting their views across in more conservative-leaning media. I begin with the cases of Kennedy and Johnson, reviewing the sources of the socialized medicine frame at the time, and then highlighting a high-profile, consequential moment for each president in his battle to undercut that interpretation of his plans.

Medicare as "Socialized Medicine"

Although some Republicans and conservative groups also applied the "socialism" frame to Democratic healthcare proposals, the American Medical Association

(AMA), an interest group advocating for physicians and the medical profession, was arguably the most prominent source of this attack throughout the mid-20th century (Berkowitz 2005, 332). Whereas some more recent polls demonstrate that "socialized medicine" may not have an entirely negative connotation in the present era, particularly among Democrats (Harvard School of Public Health 2008), the Cold War anti-communist context of this earlier time made the accusation highly damaging. When President Truman first proposed his national health-care system plan, it appeared unlikely Congress would pass it, and yet the AMA still spent over a million dollars, a staggering amount for the time period, advertising against what they termed a "government takeover" of medicine (Blumenthal and Morone 2009, 93).

As Medicare, the Federal program providing health insurance to Americans 65 and older, and earlier versions of that policy, made their way through Congress in the mid-1960s, the AMA again levied the "socialized medicine" condemnation. In 1961, the AMA had Ronald Reagan, then at the very start of his political career, make a record to be distributed and played at the group's anti-Medicare rallies (Zelizer 2015). The future president told listeners that "one of the traditional methods of imposing statism or socialism on a people has been by way of medicine," and warned if Americans did not act immediately, "we will wake to find that we have socialism . . . we are going to spend our sunset years telling our children and our children's children what it once was like in America when men were free."[3] Despite the onslaught of attacks by the AMA, several authors (Marmor 1973; Blumenthal and Morone 2009) contend that conservatives in Congress, including both Republicans and southern Democrats, are the real reason Medicare did not pass before 1965. Still, these scholars credit the AMA with significantly changing the terms of the debate around Medicare, and putting the policy's advocates on the defensive throughout this time period. I now turn to President Kennedy's major address, where he cast "socialized medicine" as a false framing of the policy by the AMA.

Kennedy "Going Public" at the Garden

The Kennedy Administration's Medical Care for the Aged plan, a proposal that eventually would evolve into Medicare, called for a small increase in Social Security contributions to help pay for the hospital and nursing home costs of those over 65. Throughout the debate surrounding Kennedy's plan, it was clear how large the AMA loomed as a source of opposition for the president and his team. When the bill failed in the Senate by two votes in July 1962, President Kennedy noted in his official remarks, "I hope we will return in November a Congress that will support a program like Medical Care for the Aged, a program which has been fought by the American Medical Association and successfully defeated" (White House Staff File Papers 1962b). Louis Harris' polling in the first sixty days of the Kennedy Administration had argued Kennedy should counter the AMA's communication about the policy in a very public manner—"It is a classic case of an issue which, if handled quietly, will die aborning in the legislative chambers. But if made a dramatic and essentially human and economic issue, it will in short order overpower the special interest groups working on Capitol Hill. We would recommend that this issue be one that the President takes directly to the people."[4] White House press conference briefing memos noted the framing of the Administration's bill as "the first step to socialism," countering, "But these were attacks on Social Security in the 1930s—the identical . . . attacks made on Health Insurance today, and from the same sources—the A.M.A., the N.A.M., and the G.O.P." (White House Staff File Papers 1962a).

Taking this contest to the people, as advised, President Kennedy gave a high-profile public address in support of the policy on May 20, 1962, at a Madison Square Garden rally sponsored by the Golden Ring Council of Senior Citizens and the National Council of Senior Citizens, in conjunction with over 30 similar rallies held around the country to show support for the president's plan. News reports put attendance at the Garden rally at over 17,000, an audience largely made up of senior citizens, with many more people gathered outside the building, and the speech was shown on all three broadcast television networks. Unlike the challenges Obama occasionally faced in securing a prime-time television time slot, here the less complex media era played to the advantage of the president, assuring Kennedy a large audience.

Kennedy's address stressed several themes to undercut the AMA's "socialism" frame: that this health-care reform reflected deeply held American values in the tradition of the New Deal; was a modest, moderate bill that shouldn't cause alarm; and was being opposed by special interests counter to the public good. He began his speech with the story of a "typical" American family, featuring a retired husband whose wife suddenly suffers a serious illness.[5] The man, the president explained, "has always wanted to pay his own way. He does not ask anyone to care for him; he wants to care for himself." But the resulting medical bills exhaust the couple's savings and that of their adult children. The president's proposed bill would pay the hospital bills, and then the citizen and the "effort that he makes, and his family, can meet his other responsibilities." Emphasizing how moderate this plan was, Kennedy stressed, "Now that does not seem such an extraordinary piece of legislation, 25 years after Franklin Roosevelt passed the Social Security Act." The president also used a comparative argument, noting that the proposed program was not as extensive as government-run health care for all in England, and "The fact of the matter is that what we are now talking about doing, most of the countries of Europe did years ago. The British did it 30 years ago. We are behind every country, pretty nearly, in Europe, in this matter of medical care for our citizens."

In direct response to critics of Medicare, the president told his audience, "And then I read that this bill will sap the individual self-reliance of Americans. I can't imagine anything worse, or anything better, to sap someone's self-reliance, than to be sick, alone, broke—or to have saved for a lifetime and put it out in a week, two weeks, a month, two months." The system rested upon the productive contributions of citizens, Kennedy argued, stating "Nobody in this hall is asking for it for nothing. They are willing to contribute during their working years. That is the important principle which has been lost sight of."

Further, Kennedy spoke about the AMA's framing of the bill and alluded to the spread of distortions: "We read that the AMA is against it, and they are entitled to be against it. Though I do question how many of those who speak so violently about it have read it." The president went on, "And I hope that one by one the doctors of the United States will take the extraordinary step of not merely reading the journals and the publications of the AMA, because I do not recognize the bill when I hear those descriptions, but instead to write Secretary Ribicoff in Washington, or to me—and you know where I live—or to Senator Anderson or to Congressman King, if you are a doctor or opposed to this bill, and get a concise explanation and the bill itself and read it." Praising doctors for all the ways serve the public, Kennedy noted, "There are doctors in New Jersey who say they will not treat any patient who receives it. Of course they will. They are engaged in an effort to stop the bill. . . . The point of the matter is that the AMA is doing very well in its efforts to stop this bill. And the doctors of New Jersey and every other state may be opposed to it, but I know that not a single doctor—if this bill is passed—is going to refuse to treat any patient." In what appeared to be a reference to the "socialism" frame without using the word explicitly, President Kennedy continued, "All these arguments were made against social security at the time of Franklin Roosevelt. They are made today. The mail pours in. And at least half of the mail which I receive in the White House, on this issue and others, is wholly misinformed."

The president cast the policy's opponents as a well-financed, powerful lobby deliberately misleading people about the substance of the bill and obstructing the will of the people: "There are so many busy men in Washington who write—some organizations have six, seven, and eight hundred people spreading mail across the country, asking doctors and others to write in and tell your Congressman you're opposed to it. The mail pours into the White House, into the Congress and Senators' offices—Congressmen and Senators feel people are opposed to it. Then they read a Gallup Poll which says 75 percent of the people are in favor of it, and they say, 'What has happened to my mail?'"

Finally, the president positioned himself on the side of progress and as fulfilling the promises of the New Deal era and his Democratic predecessors and taking them into new directions: "Every day I am reminded of how many things were left undone. . . Anyone who says that Woodrow Wilson, as great a President as he was, and Franklin Roosevelt and Harry Truman, that they did it all and we have nothing left to do now, is wrong . . . all who are committed to this great effort of moving this country forward: come and give us your help." Decades later, President Obama would also place his proposed health-reform plan in the context of the unfinished business of the Democratic presidents who went before him.

The AMA Responds to Kennedy

The AMA wasted no time defending its fear-inducing framing of the Medical Care for the Aged plan following Kennedy's speech. The association rented the exact same venue, Madison Square Garden, the following evening and even bought time on NBC to broadcast its response to the country. Addressing an empty arena, the organization's president, Dr. Edward Annis, compared the AMA's event with the president's rally, noting, "Nobody, certainly not your doctors, nobody can compete in this unfamiliar art of public persuasion against such massive publicity, such enormous professional machinery, such unexplained money and such skillful manipulation."[6] Turning Kennedy's powerful special interest argument on its head, it was inherently unfair, according to Annis, when the president's message gets "televised all over three networks, free-of-charge as a news event . . . when your doctors asking for equal time to make reply, got turned down and have to pay for a half an hour on one network to tell you the other side of the story." Presidents in Kennedy's time might have a freer hand to commandeer coveted television real estate, but in this case it opened Kennedy up to the criticism that he was using the tools of propaganda to drown out the valid concerns of the country's medical care providers, which capitalized on the trust most people have for their physicians. Annis accused Kennedy of being the one responsible for misleading the public: "If our government wants to move toward Welfare State medicine, let them tell us so honestly. Why sneak it in piece by piece on the backs of old people first?"

Media Coverage of Kennedy's Speech: Just the "Facts"

I now look at media coverage for a week after Kennedy's speech in *The New York Times* and *The Chicago Tribune*, two prominent newspapers of the time associated with different regions of the country and ideological leanings.[7]

Most articles in the two papers privileged either the president's views on Medicare or those of his opponents, as shown in Figure 6.1, with a minority of articles providing the relatively balanced account of perspectives we typically associate with objective coverage today. News coverage of Kennedy's speech was far more positive in the *Times* than the *Tribune*, as the editorial stance of each paper—in favor of and opposed to Medicare, respectively—was reflected in the space they afforded the president and his critics. Although Kennedy's arguments in favor of hospital care for the aged were certainly transmitted to readers of both the *Times* and the *Tribune* on the front page the day after the rally, the AMA's counter-rally the following evening also garnered headlines in both papers and gave the impression Kennedy's proposal was highly controversial.

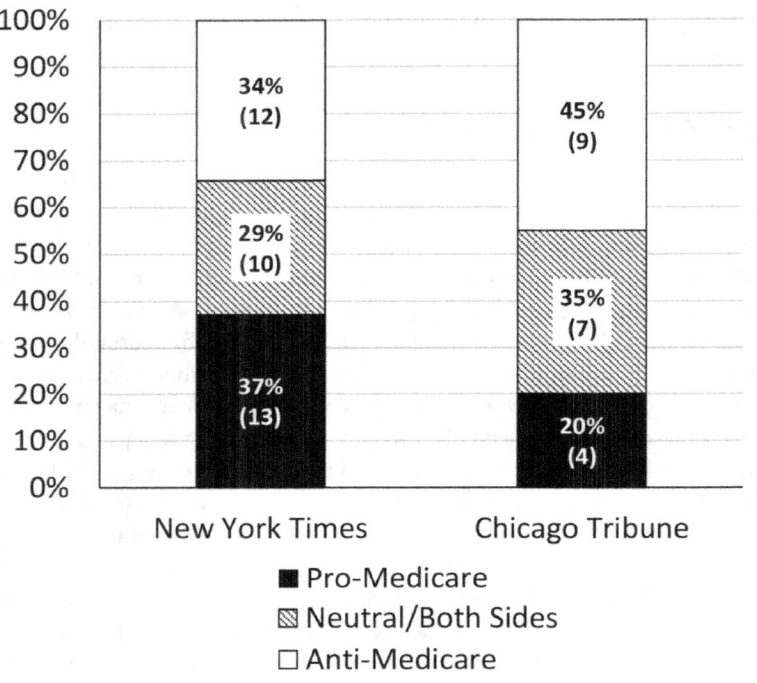

FIGURE 6.1 Coverage of Kennedy's Health Care Proposal, Week Following MSG Speech

Despite his efforts to bring the issue to the public and counter opponents' framing of his proposal, Kennedy was unable to create a groundswell of grassroots support big enough to counteract congressional resistance, and his hospital care for the elderly plan failed to pass during his time in office.

President Johnson and Securing Support for Medicare's Implementation

Under President Johnson, the prospects for Medicare's passage improved dramatically with the Democratic landslide of 1964, though the specifics of what the program would entail were still subject to debate. Johnson had initially omitted doctors' fees from his proposal precisely to prevent the charge that he was advocating "socialized medicine," but ironically, Democratic Arkansas Congressman Wilbur Mills, Chair of the Ways and Means Committee, incorporated both Republican and AMA policy alternatives into the final version of the bill, which therefore now included a voluntary insurance program to help cover doctors' fees (Dallek 2004, 198f).

Like the Kennedy Administration before it, the Johnson team felt the need to stay one step ahead of the AMA. On March 23, 1965, the president urged

Under Secretary of Health, Education and Welfare Wilbur Cohen to tell congressional leaders to push ahead on the Medicare bill as soon as possible, exhorting him to "tell them not to let it lay around. Do that! They want to, but they might not. Then that gets the doctors organized. Then they get the others organized. And I damn near killed my education bill, letting it lay around!" (Beschloss 2002, 241). For months the AMA had been filling doctors' offices with brochures featuring an "open letter from your doctor," taking the framing contest directly to Americans by telling them, "My concern is that if this compulsory King-Anderson Bill is enacted, the politicians will try to make me a socialized, government-paid doctor and you a socialized, regulated patient" (White House Central Files 1964). In the summer of 1965, the AMA spent a reported $5,000 per day in a lobbying campaign to try to defeat Medicare, adding to the astounding $50 million total the association spent in the entire battle to combat the program (Andrew 1999, 101).

Even as Medicare's passage became seemingly inevitable in the summer of 1965, Johnson and his team worried about how the AMA could continue to obstruct the program. In his memoirs, Johnson related that even after Medicare was enacted by Congress in late July 1965, "The hardest job lay ahead. There was wide speculation that doctors, with the support of the AMA, would boycott Medicare" (Johnson 1971, 217). The AMA's House of Delegates had voted the month before to let individual doctors determine for themselves whether or not they would boycott the Medicare program, and eight states went on to pass resolutions backing boycotts (Andrew 1999, 101). White House aide Horace Busby urged the president's senior staff not to go ahead with a plan to hold the bill's signing in Missouri with President Truman, because associating the new law with Truman's proposal "would be a grotesque distortion with unhappy and impolitic overtones. President Truman requested medical coverage for all the population, regardless of age—a close parallel to Great Britain's 'socialized medicine.'" Busby predicted this setting would produce "a boycott and denunciation of the ceremony by leaders of the AMA with whom we are now attempting to work" (White House Central Files 1965). Johnson did it anyway, issuing Truman and his wife the very first Medicare cards.

Perhaps because the AMA realized some form of Medicare was going to be passed in 1965, representatives of the AMA contacted the Johnson Administration several times between March and May of that year to try to arrange a meeting with the president. These requests were all denied until just before the president was to sign the bill into law (White House Central Files 1963–1966). This timing suggests that the White House had no interest in speaking to the doctors until the president was doing so from a position of power, with Medicare a done deal. The meeting was thus set for July 29, just one day before the bill's signing. Johnson's Special Assistant Douglass Cater, in a memo advising the president about the appointment, emphasized, "This is an important opportunity to urge the medical profession to cooperate with the Government in making Medicare a success. They have requested to see you. But you should take the initiative in making clear to them that the legislative struggle is over—now it is time to work together to make the new act work" (White House Central Files 1965). Internal White House communications about the AMA meeting reported, "No remarks are needed. It is an office (or Cabinet Room) meeting," and the meeting was initially listed on the president's schedule as "off record" (Appointment File 1965). However, the meeting would not remain off the record for long.

While Kennedy had very publically countered the "socialized medicine" charge, Johnson, as one might expect of the president famous for cajoling support from others with a signature mix of flattery and intimidation, maneuvered behind the scenes to force the AMA to express support for Medicare. In the course of that July 29 meeting, Johnson asked for aid organizing a program to send physicians to Vietnam, which the organization's representatives quickly agreed to. Johnson then summoned reporters to cover the AMA's backing for the Vietnam program and showered the organization with praise. Reporters asked whether the doctors would back Medicare, which historian Robert Dallek (2004, 200) argues was precipitated by the journalists being "undoubtedly primed by [White House Press Secretary Bill] Moyers." Johnson acted offended by the reporters' question, responding, "These men are going to get doctors to go to Viet Nam where they might be killed . . . Medicare is the law of the land. Of course they'll support the law." He then turned to AMA President James Appel and said, "You tell him." Appel obeyed, responding in the affirmative, saying, yes, "We are, after all, law-abiding citizens" (Califano 2015, 50f). Instead of a war of words on television in competing speeches as Kennedy had engaged in, Johnson worked to neutralize his opponents in the media spotlight, putting the AMA in a position where it would be very difficult to continue framing the Administration's policy as dangerous socialized medicine.

Later describing the July 29 meeting in his memoirs, Johnson noted, "If any of the AMA leaders came to the meeting that day primed to be difficult, I did not give them the opportunity." Johnson went on to describe how he emphasized to the group the "respect and gratitude for doctors" that Americans, including himself personally, had and how important they would be to the Medicare program, which "was going to be an inevitable part of their lives." Johnson does not mention involving reporters or photographers in this moment, but does recall, "I said I hoped they would give that cooperation, and I indicated I was sure they would" (Johnson 1971, 217f).

This public avowal of support for Medicare's implementation by the AMA then allowed Cater to go to a press conference later in the day and tell reporters that the doctors' association had "pledged their desire to be cooperative" and that the AMA felt "when an organization was permitted to come in like this it dispelled a feeling of fear of Government" (News Conference at the White House 1965). This turnaround was important, given that "fear of government" was precisely the feeling the AMA had previously sought to evoke by likening

Medicare to socialism. The organization was, by this point, torn apart by internal divisions over whether it should continue its fight against Medicare now that it was the law of the land, and President Johnson helped expose and exacerbate these fractures within the medical profession by co-opting their leadership, getting the AMA's president to explicitly support the new law's implementation, with reporters as witnesses. President Johnson used the news media to his advantage not through a major prime-time address, but instead via strategic maneuvering less readily available to presidents today.

News Coverage of Johnson's Meeting with the AMA

If one of Johnson's goals was to gain media attention for the Medicare endorsement he had cajoled out of Appel, he was more effective at shaping coverage to his liking in both *The New York Times* and *The Chicago Tribune* than the Kennedy efforts explored above. To be sure, Johnson's aims were more limited in scope then dispelling the framing of Medicare as socialized medicine generally. Instead, the president worked to prevent the AMA's leadership from being able to believably promote such a detrimental interpretation of the law any further in the public debate around Medicare. The *Times* reported President Johnson held an "unusual meeting lasting nearly 2 hours" with the leaders of the AMA, "which fought the Medicare bill with every resource at its command. The principal purposes of the meeting were, in the words of one White House source, 'to smooth the way for implementation of Medicare and convince the doctors that the Government was not planning to straitjacket the medical profession.' Apparently Mr. Johnson was successful on both counts. The association leaders agreed to cooperate with the appropriate Federal officials in administering the program and acknowledged that the meeting had done much to alleviate their suspicions about the Federal Government's intentions" (Semple 1965). The *Chicago Tribune*'s July 30 headline read, "A.M.A. Chief Vows to Obey Medicare Bill," publicizing the surprising backing of the organization even in the pages of the more right-leaning newspaper.

This expression of AMA support proved important as the summer wore on. As the *Times* reported on its front page in early August, the Association of American Physicians and Surgeons, representing 16,500 members, criticized the AMA for failing to support a boycott of Medicare after its passage. The group's leader said, "the action taken by the AMA's House of Delegates in June left it up to the individual doctor to decide whether to cooperate with the health program," and his particular organization recommended not cooperating. The *Times* noted the group "was formed in 1943 by members of the AMA to oppose socialization of medicine in America. He said that wherever socialized medicine had been tried, a deterioration has occurred in the quality of medical care" (*New York Times* 1965a). Had organized medicine presented a united front in continuing to frame Medicare as the slippery slope to socialism and engaged in a coordinated boycott, the long-fought battle over health care for the aged might have persisted.

Framing Medicare as "Socialized Medicine" in the News in the mid-1960s

Beyond this look at news coverage immediately following efforts by Presidents Kennedy and Johnson to neutralize the claims of Medicare's critics, how did the "socialized medicine" frame fare over a longer period in *The New York Times*? Along with an independent coder, I analyzed all *The New York Times* articles, including the terms "Medicare" and "socialized" or "socialist" in the years 1962–1965. The goal was to assess whether the article's content focused on the view that Medicare is/will be socialized medicine or a socialist policy (with no content undermining that viewpoint); expressed solely the view that Medicare is not/will not be equivalent to socialized medicine or a socialist policy; or featured "both sides" of the contest over whether Medicare is/will be socialized medicine. The unit of analysis was the article, due to the short nature of most of the pieces in the *Times*.[8]

Figure 6.2 demonstrates the extent to which presidents can engage in agenda-setting, focusing the media's attention on health-care reform, as President Kennedy did in advocating for the policy in early 1962, and President Johnson did in the 1964 election through Medicare's passage into law in 1965. However, it also illustrates the ways that the president's opponents could seize control of news narratives, given the substantial portion of coverage that passed on the "socialized medicine" frame without direct, explicit contradiction in the same article. For instance, on June 27, 1965, the *Times* reported, "Since 1920 the A.M.A. has fought an expensive but losing battle against 'third party encroachment' and government programs that its members fear are steps toward 'socialized medicine' . . . the underlying basic dread is that Medicare today means nationalized health care tomorrow: harassing regulations and paperwork dictated by Washington . . . they fear overcrowded hospitals and nursing homes and a waste of available medical resources" (*New York Times* 1965b).

The 1964 presidential election context led to a plurality of the coverage meeting the "balanced" or "both sides" category, perhaps an indication of how the news media of the time might be more likely to pursue "objective" reporting as we are familiar with it today, in the midst of a high-profile, national campaign battle between the two major political parties. In the other years of the analysis, when Medicare was framed as either "socialized medicine" or *not* "socialized medicine" in an article, it was not uncommon for that framing to be presented unchallenged. Again we are confronted with what "objectivity" might have meant to journalists in the mid-1960s, emphasizing reporting just the "facts" as provided by prominent political actors and not the "balanced" style stressed by the mainstream media today. As seen in the pie chart in Figure 6.2, a majority of the *Times* articles presented one side of the "socialized medicine" framing contest, but not both side by side.

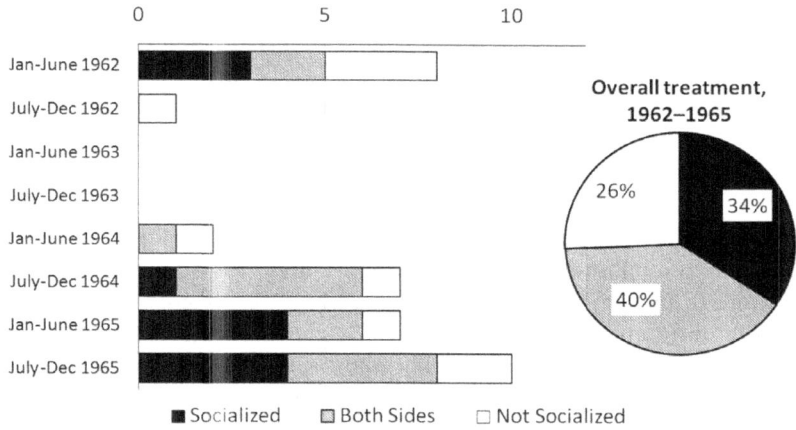

FIGURE 6.2   Number of Articles in Which Medicare Was Discussed as "Socialized Medicine" in *The New York Times*, 1962–1965

The Affordable Care Act, "Socialized Medicine," and "Death Panels"

Decades after Medicare's passage, as President Obama and his supporters in Congress worked to pass the ACA, "socialized medicine" once again plagued a Democratic president's health-care reform plans. This time, however, the frame did not come from the AMA, which the Obama Administration had worked early on to bring into the fold with various concessions, along with other special interests that had the potential resources to spend millions derailing health-care reform, such as the pharmaceutical industry (Starr 2013, 205, 224). Still, as Starr (2013, 9) informs us, part of the legacy of the AMA and other opponents of health-care reform over time has been "ideas and language that American conservatives summon when they oppose proposals for government financing of health insurance." Chapter 2 provided explicit examples of Mitt Romney, Michele Bachmann, and Fox News program hosts talking about "Obamacare" as socialism or socialized medicine over the years the policy was debated and implemented into law. In the summer of 2009, chairman of the Republican Party Michael Steele accused the Democratic "Obama-Pelosi-Reid-Waxman cabal" of pushing a health-care plan that equated to socialism (*CBS News* 2009). Senator Orrin Hatch (R-UT) told reporters that fall that the health-care proposals before Congress were a "step-by-step approach to socialized medicine," which threatened the very structure of competitive democratic politics, because "if they get there, of course, you're going to have a very rough time having a two-party system in this country because almost everybody's going to say, 'All we ever were, all we ever are, all we ever hope to be depends on the Democratic Party. That's their goal" (O'Brien 2009). The liberal group Media

Matters amassed a laundry list of media personalities discussing the proposed reforms as socialized medicine throughout 2009 (Media Matters for America 2009a). Many Republican politicians adhered to talking points put together by strategist Frank Luntz that encouraged casting the plan as "a government takeover of health care" (Adair and Holan 2010), phrasing that also implied the socialism charge.

Cries of socialism regarding health-care reform became particularly loud over the summer of 2009, as media outlets gave a great deal of dramatic coverage to citizens opposing health-care reform in those and other extreme terms, at town hall meetings held by various members of Congress. Many of the protesters were encouraged to disrupt the meetings by grassroots Tea Party organizations and conservative media personalities (Beutler 2009; Urbina 2009). In response, President Obama held his own town hall meetings (with far more supportive, pre-screened crowds) during which he repeatedly sought to debunk such claims. Whereas Kennedy was able to focus his energies on a single major rally appearance that was carried on all the major media networks, as Heith (2013) illustrates, today the fragmented nature of the modern media can incentivize presidents to instead travel around the country giving speeches in support of their agenda to reach audiences with their message, as Obama did here. The Obama team also took advantage of communications tools Kennedy and Johnson did not have access to, such as setting up a "Health Insurance Reality Check" website aimed specifically at countering the more outrageous claims of opponents.

In his town hall meetings, portions of which were broadcast on cable news networks, Obama directly addressed the damaging frames of health-care's opponents. On August 14 in Montana, the president responded to a question about how the proposed changes might compare to Canada or Britain's health-care system by noting those countries have "what people I guess would call a socialized system in the sense that government owns the hospitals, directly hires doctors" (White House 2009b). Obama said he was not in favor of such a system for the U.S. "And so when you start hearing people saying, you know, we're trying to get socialized medicine and we're trying to have government bureaucrats meddle in your decision-making between you and your doctor, that's just not true."

A few days later in Colorado, the president replicated Kennedy's communications strategy of framing his proposal as akin to established, well-liked policies hard-won by his Democratic predecessors, though Obama had a longer history to refer to. Opponents of reform, according to President Obama, had always sought to frighten the public to prevent change, declaring:

> That's what happened when FDR tried to pass Social Security—they said that was socialist. They did—verbatim. That's what they said. They said that everybody was going to have to wear dog tags and that this was a

plot for the government to keep track of everybody. When JFK and then Lyndon Johnson tried to pass Medicare, they said this was a government takeover of health care; they were going to get between you and your doctor—the same argument that's being made today.

(White House 2009c)

This sentiment was reiterated in Obama's September 9, 2009, prime-time televised address before Congress, where he highlighted the government's role in helping ensure citizens' well-being as integral to "the history of our progress. In 1935, when over half of our seniors could not support themselves and millions had seen their savings wiped away, there were those who argued that Social Security would lead to socialism, but the men and women of Congress stood fast, and we are all the better for it. In 1965, when some argued that Medicare represented a government takeover of health care, members of Congress—Democrats and Republicans—did not back down."[9]

News Coverage of the ACA as "Socialized Medicine"

I searched *The New York Times*, *The Washington Post*, *The New York Post*, and CNN.com for any mentions of "socialized medicine" between the dates of August 1, 2009 and March 24, 2010, to capture the time period as health-care reform plans were debated in Congress through the ACA's passage into law.[10] These outlets give us a preliminary sense of how the frame fared in the more complicated contemporary news environment, including prestige press outlets, tabloid newspapers, and online news sources affiliated with cable news. The method of analysis was the same as in the Medicare case as to whether framing the policy as socialized medicine was substantiated, undermined, or "both sides" were relayed, with the unit of analysis again the article.

The assessment of coverage of "socialized medicine" in *The New York Times*, *The Washington Post*, and CNN.com depicted in Figure 6.3 shows that these mainstream news outlets were most likely to publish pieces that either dispelled the socialism frame or presented both sides of the contest. For media organizations more committed to "objective" reporting, this reflects the altered news norms since the 1960s that now prioritized "accuracy" and "balance" as key journalistic values. Those values are not, as evidenced by the figure, held in high esteem by *The New York Post*, perhaps because it is a tabloid newspaper. Devoting far less overall attention to health-care policy than the other outlets analyzed, the conservative-leaning *New York Post* deemed it sufficient to remind readers roughly once a month in the fall of 2009 that Obama and the Democrats were forcing socialized medicine on the country. Here we get a glimpse of how partisan media sources might largely ignore the president's takedown of his detractors' frames.

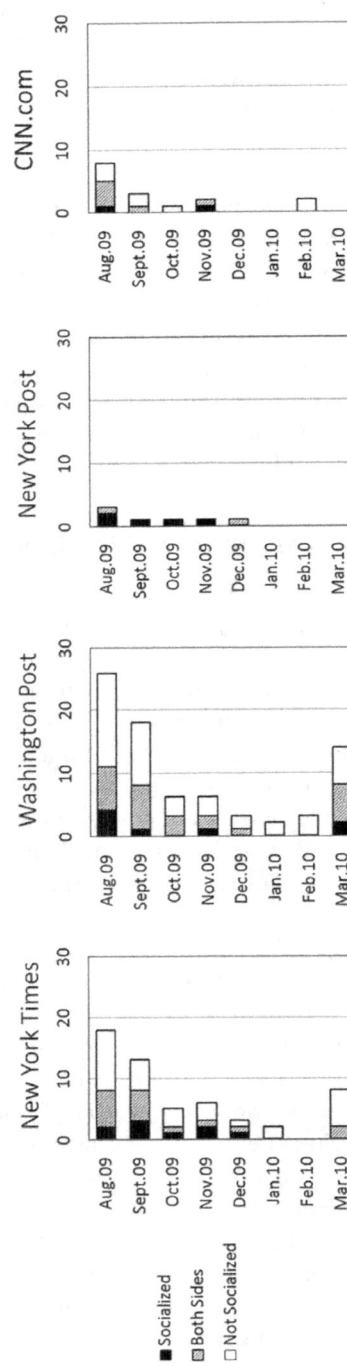

FIGURE 6.3 Treatment of ACA as "Socialized Medicine" by Month across News Outlets, August 2009–March 2010

However, open-ended Gallup polls in September 2009 and March 2010 found that only 3% and 4%, respectively, of those who said they would urge their member of Congress to vote against the ACA provided their main reason as "socialism" or "socialized medicine." The most popular responses instead were that the bill would raise costs and make insurance more expensive (Gallup 2016). Even among the law's opponents in the public then the "socialized medicine" frame did not appear to circulate widely, perhaps thanks to the president's communications, or because it no longer carries the same sting it did in the mid-20th century.

The "Death Panels" Controversy

In addition to raising the age-old specter of socialized medicine, Republicans and conservative groups that stood against the plan that would become the Affordable Care Act developed new lines of fear-inducing attacks, including framing end-of-life care provisions as government administered "death panels." That interpretation appears to have originated with Betsy McCaughey, a former Lieutenant-Governor of New York, who appeared on a conservative radio program in the summer of 2009 and stated, "Congress would make it mandatory—absolutely require—that every five years people in Medicare have a required counseling session that will tell them how to end their life sooner" (Lieberman 2009). The "death panels" term itself was coined by Sarah Palin in her infamous Facebook post on August 7, 2009, where she wrote, "The America I know and love is not one in which my parents or my baby with Down Syndrome will have to stand in front of Obama's 'death panel' so his bureaucrats can decide, based on a subjective judgment of their 'level of productivity in society,' whether they are worthy of health care. Such a system is downright evil."[11] Framing end-of-life care in health-care reform as "death panels" ultimately had a significant policy impact: the relevant provisions were dropped from the ACA before it was passed, and not until 2016 did Medicare begin reimbursing beneficiaries for end-of-life planning conversations with their doctor (Associated Press 2016).

Factcheck.org (2009) deemed Palin's words inaccurate, the *St. Petersburg Times'* PolitiFact.com awarded "death panels" its 2009 "Lie of the Year" designation (Holan 2009), and media watchdog groups noted numerous instances in which the mainstream press debunked the claim (Media Matters for America 2009b). In today's media context, we often assume that widely rejected narratives like these originate and spread from the bottom up on the Internet. But in this case, what was generally pilloried as a false framing of the policy was generated by a prominent political figure. An extreme frame might gain a lot of traction on the web, but one can still identify a top-down dimension to the communication process—a politician like Sarah Palin, with a bright media spotlight and sizeable public following was able to get the ball rolling. Subsequently, some prominent, mainstream Republican politicians also adopted this framing:

for instance, Senator Chuck Grassley (R-IA) stated just a few days later that we "should not have a government-run plan to decide when to pull the plug on grandma" (Lerer 2009).

One of the core assumptions of the concept of presidential framing resilience is that there are, in fact, presidential frames being offered by the Administration rather than silence. Despite the speed of the 21st century news cycle, the Obama Administration's moves to dispel the death panels frame in the wake of Palin's Facebook posting were slow and minimal. The White House waited four days to respond to these particular attacks, with communications director Dan Pfeiffer explaining, "We thought it was absurd and there was a perhaps naive view on our part that, if a major political figure says something that is entirely untrue and ridiculous, the press would treat it as untrue and ridiculous" (Auletta 2010).

President Obama did first address the "death panels" charge at one of the same health-care town hall events that he used to refute the socialism criticisms. In New Hampshire on August 11, 2009, Obama spoke about some of the "wild representations" about the bill, stating:

> The rumor that's been circulating a lot lately is this idea that somehow the House of Representatives voted for "death panels" that will basically pull the plug on grandma because we've decided that we don't—it's too expensive to let her live anymore. (Laughter.) And there are various—there are some variations on this theme. It turns out that I guess this arose out of a provision in one of the House bills that allowed Medicare to reimburse people for consultations about end-of-life care, setting up living wills, the availability of hospice, et cetera. So the intention of the members of Congress was to give people more information so that they could handle issues of end-of-life care when they're ready, on their own terms. It wasn't forcing anybody to do anything. This is I guess where the rumor came from. The irony is that actually one of the chief sponsors of this bill originally was a Republican—then House member, now senator, named Johnny Isakson from Georgia—who very sensibly thought this is something that would expand people's options. And somehow it's gotten spun into this idea of "death panels." I am not in favor of that. So just I want to—(applause.) I want to clear the air here.
>
> *(White House 2009a)*

Additionally, in his aforementioned September 9, 2009 televised address, the president had stated, "Some of people's concerns have grown out of bogus claims spread by those whose only agenda is to kill reform at any cost. The best example is the claim made not just by radio and cable talk show hosts, but by prominent politicians, that we plan to set up panels of bureaucrats with the power to kill off senior citizens. Now, such a charge would be laughable if it weren't so cynical and irresponsible. It is a lie, plain and simple." As Kennedy had in 1962, the president used his prime-time televised address on health-care reform as an opportunity to directly tackle the more extreme frames of his opponents.

"Death Panels" Dismantled in the News

Again looking at *The New York Times*, *The Washington Post*, *The New York Post*, and CNN.com, I searched for any mentions of "death panel" or "death panels" between the same dates of August 1, 2009 and March 24, 2010. Each instance in which "death panels" appeared in the coverage was coded as to whether they were depicted as a valid, legitimate concern about the policy; as an illegitimate, inaccurate concern about the policy; or as neutral/mixed assessment of their accuracy. The unit of analysis was the paragraph, to allow for a better indication of how the misconception fared within the content of these articles, many of them quite lengthy.[12]

Across all four outlets, the most content about "death panels" in the Affordable Care Act appeared when Sarah Palin first launched the term into the public debate in August 2009. Some observers argue objectivity in the news today entails "he said, she said" style reporting, in which journalists relay both sides of a political debate as though they are equally valid, even when one side has far more evidence in support of it than the other (Rosen 2009). Lawrence and Schafer (2012) have argued this tendency inhibited the mainstream media's ability to effectively debunk Palin's "death panels." However, at least in these four news sources, this framing of the law's provisions was rejected in the majority of their content involving that term in this early period. This was true even of the conservative-leaning *The New York Post* that had treated "socialized medicine" far more favorably. The correction was often made explicitly by the journalist in the news item—for instance, an article on public opinion and the health-care proposal on September 25, 2009, in *The New York Times* noted, "there is abundant evidence that critics of the bill made progress over the summer while the White House stayed largely silent: about one in four respondents said they believed that health-care legislation would create organizations to decide when to stop providing medical care to the elderly—so-called death panels—despite an all-out effort by Mr. Obama to debunk the claim, *which is false*" [my emphasis] (Nagourney and Sussman 2009).

But as time went on and "death panels" were less likely to appear in the news overall, the media outlets were also less steadfast in consistently undermining them. Although a relatively small number of instances, in December 2009 in the *Times* and February 2010 in *The New York Post* and *The Washington Post*, depictions of "death panels" as illegitimate were either surpassed or matched by neutral or legitimate portrayals. This may help explain some researchers' findings that even when the press corrects inaccuracies, it does not, in the long term, dispel public belief in the falsehood (Nyhan and Reifler 2010). The effectiveness of corrections may fade because they are no longer being made on a consistent, prominent basis in comparison to restating the original misconception.

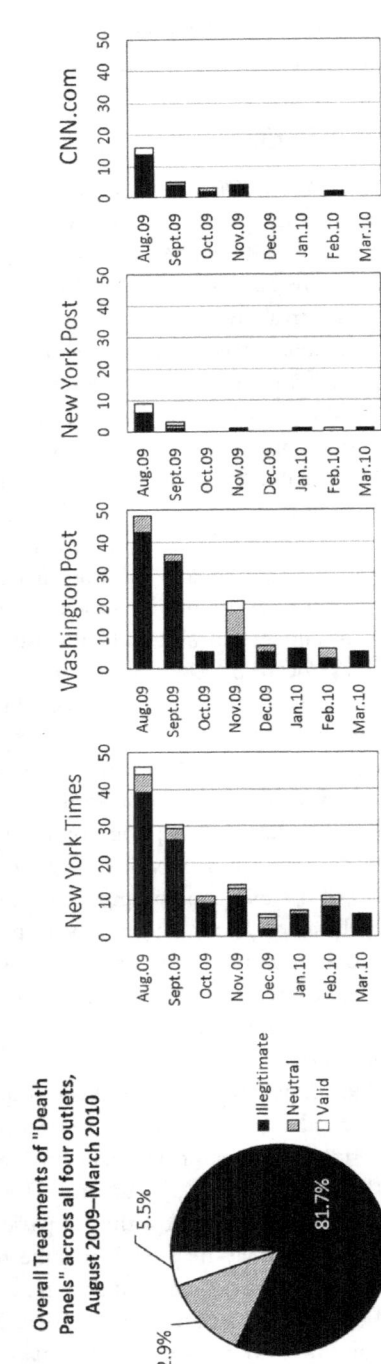

FIGURE 6.4 Treatment of "Death Panels" by Month across News Outlets, August 1, 2009–March 24, 2010

The more emphatic rejection of the "death panels" frame compared to that of "socialized medicine" could be explained in a number of ways. Potentially the long history of applying "socialized medicine" to health-care reform efforts even prior to Medicare meant the press did not feel as strong a responsibility to undercut it as a brand-new charge. Although Palin's "death panels" assertion was grounded in established arguments about health-care rationing and declining quality of care stemming from greater government involvement, her invention of this novel, dramatic term propelled the outlets analyzed here to contradict those claims early on. Admittedly too, "death panels" are more extreme, exaggerated, and inflammatory than "socialized medicine," and so the difference in the quality of the frames may have also affected the news media's treatment of them.

A Small Window into Social Media and "Death Panels"

If the mainstream news media was largely rejecting the death panels' frame, what was the conversation like on social media? I searched Twitter for tweets involving the phrase "death panel" or "death panels" from December 23 to 24, 2009. On December 24, the Senate voted 60 to 39 to pass the health-reform bill, leaving only the step of reconciling a compromise with the version passed by the House of Representatives before the ACA could become law. How were people using Twitter at this key moment in the process talking about the possibility of death panels in the bill? Leading up to this date, media and political actors also helped thrust the death panels' frame back into the spotlight. The week before, Politifact.com had issued its designation of death panels as its "lie of the year." On the evening of December 22, Sarah Palin posted on Facebook accusing "Harry Reid's Senate" of incorporating a provision requiring a two-thirds vote to amend or repeal the Independent Payment Advisory Board, "which is a panel of bureaucrats charged with cutting health care costs on the backs of patients—also known as rationing." According to Palin, "Though Nancy Pelosi and friends have tried to call 'death panels' the 'lie of the year,' this type of rationing—what the CBO calls 'reduc[ed] access to care' and 'diminish[ed] quality of care'—is precisely what I meant when I used that metaphor."[13] The Cato Institute, LifeNews.Com, and *The Weekly Standard* all helped promote this view that Palin had ultimately been proven right about "death panels" in the bill (Ertelt 2009; McCormack 2009; Reynolds 2009) which some liberal critics argued was not only inaccurate, but also rewriting the history of Palin's original charges (Media Matters for America 2009c).

Similar to the Twitter content included in Chapter 4, many of the tweets appeared driven by news coverage, particularly of Politifact's "lie of the year" award and Palin's Facebook post. As shown in Figure 6.5, 52% of the 328 tweets depicted "death panels" as an illegitimate concern, 28% as legitimate, and 20% offered a mixed assessment on their accuracy. Clearly this is a very limited time frame and only a minute sample of the conversation going on via social media

	Number of Tweets	%
Valid	91	28%
Illegitimate	171	52%
Neutral	66	20%
Total	**328**	**100%**

FIGURE 6.5 Treatment of "Death Panels" Frame on Twitter, December 23–24, 2009

regarding the "death panels" frame. Still, we might note that a small majority of these tweets harmonized with Obama's efforts to dismantle the death panels' frame. Further studies of more social media content across a longer time span would be needed to investigate this dimension of the case fully, but just as the bill was passed by the Senate, the president's communication project on death panels was largely affirmed rather than undercut by what people were sharing on Twitter.

Public Opinion on Death Panels

Although overall, "death panels" were overwhelmingly rejected in the news outlets analyzed here, the ability of the president to counter this framing might be limited by the fragmented media environment he faced and the bevy of ways citizens can choose to get their information. A September CNN poll (2009) found 41% of respondents answered yes to the question, "If Obama's plan became law, do you think senior citizens or seriously ill patients would die because government panels would prevent them from getting the medical treatment they needed?" though a clear majority of 57% disagreed that this would happen. A full three years after that poll, four in ten Americans continued to believe in death panels (Viebeck 2012), and that percentage stayed remarkably consistent over the first few years of the ACA's existence (DiJulio et al. 2014). A Vox 2015 poll found 12% of Democrats and 26 % of Republicans believed part of the law entailed "a government panel helps make decisions about patients' end-of-life care" (Kliff 2015), suggesting the belief lost at least a little bit of traction over time. Although most of these polls did not use the "death panels" term specifically, they show how effectively opponents' framing impacted perceptions of the policy, even when the provisions that seemed to spark the charge were left out of the law. Americans today express perilously low levels of trust in the news media in comparison to Kennedy and Johnson's day (Gallup 2012), and thus, although journalists might join the president's effort to discredit opponents' frames, it may be of limited persuasiveness.

Additionally, just as President Kennedy enjoyed less favorable treatment for his health-care views in *The Chicago Tribune*, the tremendous proliferation of media outlets providing information to citizens today, with different ideological leanings and standards of what is "fit to print," points to ever more venues where audiences are potentially exposed to questionable information. Pew Center data revealed 46% of regular Fox News watchers believed the "death panels" claim compared to 58% of regular MSNBC viewers that rejected it (Lawrence and Schafer 2012). If you get your news primarily from Sarah Palin's social media accounts, you might have a very different understanding of events than if you rely on a mainstream news outlet. Although this is one of the obvious challenges of 21st century presidential communication, we might keep in mind Kennedy's admonitions about those Americans who primarily got their information from AMA publications.

Conclusion

Does the news media of today help perpetuate extreme or false framings of issues and events more so than the press of the past? Some observers seem to think so. In a *New York Times* op-ed in November of 2009, Congressman Earl Blumenauer, Democrat from Oregon, author of the bill's end-of-life provisions that engendered such a controversy, argued, "The 'death panel' episode shows how the news media, after aiding and abetting falsehood, were unable to perform their traditional role of reporting the facts. By lavishing uncritical attention on the most exaggerated claims and extreme behavior, they unleashed something that the truth could not dispel" (Blumenauer 2009). But this chapter's comparison of how the news treated what presidents sought to debunk as false framings of their health-care proposals over time indicates that, at least in some cases, the "traditional role" of the media might be better fulfilled today than it was decades ago. As later scrutiny of the journalism of the past has made clear, at times we fall victim to a nostalgia for an idealized news media that never truly existed, considering the whitewashed version of American politics many outlets presented to the public in the mid-20th century, failing to fully inform the nation on important topics such as the realities of the early Vietnam War and consequential personal failings of powerful politicians.

More than this though, this chapter's focus suggests that presidential framing resilience, when considered in the context of being able to derail damaging, intemperate frames promulgated by opponents to defeat health-reform efforts, is more apparent in mainstream news sources today than in the 1960s. Unquestionably, there are limits to the comparisons that can be made between these three presidents challenging critics' frames due to the differing time periods, strategies employed, and media outlets analyzed. However, in this preliminary stab at exploring presidential efforts to correct what they see as misreadings of health-care reform and subsequent news coverage, there are remarkable similarities in how Democratic presidents have sought to counter opponents. These leaders all framed health-care reform as an unfulfilled promise to the American people, carrying out a revered progressive agenda that began with FDR, and cast the policy change as moderate and embodying widely shared values in the U.S. The presidents looked at here sought to cast their opponents as the fanatical, un-American voices in the debate, as Kennedy and Obama did, or to put them in a position where the patriotic move was to support the Administration's stand on health care, as Johnson did.

Throughout the chapters of this book, I have explored the concept of presidential framing resilience and how the 21st century president can foster or inhibit his or her advantages in shaping interpretations in the news. The historical comparative case of socialized medicine and death panels raises the possibility that, with respect to some communication goals, presidents today can better shape news coverage to their liking than some of their predecessors, who dealt with a much smaller number of influential media outlets. Obama's counters to his health-care plan being framed as "socialized medicine" and instituting "death panels" were more likely to enjoy support in the news outlets I analyzed than those of the Democratic presidents dismissing "socialized medicine" in the 1960s. Part of this might be for reasons out of the president's direct control, such as altered news norms about objectivity. But the president exploits those norms, in this case quite effectively, by clearly articulating that there is another side to this framing contest over socialist policies and government-rationed care.

Unlike Kennedy and Johnson though, Obama had to face the ways a framing such as "death panels" can circulate far more widely via nonmainstream sources of political information, such as the Internet and social media, reaching far more Americans than AMA pamphlets left in doctors' offices. Even the most categorical corrections of such frames by journalists and commentators in the more traditional news media may fail to reach persuadable ears in such corners. Taking into consideration then both this comparative historical look at presidential framing of health-care reform and all the framing contests surrounding the various facets of the Affordable Care Act, I now turn to a concluding chapter about the lessons of this inquiry for our understanding of the presidency, the news media, and 21st century political communication.

Notes

1 The full text of Truman's message can be found here: http://www.trumanlibrary.org/publicpapers/index.php?pid=483&st=&st1=.
2 Though George Lakoff (2004, 38) warns that "simply negating the other side's frames only reinforces them," in this case, as presidents sought to invalidate what they saw as factually incorrect framings of their policy, it may be one of those instances where this was a necessary and effective strategy.
3 Audio of the record can be found here: https://www.youtube.com/watch?v=AYrlDlrLDSQ.
4 Archival research at the John F. Kennedy Presidential Library in Boston, MA and the Lyndon B. Johnson Presidential Library in Austin, TX has helped to inform these sections of the chapter.
5 The entirety of President Kennedy's address can be found here, at the American Presidency Project: http://www.presidency.ucsb.edu/ws/?pid=8669.

6 Video of Annis' AMA address can be found here: https://www.youtube.com/watch?v=vFesycofKk4.
7 The *Tribune* did not endorse a Democrat for president in its history until Obama in 2008 ("Tribune 2008 presidential endorsement" 2008).
8 See Appendix A.6 for a more detailed discussion of the coding and intercoder reliability.
9 Video of the address can be found here: https://www.whitehouse.gov/video/President-Obama-Address-to-Congress-on-Health-Insurance-Reform.
10 See Appendix A.6 for a more detailed explanation of how these articles and transcripts were accessed and analyzed.
11 Palin's original post can be found here: https://www.facebook.com/note.php?note_id=113851103434&ref=mf.
12 See Appendix A.6 for intercoder reliability statistics for this section.
13 Palin's entire post can be seen here: https://www.facebook.com/note.php?note_id=213042303434

References

Adair, Bill and Angie Drobnic Holan. 2010. "Politifact's Lie of the Year: 'A Government Takeover of Health Care'." *Politifact*, December 16. Accessed July 15, 2016. http://www.politifact.com/truth-o-meter/article/2010/dec/16/lie-year-government-takeover-health-care/.

American Presidency Project. 1945. "Harry S. Truman: Special Message to the Congress Recommending a Comprehensive Health Program." November 19. Accessed September 26, 2016. http://www.presidency.ucsb.edu/ws/?pid=12288.

Andrew, III, John A. 1999. *Lyndon Johnson and the Great Society*. Chicago: Ivan R. Dee.

Appointment File, Diary Backup. 1965, July 29. Austin, TX: Lyndon B. Johnson Library.

Associated Press. 2016. "Patients Seek End-of-Life Talks Once Labeled 'Death Panels'." *CBS News*, May 23. Accessed July 15, 2016. http://www.cbsnews.com/news/patients-seek-end-of-life-talks-once-labeled-death-panels/.

Auletta, Ken. 2010. "Non-Stop News." *The New Yorker*, January 25. Accessed July 15, 2016. http://www.newyorker.com/magazine/2010/01/25/non-stop-news.

Berkowitz, Edward. 2005. "Medicare: The Great Society's Enduring National Health Insurance Program." In *The Great Society and the High Tide of Liberalism*, eds Sidney M. Milkis and Jerome M. Mileur, 320–350. Amherst: University of Massachusetts Press.

Beschloss, Michael R. 2002. *Reaching for Glory: Lyndon Johnson's Secret White House Tapes, 1964–1965*. New York: Simon & Schuster.

Beutler, Brian. 2009. "Tea Party Town Hall Strategy: 'Rattle Them,' 'Stand Up and Shout'." *Talking Points Memo*, August 3. Accessed July 15, 2016. http://talkingpointsmemo.com/dc/tea-party-town-hall-strategy-rattle-them-stand-up-and-shout.

Blumenauer, Earl. 2009. "My Near Death Panel Experience." *The New York Times*, November 14. Accessed July 15, 2016. http://www.nytimes.com/2009/11/15/opinion/15blumenauer.html?pagewanted=all &_r=0.

Blumenthal, David and James Morone. 2009. *The Heart of Power: Health and Politics in the Oval Office*. Berkeley: University of California Press.

Califano, Joseph A. 2015. *The Triumph and Tragedy of Lyndon Johnson: The White House Years*. New York: Simon & Schuster.

CBS News. 2009. "Steele Calls Obama Health Plan 'Socialism.'" *CBS News*, July 20. Accessed July 15, 2016. http://www.cbsnews.com/news/steele-calls-obama-health-plan-socialism/.

CNN Poll. 2009, September 11–13. Accessed July 15, 2016. http://i2.cdn.turner.com/cnn/2009/images/09/14/rel14b2.pdf

Dallek, Robert. 2004. *Lyndon B. Johnson: Portrait of a President.* New York: Oxford University Press.

DiJulio, Bianca, Jamie Firth, and Mollyann Brodie. 2014. "Kaiser Health Policy Tracking Poll: December 2014." *Kaiser Family Foundation*, December 18. Accessed July 14, 2016. http://kff.org/health-reform/poll-finding/kaiser-health-policy-tracking-poll-december-2014/.

Ertelt, Steven. 2009. "Sarah Palin: Death Panels in Senate Health Care Bill Worse Than We Thought." *LifeNews.com*, December 23. Accessed July 15, 2016. http://www.lifenews.com/2009/12/23/bio-3023/.

Factcheck.org. 2009. "Palin vs. Obama: Death Panels." August 14. Accessed July 15, 2016. http://www.factcheck.org/2009/08/palin-vs-obama-death-panels/.

Gallup. 2012. "U.S. Distrust in Media Hits New High." September 21. Accessed July 15, 2016. http://www.gallup.com/poll/171740/americans-confidence-news-media-remains-low.aspx.

Gallup. 2016. "In Depth: Topics A to Z, Healthcare System." Accessed July 15, 2016. http://www.gallup.com/poll/4708/healthcare-system.aspx.

Harvard School of Public Health. 2008. "Poll Finds Americans Split by Political Party over Whether Socialized Medicine Better or Worse than Current System," February 14. Accessed July 15, 2016. http://www.hsph.harvard.edu/news/press-releases/poll-americans-split-by-political-party-over-socialized-medicine/.

Heith, Diane J. 2013. *The Presidential Road Show: Public Leadership in an Era of Party Polarization and Media Fragmentation.* Boulder: Paradigm Publishers.

Holan, Angie Drobnic. 2009. "PolitiFact's Lie of the Year: 'Death Panels'." *PolitiFact*, December 18. Accessed July 15, 2016. http://www.politifact.com/truth-o-meter/article/2009/dec/18/politifact-lie-year-death-panels/.

Johnson, Lyndon Baines. 1971. *The Vantage Point: Perspectives of the Presidency, 1963–1969.* New York: Holt, Rinehart, and Winston.

Kliff, Sarah. 2015. "Obamacare is 5 Years Old, and Americans are Still Worried about Death Panels." *Vox*, March 23. Accessed July 15, 2016. http://www.vox.com/2015/3/23/8273007/obamacare-poll-death-panels.

Lakoff, George. 2004. *Don't Think of an Elephant! Know Your Values and Frame the Debate.* White River Junction: Chelsea Green.

Lawrence, Regina G. and Matthew L. Schafer. 2012. "Debunking Sarah Palin: Mainstream News Coverage of 'Death Panels'." *Journalism* 13: 766.

Lerer, Lisa. 2009. "Grassley on Death Panels: 'You have Every Right to Fear'." *Politico*, August 12. Accessed July 15, 2016. http://www.politico.com/blogs/politicolive/0809/Grassley_on_death_panels_You_have_every_right_to_fear.html.

Lieberman, Trudy. 2009. "Straight Talk, Part I." *Columbia Journalism Review*, August 13. Accessed July 15, 2016. http://www.cjr.org/campaign_desk/straight_talk_part_i.php?page=all&print=true.

Marmor, Theodore R. 1973. *The Politics of Medicare.* Chicago: Aldine Publishing Company.

McCormack, John. 2009. "Sarah Palin and Death Panels: A Brief History." *The Weekly Standard*, December 23. Accessed July 15, 2016. http://www.weeklystandard.com/article/272939.

Media Matters for America. 2009a. "Updated Report: Conservative Media Push 75-Year-Old 'Socialized Medicine' Smear against Health Care Teform." August 19.

Accessed July 15, 2016. http://mediamatters.org/research/2009/08/19/updated-report-conservative-media-push-75-year/153531.

Media Matters for America. 2009b. "Report: The Media Have Debunked the Death Panels: More Than 40 Times Over," August 15. Accessed July 15, 2016. http://mediamatters.org/research/2009/08/15/report-the-media-have-debunked-the-death-panels/153367.

Media Matters for America. 2009c. "Morris Falsely Asserted Medicare Advisory Board is 'Death Panel' that Will Deny Treatment for Broken Hips, Colon Cancer." December 23. Accessed July 15, 2016. http://mediamatters.org/research/2009/12/23/morris-falsely-asserted-medicare-advisory-board/158468.

Nagourney, Adam and Dalia Sussman. 2009. "In Poll, Public Wary of Obama on War and Health." *The New York Times*, September 24. Accessed July 15, 2016. http://www.nytimes.com/2009/09/25/us/politics/25poll.html.

New York Times, The. 1965a. "Medicare Boycott Urged for Doctors." August 5, 1.

New York Times, The. 1965b. "A.M.A. Tries New Prescription on Medicare." June 27.

News Conference at the White House With Joseph Laitin, Horace Busby, and Douglass Cater. 1965. (PSNC #25-a – PSNC #33-a, July 29, 4:22 PM). Austin: Lyndon B. Johnson Library.

Nyhan, Brendan and Jason Reifler. 2010. "When Corrections Fail: The Persistence of Political Misperceptions." *Political Behavior* 32: 303–330.

O'Brien, Michael. 2009. "Senator Hatch: Healthcare Reform Bills Threaten Survival of Two-Party System." *The Hill*, November 2. Accessed July 15, 2016. http://thehill.com/blogs/blog-briefing-room/news/65853-hatch-health-bills-threaten-two-party-system

Reynolds, Alan. 2009. "Death Panels? Sarah Palin Was Right." *Cato at Liberty*, December 22. Accessed July 15, 2016. http://www.cato.org/blog/death-panels-sarah-palin-was-right.

Rosen, Jay. 2009. "He Said, She Said Journalism: Lame Formula in the Land of the Active User." *Press Think*, April 12. Accessed July 15, 2016. http://archive.pressthink.org/2009/04/12/hesaid_shesaid.html.

Semple, Jr., Robert B. 1965. "Truman to Watch Medicare Signing." *The New York Times*, July 30, 10.

Starr, Paul. 2013. *Remedy and Reaction: The Peculiar American Struggle Over Health-care reform*. New Haven: Yale University Press.

Tribune 2008 Presidential Endorsement. 2008. *The Chicago Tribune*, October 19. Accessed July 15, 2016. http://articles.chicagotribune.com/2008-10-19/news/chi-tribune-2008-presidential-endorsement_1_endorsement-obama-first-african-american-president.

Urbina, Ian. 2009. "Beyond Beltway, Health Debate Turns Hostile." *The New York Times*, August 7. Accessed July 15, 2016. http://www.nytimes.com/2009/08/08/us/politics/08townhall.html?_r=0.

Viebeck, Elise. 2012. "Poll: Four in 10 Believe in Obama Healthcare Law 'Death Panels.'" *The Hill*, September 26. Accessed July 15, 2016. http://thehill.com/policy/healthcare/258753-poll-four-in-10-believe-in-health-law-death-panels.

White House Central Files. 1964. *LE/IS 1*, September 5–26. Austin: Lyndon B. Johnson Library.

White House Central Files. 1965. *LE/IS1*, June 1-August 31. Austin: Lyndon B. Johnson Library.

White House Central Files, Executive. 1963–1966. *IS 1 Accident-Hospital-Medical-Health*, November 22, 1963–March 23, 1966. Austin: Lyndon B. Johnson Library.

White House Staff File Papers of Pierre Salinger. 1962a. Presidential Press Conference Memo. May 23. Boston: John F. Kennedy Library.

White House Staff File Papers of Pierre Salinger. 1962b. Remarks of the President, The Fish Room. July 17. Boston: John F. Kennedy Library.

White House, The. 2009a. "Remarks by the President at Town Hall on Health Insurance Reform in Portsmouth, New Hampshire." August 11. Accessed July 15, 2016. https://www.whitehouse.gov/the-press-office/remarks-president-town-hall-health-insurance-reform-portsmouth-new-hampshire.

White House, The. 2009b. "Remarks by the President in Town Hall on Health Care, Belgrade, Montana." August 14. Accessed on July 15, 2016. https://www.whitehouse.gov/the-press-office/remarks-president-town-hall-health-care-belgrade-montana.

White House, The. 2009c. "Remarks by the President in Town Hall on Health Care Grand Junction Colorado." August 15. https://www.whitehouse.gov/the-press-office/remarks-president-town-hall-health-care-grand-junction-colorado.

White House, The. 2009d. "Remarks by the President on Health Insurance Reform in St. Charles, MO." March 10. Accessed July 15, 2016. https://www.whitehouse.gov/the-press-office/remarks-president-health-insurance-reform-st-charles-mo.

Zelizer, Julian E. 2015. "How Medicare Was Made." *The New Yorker*, February 15. Accessed July 15, 2016. http://www.newyorker.com/news/news-desk/medicare-made.

7
CONCLUSION

I began this book with an argument that despite the present-day fragmented political and communications context, the president still retains significant ability to frame major controversial issues for the media and the American people. My purpose in looking at how framing contests surrounding the Affordable Care Act between President Obama and his opponents played out in major U.S. news outlets was to gain a more nuanced understanding of how the 21st century presidency might influence media coverage. Too often we may be prone to assumptions about how instances like the proliferation of the name "Obamacare" reflects presidential helplessness in the face of criticism, or that rumors such as death panels spread like wildfire, unobstructed, in contemporary discourse. This kind of conjecture obscures the harder to detect ways we can see the power of presidential communication in the news. To borrow language from the presidential scholar Fred Greenstein (1994) and put it toward a very different purpose, scrutinizing news narratives for presidential frames can reveal the "hidden hand" of the presidency in constructing news coverage. That influence can be quite subtle, as we have witnessed in many of the cases in this book, but it is far from unimportant.

Effective presidential communication on contentious domestic policies today is unlikely to look like the utter dominance of the news that we associate with past media-savvy presidents, or recent executives' considerable power to frame foreign policy crises. It is more likely to be uneven, sometimes spectacularly disrupted with a later return to prominence, occasionally diverted in new directions, some beneficial for the president's communication project, others not. Analyzing news through the lens of framing can help us discern how presidential interpretations ripple throughout the media system. Even where the president's opponents appear to have the upper hand in framing contests, we might recognize faulty presidential frames as helping to feed those setbacks, with challengers still reactive to the Administration's communications. While presidents might work to avoid engendering this impact via their framing strategies whenever possible, there are times when the inadvertent effects of presidential frames on the news can end up working to the president's advantage. Taken as a whole, the 21st century presidency has substantial ability to frame controversial domestic policy issues in the news, with many of its challenges self-imposed, and yet there is still an element of unpredictability in the contemporary news landscape that makes it hard for any administration to predetermine all the implications of inserting their frames into public debate.

I introduced three new concepts to aid our understanding of what effective presidential communication in the 21st century might look like: presidential framing resilience, presidential framing side effects, and presidential frame refraction. These concepts were meant to capture presidential influence over the news, as well as the limits to that influence. I have emphasized the role of presidential agency, of the ways the president and his or her team can empower or impair their proficiency in obtaining favorable coverage for their frames in the news. At the same time, the cases throughout the book make plain the factors beyond the president's control that may impact the outcome of framing contests in the news.

There are limitations to the value of studying any single administration or policy issue. However, the case of the Obama Administration and the Affordable Care Act offers a formidable set of challenges for presidential framing effectiveness. Media actors would not accept favorable depictions of health-care reform at face value the way they might assertions of national security threats, and the political environment produced little of the kind of consensus that can cause mainstream news outlets to defer to the Administration.[1] The foundation of the Republican Party's opposition to the Obama presidency has largely been centered around resisting "Obamacare." Even Hillary Clinton and Bernie Sanders, the primary candidates for the Democratic Party's 2016 presidential nomination, although expressing general support for the law, ran on platforms proposing major changes to it, including a public option or a single-payer program. The news media has changed so strikingly not only in the dramatic diversification of platforms and technologies, but also in terms of how many venues can exert an influence on the rest of the news system through their coverage, in contrast to even just a decade ago. The speed of the news cycle, the proliferation of outlets with very loose ties to journalistic ethics, and the vast differences in how popular news sources may cover the same story for their distinct and possibly insulated audiences all lead to reasonable expectations that the 21st century news landscape is too wild and unmanageable a space in which presidents can effectively convey their messages.

What I have sought to do through the resilience, side effects, and refraction concepts and the cases of the preceding chapters is to identify those ways that the president's ability to shape our interpretations of issues persists, but that the indisputable challenges of this media moment require us to reimagine when and how that influence might manifest itself. We need to adjust our expectations to make them more realistic about what presidential communication influence looks like now. Looking back at the individual framing contests throughout the book, what are some of the connections and lessons we might draw about what makes for effective presidential framing of contentious domestic policies in the news in this media moment?

The Manifestations of Resiliency: Toughness, Adjustability, Staying Power

"Obamacare" is not the name the president chose for his signature health-care policy. From the outset then, the framing contest over the nickname originated from the president's lack of control over this issue. But as I explored in Chapter 2, after the Obama team sought to reframe the term what began as a small uptick in positive content about the ACA alongside the use of "Obamacare" over the long term completely upended who was using "Obamacare" in the news. When I looked at "Obamacare" across the three national networks' Sunday morning news programs over a year after the "I Like Obamacare" campaign, a majority of the times it was employed health-care reform was discussed in a positive or neutral light. We can see both the spreadability of the Administration's favorable framing of "Obamacare" as supporters adopted their message, as well as the staying power of that frame over time in the news. Not all of my cases have demonstrated that trajectory of presidential frames steadily gaining influence. Early successes in the cases of framing the individual mandate's enforcement mechanism as a penalty in the news, and HealthCare.gov as hampered by glitches, eventually gave way to significant setbacks and privileging of opponents' frames. In the case of the "penalty" frame, this was a short-lived bump in the road fostered by the Supreme Court's unusual entry into the framing contest. In the case of "glitches," the president was not even able to sustain a preferred position for his frames in the news through the first week of the launch of the website's insurance exchanges. The notion of presidential framing resiliency captures the uneven path the Administration's frames can take in the news, but also the enduring impression that they leave. In the fall of 2013, the Obama team was not flooding the country with messages about how those who did not procure insurance would face a penalty and not a tax, but in the media coverage analyzed in Chapter 3, that is how it was described in the news because that was how the Administration had originally discussed it. It is easy to see how such forms of subtle influence can be overlooked.

The "toughness" of presidential frames is also supported by some of the surprising places I have identified them as translating into the news. Even in the unfriendly territory of Fox News and *The New York Post*, the effort to reframe

"Obamacare" as a positive appeared to have an impact. Across the print and online outlets I analyzed, news articles overwhelmingly corroborated the president's dismantling of the "death panels" frame. Furthermore, comparing presidential opponents' ability to frame health-care reform as "socialized medicine" over time points to the advantages news outlets during Obama's tenure afforded his challenge to these charges in comparison to news outlets during the Kennedy and Johnson Administrations. The small sample of tweets reviewed in Chapters 4 and 6 did not conform to conventional wisdom regarding political content on social media, tending toward the extreme and inaccurate. Instead, they spread the word that death panels were an illegitimate concern about the ACA on the December 2009 dates, and accused the mainstream news media of being the source of hysteria and hyperbole by purveying the "Obama's Katrina" narrative in the middle of November 2013.

What the President Can Control and What He Cannot

From the outset, I have described this presidential framing resilience as conditional. The two framing contests in which the president appeared to most hamper his ability to shape news narratives were those regarding HealthCare.gov and dropped insurance plans. Both cases required the Obama team to react quickly to emerging problems surrounding the ACA, a formidable communications challenge. How much advance notice the Administration had and how prepared it was for the appearance of these events is difficult to discern. It is perhaps no accident that the framing contests the Obama Administration performed best in were those they had the greatest amount of time to anticipate and plan for, as in the "Obamacare," tax/penalty, and socialized medicine/death panel cases.

What we do know, however, is that in both of the more problematic instances, the frames disseminated by the Obama team to mitigate the political damage of the controversies did not come across as a clear and consistent defense of the president's actions, but instead a jumble of incoherent excuses and alibis. Even many committed Democratic supporters of President Obama and the ACA could not bring themselves to spread those presidential frames in the media. In fact, one of the markers of how unsuccessful that these frames were is that in both the website and dropped plans examples, the president and his surrogates themselves had to back away from continuing to echo them in the news! The delayed apologies from senior Administration officials and, in the case of dropped plans, from the president himself, appeared to not only acknowledge mishandling of the actual policy problem, but also to signal a surrender in the framing contest. Presidential frames would no longer be repeated, tweaked, or advanced. Instead there was acceptance of the political cost that opponents' frames encouraged. By contrast, the president's most successful frames in the various contests were clear, emphatic, compelling, and easily repeatable by sympathetic political elites.

Obama does care. If you irresponsibly don't get insurance, you will be fined. Death panels are a lie.

Crafting frames that fit with current norms of journalism is also key to enhancing presidential framing resilience. The more easily the president's frames slide into established means of covering politics in the U.S. media, the greater the likelihood they will dominate framing contests in the news. Before the Obama team co-opted "Obamacare," journalists did not seem to know what to do with the term—some were already using it sporadically to describe the policy, others refusing to do so. The president's reframing of the term brought clarity to what an "objective" stance on the nickname would be. By contrast, those outlets most strongly committed to a professional code of ethical journalism at times avoided echoing presidential frames so as not to endorse one side of a framing contest. This would explain *The New York Times* propensity for using "tax penalty" to describe the mandate's repercussions long after the Court's 2012 ruling faded from the headlines.

When the president cast "death panels" as an irresponsible rumor, the news media's view of themselves as an arbiter of what separates fact from fiction for the public was engaged, and outlets independently countered Sarah Palin's claim in a way they are often criticized for not doing in other contexts, such as in the case of climate-change skeptics. This coverage is all the more remarkable for how it deviates from the news treatment granted to 1960s presidential efforts to deny Medicare was "socialized medicine." But when it comes to present-day news norms, events sometimes privilege presidential opponents' frames. HealthCare.gov's flawed rollout was such a simple, entertaining story that it even inspired *Saturday Night Live* skits parodying Kathleen Sebelius offering website tips on how to navigate the system. Obama's eventual assertions that he had not known the extent of the website problems fit easily with a preexisting media narrative depicting the president as a bystander in his own Administration. The cynical, negative lens through which reporters often cover politicians (Patterson 2003) made accusations the president had lied to the public about whether they could keep their insurance plans under the ACA an effortless narrative for the press.

The Unexpected Implications of Presidential Framing: Side Effects and Refraction

The nonlinear path for most presidential frames in the news in the domestic policy context is further fleshed out by presidential side effects and presidential frame refraction. The former concept draws attention to how presidential frames can be tremendously influential in the news, distinct from their intended impact. If the Administration reframed "Obamacare" in order to empower its supporters to use and spread that positive message, it was tangential to their purpose that the name was now classified as an objective one, in turn causing reporters to use it freely in place of the Affordable Care Act. The president's influence even in the 21st century media system is so great that he can alter the parameters of what constitutes ethical journalism. In another, less dramatic case, the timing of the emergence of the "dropped plans" framing contest in the pages of *The New York Times* and *The Washington Post* suggests that those two influential papers held off on reporting about this controversy until the White House had responded to the accusations of presidential malfeasance. On the one hand, this benefited the president, that he was not being framed as a liar in those papers absent a counter-interpretation from the Administration. On the other hand, the Obama Administration response also gave credence to the story and generated more coverage of an issue the president would prefer went away entirely.

Across the assorted framing contests, we can see the promise and peril of presidential frame refraction for the president's communications goals. In some cases, the ways presidential frames were deflected from their original paths were damaging to the president's standing in the framing contests. Chief Justice John Roberts weighing in on the individual mandate not only invested presidential opponents' tax frame with a new sense of legitimacy, but he also altered how the president's penalty frame could be cast in its past and future usage, most harmfully as obfuscation by the Administration. In the case of HealthCare.gov, Obama had tied himself to the "glitches" frame so decisively that when he later qualified his actions, the news media read his earlier behavior as incompetence on a par with President Bush's mismanagement of Hurricane Katrina. Supporters too can engage in presidential frame refraction, to the president's political benefit. With President Obama under siege by accusations he had broken his promise to the American people that they could keep the insurance plans they liked under health-care reform, MSNBC took a wobbly presidential frame, wherein the Administration washed its hands of responsibility for the cancellations and vaguely shifted culpability to insurance companies, and turned it into a full-throated condemnation of a shady, predatory insurance industry. For political and policy reasons, the Obama Administration did not have the freedom to throw insurers under the bus, but they certainly benefited from news narratives on MSNBC that turned the industry into the real villains of the story.

Future Areas for Inquiry

The concepts of presidential framing resilience, refraction, and side effects might be applied to other cases to better determine their usefulness beyond the circumstances of the Obama Administration and the Affordable Care Act. We might take a fresh look at political setbacks for the president—such as failure to gain passage of a preferred domestic policy or an emerging White House scandal—in light of these concepts, to identify how even in seeming defeat, the president can drive public conversations and media coverage of what is happening. Analysis of how presidential frames evolve and alter news content could inspire a reevaluation of what we typically consider negative news about an Administration, or times when the White House "loses control of the narrative." Further, presidential framing resilience could potentially endure beyond a single Administration; presidential communications supporting even unsuccessful executive endeavors might importantly shape debates that emerge the next time a policy window opens.

Future projects might also evaluate the effectiveness of presidential frames and the strategies behind them as incorporating not only considerations about what the message will look like today, but how it will play in the media months, or even years, into the future. We might refine our understanding of what nurtures or obstructs the spread of presidential frames by supporters and media actors across a variety of 21st century media platforms. Testing for presidential framing resilience in other forms of policy, domestic and foreign, might shed greater light on the extent to which the contemporary media moment empowers or constricts presidential communication.

Conclusion

My findings suggest that even in the demanding context of framing contests concerning a controversial domestic policy overhaul in a fragmented media environment, the president enjoys substantial advantages in getting his frames into the news. To be sure, the complexities of the contemporary news landscape mean the president and his or her team cannot always be assured of how this communications influence will manifest itself in coverage, and presidential frames can be taken in new and unexpected directions by supporters, opponents, and journalists alike. By largely emphasizing the constraints today's media system places on presidential communication, we may lose sight of the ways, however nuanced or subtle, today's news context enhances the president's framing prospects, in some ways offering support for presidential communications even more fully than in the past.

Although the president's ability to lead the public, shape political debates, and impact news coverage has increasingly come into question in recent years, the framing contests at the heart of this book offer some confirmation of the centrality of the presidency in the American political system. While our range of media options has exploded, opponents are bolder than ever in undercutting the president's version of events, and journalists cover politics with a more jaundiced eye, the president still has tremendous control over how we think and talk about some of the most important issues facing our nation.

Note

1 See for instance Zaller's (1992) model of one-sided information flow, Entman's (2004) discussion of hegemony vs. indexing and his cascading activation model, and Bennett et al.'s (2007) analysis of how dissenting views that are perceived as having little likelihood of derailing a policy receive little news attention.

References

Bennett, W. Lance, Regina G. Lawrence, and Steven Livingston. 2007. *When the Press Fails: Political Power and the News Media from Iraq to Katrina*. Chicago: University of Chicago Press.

Entman, Robert M. 2004. *Projections of Power: Framing News, Public Opinion, and U.S. Foreign Policy*. Chicago: University of Chicago Press.

Greenstein, Fred I. 1994. *The Hidden-Hand Presidency: Eisenhower as Leader*. Baltimore: The Johns Hopkins University Press.

Patterson, Thomas E. 2003. *The Vanishing Voter: Public Involvement in an Age of Uncertainty*. New York: Vintage.

Zaller, John R. 1992. *The Nature and Origins of Mass Opinion*. Cambridge, UK: Cambridge University Press.

Appendix

A.1: Common Elements for All Chapter Analyses

All news articles and transcripts were accessed via Lexis-Nexis. Search terms in most cases were made as broad as possible to catch as much coverage dealing with the subject of focus as possible. Some differences between cable news outlets may be attributable to what programs each outlet makes available to the Lexis-Nexis database; Fox News appears to make fewer transcripts of their programming available than CNN, for instance. I included both objective, neutral news content and opinion pieces/programs in each chapter's analysis, to give a sense of the collective coverage consumers of U.S. news would be exposed to, and because most citizens are unlikely to delineate psychologically what information came from "news" and what came from "commentary" in recalling it later. *The New York Times* was included in the news analysis in every chapter; see Boydstun (2013) and Lee (2014) on how the *Times* also plays an agenda-setting role for the rest of the press and is generally representative of a wide array of other outlets.

In several chapters I have categorized the sources of frames and/or users of particular words. Several of these categories are straightforward, such as Democratic or Republican politicians, others may need further explanation. Individuals who worked directly for a public official and could be considered a spokesperson for them were categorized as Republican or Democratic surrogates—David Axelrod, who worked as a senior advisor and campaign strategist for President Obama, for instance, would be an example of a Democratic surrogate. Those on cable news whose primary job was to convey news and information to viewers, such as CNN anchor Wolf Blitzer, were categorized as journalists, and those whose primary role was to convey opinion and subjective analysis, such as Fox News personality Eric Bolling, were categorized as commentators/pundits. The category of "other" was applied to those who did not fit properly into the other classifications, such as political satirists Jon Stewart or Stephen Colbert.

In evaluations of the news content for each chapter that required a subjective judgment, both I and a trained independent coder unfamiliar with the propositions of the work conducted the analysis. Intercoder reliability statistics are discussed in the chapter-specific appendices; all indicate strong intercoder reliability. Any remaining differences in coding results were reconciled through discussion between me and the independent coder to produce the final set of results that are presented. For simplicity's sake, percentages were often rounded to the nearest percentage point, resulting in some columns in the figures not adding up to 100%.

A.2: Chapter 2

Articles and transcripts for the first section of this chapter, before and after the Obama team's March 2012 re-appropriation campaign around "Obamacare," came from a Lexis-Nexis search for news in the selected outlets containing the term "Obamacare" from December 23, 2011 to March 22, 2012 and from March 23, 2012 to June 23, 2012, yielding 143 *New York Times* and 65 *New York Post* articles, and 339 CNN and 362 Fox News transcripts.

A trained independent coder replicated a portion of the news analysis for the print outlets, regarding whether the tone surrounding the usage of Obamacare was positive, negative, or neutral on the Affordable Care Act. The coding protocol stressed that our goal was to only record whether the health-care policy itself was being cast in a positive, negative, or neutral way, not whether President Obama, the Democratic Party, or some other actor or institution alone was being depicted positively or negatively. For *The New York Times*, intercoder percentage agreement for the first time period was 91.6% and Cohen's kappa=0.8117, and for the second time period 94% agreement and Cohen's kappa=0.8716. For *The New York Post*, the first time period percentage agreement was 95.2% and Cohen's kappa=0.8495, and in the second, 91.4% agreement and Cohen's kappa=0.8501.

Transcripts for the second section, regarding the use of "Obamacare" on the Sunday news programs came from a Lexis-Nexis search for news on the three major network programs containing the term "Obamacare" from March 23, 2010 through March 24, 2014. The results included 83 episodes of *This Week* on ABC, 56 episodes of *Face the Nation* on CBS, and 81 episodes of *Meet the Press* on NBC. Intercoder percentage agreement for the positive/negative/neutral portrayals of health-care reform alongside "Obamacare" was roughly 99%—there were only nine cases we differed on—and Cohen's kappa was 0.9866.

A.3: Chapter 3

Using Lexis-Nexis, for each time period I used the search terms "Obama" AND "health care" OR "mandate" AND "penalty" OR "fine" OR "tax" in an attempt to capture as many references to the policy as possible. This encompassed a total of 220 *New York Times* articles, 240 *The Washington Post* articles, 19 *New York Post* articles, 189 CNN transcripts, and 103 Fox News transcripts. Each time that one of the framing devices ("tax," "penalty," "fine" or some combination thereof) was uttered or written in the news is captured in the totals in the figures. The unit of analysis was the sentence.

A.4: Chapter 4

For the first week of October 2013, articles and transcripts were acquired through a very broad Lexis-Nexis search of the terms "Obama" and "health," in order to capture any possible mention of the HealthCare.gov rollout. However, these wide-ranging parameters meant that the volume of coverage produced allowed for only the single week of news content to be included in the analysis. The unit of analysis was the paragraph, as the way Lexis-Nexis transcribes news articles and programs typically consists of short paragraphs, allowing for some uniformity across different types of outlets; a paragraph level of analysis is also recommended by Matthes and Kohring (2008) and Entman (2012).

The coding protocol was as follows: Please identify any paragraph that discusses HealthCare.gov not working properly as including the White House's preferred frames, the opposition's preferred frames, or a mix of the two. The White House's preferred frames may include any of the following or content with similar meaning:

- High demand for health care and site/too many users/heavy traffic/high volume.
- Just a glitch or glitches (minor technical problems).
- The White House or the government or officials are actively working to fix the problems.
- As long as visitors can get on the website to get information, it is fine if they don't sign up until later/their signing up is delayed.

The opposition's preferred frames may include any of the following or content with similar meaning:

- Problems in the website or health-care exchanges reflect and are connected to *flaws in the health-care policy itself.*
- Significant, fundamental flaws in the design of the website and/or the program (major technological problems).

- President or the Administration or the government as negligent, insufficiently addressing the problems.
- Questioning or undermining of "too much traffic/demand" explanation.

For the news content from October 1 through October 7, 2013, the intercoder percentage agreement was 91.4%. I asked the independent coder to independently review the 36 instances in which we disagreed as to the appropriate coding, after which there were only 12 out of 419 instances in which we disagreed, for a 97.1% agreement.

For the second section of the chapter, I searched Lexis-Nexis for coverage that included the words "Obama" and "Katrina" in the selected outlets between November 11, 2013 through November 25, 2013. The coding protocol used for assessing the treatment of the "Obama's Katrina" analogy required coders to determine whether it was treated as either a legitimate, reasonable comparison; whether the comparison was rejected or discredited; or whether a mixed, neutral, or unclear take was conveyed on the comparison. The initial percentage agreement for all of the news coverage was 86.4%, and in the second round of coding of the 15 instances on which we had initially disagreed, we now only differed on one item, for a 99% intercoder percentage agreement. The initial percentage agreement for the Twitter content for November 15, 2013, consisting of 854 tweets, was 94%, and in the second round of coding of the 52 instances on which we disagreed, we now differed on 17 items, for a 98% intercoder percentage agreement and Cohen's kappa was 0.9569. Most of the differences in the determinations stemmed from the nature of the tweets; unlike most news coverage, the short format, cultural references, and occasional incoherence sometimes made the coding process difficult.

A.5: Chapter 5

Articles and transcripts were acquired through a Lexis-Nexis search of the terms "Obama AND health AND plans AND dropped OR cancelled OR canceled OR cancellation" for the listed dates in order to capture any possible mention of the conflict over the dropped plans. In total, the analysis includes 52 *New York Times* articles, 119 *The Washington Post* articles, 163 Fox News transcripts, and 79 MSNBC transcripts. The unit of analysis was the paragraph.

The coding protocol was as follows: Please identify any paragraph that discusses the dropped/cancelled health-care plans, incorporating either of the following frames or a mix of the two. Frame 1—Obama as Lying may include any of the following or content with similar meaning:

- Refers to the president lying when he said Americans could keep their plans.
- Refers to the president as not being truthful when he said Americans could keep their plans, or something with equivalent meaning, such as "not forthright" or "dishonest."

- Refers to the president breaking his promise/pledge when he said Americans could keep their health-care plans if they liked them.
- Refers to a threat to the president's credibility because of the broken pledge.

Frame 2—Defending Obama may include any of the following or content with similar meaning:

- Refers to plans not really being cancelled or dropped in the way described by critics, for example, that in reality, people are being transitioned to other plans or the policies are being replaced with better plans.
- Indicates this is the fault of insurance companies, not the law itself, and not the fault of the president.
- Refers to what the president said as technically true; or that indicates this is not really a broken promise. Possible explanations might include: (1) nothing in the law states that Americans could not keep their existing plans; (2) President Obama was only talking about plans that people bought before the law was passed; (3) these plans can hardly be considered insurance, they're so terrible and woefully inadequate.

Frame 3—Mixed:

- Any paragraph that includes elements of both Frame 1 and Frame 2.

Intercoder percentage agreement was 95.7% for *The New York Times* (Cohen's kappa=0.9199); 96.5% for *The Washington Post* (Cohen's kappa=0.9219); 97.7% for Fox News (Cohen's kappa=0.9216); and 97.7% for MSNBC (Cohen's kappa=0.9471).

A.6: Chapter 6

For both the "socialized medicine" and "death panels" frames, coding involved determining whether this was depicted as a valid, legitimate concern about the policy; an illegitimate, inaccurate concern about the policy; or whether there was a mixed or neutral assessment on its accuracy. An independent coder reviewed all of the same coverage of Medicare as socialized medicine in *The New York Times* 1962–1965 for the three-year period, resulting in an intercoder percentage agreement of 91.4%. An independent coder also reviewed the news coverage involving death panels between August 1, 2009 and March 24, 2010, resulting in an agreement rate of 95.2%. Finally, intercoder percentage agreement for the 328 tweets involving "death panel" or "death panels" on December 23 through 24, 2009 was 95%, Cohen's kappa=0.9245.

References

Boydstun, Amber E. 2013. *Making the News: Politics, the Media, and Agenda Setting.* Chicago: University of Chicago Press.

Entman, Robert M. 2012. *Scandal and Silence: Media Responses to Presidential Misconduct.* Cambridge, UK: Polity Press.

Lee, Han Soo. 2014. "Analyzing the Multidirectional Relationships Between the President, News Media, and the Public: Who Affects Whom?" *Political Communication* 31: 259–281.

Matthes, Jörg and Matthias Kohring. 2008. "The Content Analysis of Media Frames: Toward Improving Reliability and Validity." *Political Communication* 58(2): 258–279.

INDEX

24-hour news networks 8, 23, 27

ABC: *Evening News* 79–81; HealthCare.gov 83, 86; *Jimmy Kimmel Live* 17; in modern media world 7; policy promises 108; *This Week* 33–7, 43, 47
Abdullah, Halimah 56
accuracy issues in reporting 55
Adair, Bill 126
adversarial relationship between press and politics 8
All in With Chris Hayes 102–3
aloof, and disengaged, Obama as 77
Alter, Jonathan 88 n.5
Alterman, Eric 95
Altheide, David L. 9
American Medical Association 115–16, 119, 120–3, 125
American Presidency Project 55, 114
American Prospect 109 n.3
Andrew III, John A. 121
Andrews, Wyatt 79
Annis, Dr. 119
Anti-Injunction Act (1867) 60 n.9
apologies 75, 106, 109, 144
Appel, James 122, 123
approval ratings 46, 77, 85
Associated Press 34
Atkinson, Mary Layton 10, 20
Atlantic Wire, The 39 n.2
"attack dog" journalism 96
Auerbach, David 74, 88 n.5

Auletta, Ken 130
Axelrod, David 19, 56, 149
Azari, Julia R. 8

Bachmann, Michele 25, 27, 57, 125
Baier, Bret 81
Baker, Dean 102
balanced news coverage 96, 101, 124
Baldwin, Brooke 57
Balkin, Jack M. 59 n.2
Balz, Dan 68, 85
Barnett, Randy E. 60 n.5
Baucus, Max 60 n.8, 76
Begala, Paul 83
Belt, Todd L. 8
Bennett, W. Lance 7, 9, 50, 81, 146
Benoit, William 71
Berkowitz, Edward 116
Bernstein, Jonathan 95
Beschloss, Michael R. 121
Between Two Ferns 65
Beutler, Brian 126
Biden, Joe 75, 78
"big government," health-care reform framed as 21 *see also* "socialized medicine"
Bimber, Bruce 8
Black Jr., Charles L. 47
Blake, Aaron 19
Blaney, Joseph R. 71
Blitzer, Wolf 31, 83, 149
blogs 8, 96–7

Blumenauer, Earl 135
Blumenthal, David 116
Boehner, John 79, 97
Boerma, Lindsey 2
Bolling, Eric 27, 84, 150
Botelho, Greg 74, 78
Boydstun, Amber E. 8, 149
Breyer, Justice Stephen 60 n.9
Brooks, David 25
Bruce, Mary 56
Busby, Horace 121
Busby, Robert 9, 71
Bush, George H.W. 95, 96
Bush, George W. 5, 7, 55, 61 n.19, 66, 79, 82, 84, 85, 95, 146

cable news: HealthCare.gov 84, 85; in modern media world 7, 8; and the name "Obamacare" 24, 25–6, 27, 29–30; policy promises 101, 104–5; "socialized medicine" 126; tax vs. penalty framing 50, 57, 58 *see also specific outlets*
Califano, Joseph A. 122
Callaghan, Karen 9
Camia, Catalina 71
campaign promises, upholding 47–8, 56, 58, 93–112
Campbell, Andrea Louise 44
Cappella, Joseph 8, 10, 49, 76
care, as emphasis of presidential framing of Obamacare 21
Carney, Jay 55, 69–70, 98, 105
Carter, Jimmy 21
cascading activation model 7
Casillas, Christopher J. 46
Cater, Douglass 121–2
Cato Institute 133
CBS: *Evening News* 79–81; *Face the Nation* 33–7; HealthCare.gov 83, 85; in modern media world 7; policy promises 94, 108; "socialized medicine" 125; *This Morning* 2
Center for Public Integrity 103
Chadwick, Andrew. 8
Chait, Jonathan 100
Chao, Henry 72
Chicago Tribune 119–20, 123–4, 134
Chong, Dennis 10
Cillizza, Chris 19, 108
Clement, Scott 68
climate-change 45, 145
Clinton, Bill 21, 94, 99, 101, 108

Clinton, Hillary 142
Clinton Administration 48
CNN: "death panels" 131–3, 134–5; HealthCare.gov 69, 72–3, 74, 79–81, 83, 84; and the name "Obamacare" 23, 28–9, 31–3; policy promises 108; "socialized medicine" 127–9; tax vs. penalty framing 49–50, 54, 57
coding procedures 10, 24, 79, 81, 101, 124, 131, 150–3
cognitive linguistics 21
Cohen, Jeffrey E. 6, 7, 8, 77
Cohen, Wilbur 121
Colbert, Stephen 150
Cold War 116
columnists 25
communication strategies 75, 98, 101, 109, 126
compassionate government imagery 19
conditional, framing as 67, 87, 101, 144–5
congressional hearings 71, 73, 75, 97
congressional oversight powers 46, 71
conservative vs. liberal news 50, 53, 57, 85, 101–2, 104–5, 127, 131
Constitution 27
Contorno, Steve 88 n.9
contradictions 48, 74
Cornyn, John 72, 97
corrections 131 *see also* apologies
Costello, Carol 31
Cowley, Geoffrey 109 n.2
Cox, Amanda 19
Craighill, Peyton M. 85
Cutter, Stephanie 19–20
cybersecurity 73

Dahl, Robert 47
Daily Show, The 54
Dallek, Robert 120, 122
D'Angelo, Paul 9
Dann, Carrie 73
Davis, Richard 8, 47, 54
"death panels" 50, 114, 129–35, 144, 145
"death tax" vs. "estate tax" 20
DeGette, Diana 76
democratization of presidential communication 22–3
Democrats: and HealthCare.gov 75–7, 83–4, 86, 87; health-care reform 113–14; and the name "Obamacare" 28–9, 30, 32, 34–5, 37–9, 40 n.8, 40 n.10; policy promises 99–100, 103, 109; "socialized medicine" 115–16,

120–1; supporting presidential frames 144; tax vs. penalty framing 52–3, 56
Dennis, Steven T. 75
Denton, Robert E. 9
Desilver, Drew 88 n.4
Dickinson, Greg 96
digital campaigning 8, 22 *see also* Internet; social media
DiJulio, Bianca 45
direct contact with public 8–9
direct quotes 53
Dost, Meredith 47
Douthat, Ross 25
dropped plans 93–112, 144
Druckman, James N. 10, 24
Dumain, Emma 19
Dutton, Sarah 85
Dwyer, Devin 19

Edelman, Murray 45
editorial policies 57, 119
Ed Show, The 101–2
Edwards III, George C. 6, 9, 39 n.3
Eilperin, Juliet 88 n.5
Ellis, Richard J. 77
e-mail 9, 19–20
end-of-life care 129–35
Energy and Commerce Committee 72, 73, 75, 76, 97
Enroll America 46
Ensign, John 60 n.13
entertainment programming 65
Entman, Robert 7, 9, 10, 21, 53, 66, 71, 86, 147 n.1
Epstein, Reid J. 40 n.10
errors in reporting 54–5
Ertelt, Steven 133
Eshbaugh-Soha, Matthew 6
Eshoo, Anna 75
ethical journalism 145, 146

Facebook 129, 130, 133
Face the Nation (CBS) 33–7
Factcheck.org 129
fair coverage standards 24
Families USA 47
Farnsworth, Stephen J. 7, 9, 71, 82
Farrar-Myers, Victoria A. 9
Fehrnstrom, Eric 48
Feldman, Lauren 8
fines vs. taxes, language of 46
Finnegan, Lisa. 7
Fishel, Jeff 95

Five, The (Fox News) 33, 58, 84
flip flopping 61 n.19
Fox News: "death panels" 135; *The Five* 33, 58, 84; *Fox Special Report with Bret Baier* 81; HealthCare.gov 79–81, 83, 84, 86; in modern media world 7; and the name "Obamacare" 23, 27–9, 32–3; policy promises 100–7; tax vs. penalty framing 49–50, 54, 56, 57, 58; and the toughness of presidential frames 143–4
frame diffusion 104
framing, defined 9–10
framing contests 10
franked mailings, non-partisan nature of 19
Frates, Chris 74
Fried, Charles 48
Friedman, Thomas 25
Frumin, Aliyah 78
Fudge, Martha 99–100
Fuller, Jaime 7
Funny or Die 65, 66

Galifianakis, Zach 65
Gallup 60 n.4, 108, 129
Gamm, Gerald 6
Geraghty, Patrick J. 98
Gingrich, Newt 25, 48
Godrej, Farah 21
Goldstein, Amy 68, 88 n.5
Good Morning America 84
Gore, Al 55, 61 n.19
government shutdown 68, 70, 93
Grassley, Chuck 129
Green, Al 75
Green, David 21
Greenstein, Fred I. 141
Gregory, David 34, 85, 99
Gutfeld, Greg 84
Guthrie, Samantha 81
Gutierrrez, Luis 40 n.8

Haberkorn, Jennifer 71
Hagan, Kay 99
Hallin, Daniel C. 7
Hamilton, James T. 77
Hannity, Sean 104
hard news vs. soft news 50, 53
Harper, Gregg 72
Harris, Louis 116
Harris polls 45
Harvey, Paul 39 n.5
Hatch, Orrin 60 n.13, 125

Hayes, Steve 81, 103
HealthCare.gov: compared to Hurricane Katrina 82–4; "glitches" frames 68–9, 71, 72, 74, 81, 143, 146; need for quick response 144; penalty/fine language (vs. tax) 48; quick remedies promised 70–1; traffic from *Between Two Ferns* 66; website problems 38, 49, 58, 65–92
health-care reform: domestic policies face greater challenges to authority 7; earlier framings of 21, 115–25; history of 113–40; as major 2012 reelection issue 23; opponents 19; overview 5–6; overwhelming demand 69–70; public support for 44–5; tax vs. penalty framing 43–64
Heith, Diane J. 6, 8, 126
Hendricks, John Allen 8, 9
Herbst, Susan 22
Heritage Foundation 48, 60 n.10
Hicks, Josh 56
Hill, The 40 n.10
Hillarycare 18, 48
Holan, Angie Drobnic 126
Holian, David B. 21
Holley, Joe 39 n.5
Holloway, Rachel L. 9
Hopper, Jennifer Rose 9
Huelskamp, Tim 72
Huey-Burns, Caitlin 100
"human rights" 21
Hurricane Katrina 66, 67, 79, 81–5, 87, 144, 146

"I Like Obamacare" campaign 19, 23–4, 29, 34, 38
incorrect reporting 54–5
Ingold, Beth 9
inheritance tax 20
insurance industry, blaming of 98–9, 102–3
intercoder reliability 10
Internet: Obama's use of 70, 72, 77, 136; participation of citizens and presidential surrogates 22; and rejected narratives 129 *see also* e-mail; social media
intraparty conflict 76
Iran-Contra scandal 77, 78, 96
Iraq war 95
Isakson, Johnny 130
"isolationism" 21
Iyengar, Shanto. 8

Jackson, David 103
Jacobs, Larry R. 6, 21
Jacobson, Gary C. 5, 45
Jamieson, Kathleen Hall 10, 49, 55, 76, 96
Jarrett, Valerie 98, 105
Jenkins, Henry 22
job approval numbers *see* approval ratings
Johnson, Lyndon Baines 20, 95, 114, 115, 120–3, 124, 127, 136
Johnson, Ron 97
Jones, Jeffrey M. 60 n.4
Jones, Jeffrey P. 40 n.6
journalism: hyper-adversarial political journalists 8, 21; modernization/globalization of 7; source reliability in news media 24; using social media to avoid scrutiny of 8
juxtaposed analyses 57

Kaiser Family Foundation (KFF) 37, 45, 46, 60 n.4
Kelly, Megyn 104
Kennedy, John F. 114, 115, 116–19, 122, 124, 127, 130–1, 134–5, 136
Kennedy, Kelly 71
Kent, Tom 40 n.9
Kernell, Samuel 6
Kimmel, Jimmy 17, 20
Klein, Ezra 100
Kliff, Sarah 46, 88 n.4, 134
Krugman, Paul 25
Kumar, Martha Joynt 6, 8
Kuypers, Jim A. 7, 9, 10

Lakoff, George 9, 21, 66, 136 n.2
Landrieu, Mary 99
language and framing 21, 44–5
Laurence, Jonathan. 8
Lawrence, Regina G. 131, 135
Lead with Jake Tapper, The 72, 74
Lee, Han Soo 7, 149
Lee, Jesse 7, 98, 109 n.4
Lerer, Lisa 130
Lesniewski, Neils 76
Letters to the Editor 29
Levendusky, Matthew 8, 100, 104
Lew, Jack 56, 81
Lewinsky scandal 108
Lexis-Nexis 149
"liberal" 21
liberal vs. conservative news 50, 53, 57, 85, 101–2, 104–5, 127, 131

Lichter, S. Robert 9, 71
Lieberman, Trudy 129
Liesman, Steve. 37
LifeNews.Com 133
Lillis, Mike 98
linguistic reclamation projects 21
Lipton, Eric 88 n.5
Livingston, Steven 7
LoGiurato, Brett 71
Los Angeles Times, The 34, 40 n.9
lying, framing of 87, 93–5, 100–7, 108

Madison, Lucy 19
Major, Mark. 7
Manchin III, Joe 76, 99
Marbury v. Madison (1803) 61 n.19
Marmor, Theodore R. 116
Maron, Marc 87 n.1
Marshall, Chief Justice John 61 n.19
Marshall, Thomas R. 46, 47
mass media, modernization/globalization of 7, 8
McCalmont, Lucy 75
McCaughey. Betty 129
McCombs, Maxwell 9
McConnell, Mitch 56
McCormack, John 133
McDermott, Jim 103
McMorris-Rogers, Cathy 73
Media Matters for America. 125–6, 133
Medicaid 59 n.3
Medical Care for the Aged plan 119
Medicare 17, 114, 116, 120–3, 124, 127, 145
Medicare Act (1965) 114
Medicare.gov 69
Meet the Press (NBC) 33–7, 81, 97, 98–9
Merkley, Jeff 99
Metzger, Gillian E. 60 n.12
midterm elections 109 n.2
Milbank, Dana 79
Miles, Matthew R. 7
Millman, Jason 71
Mills, Wilbur 120
Morone, James 116
Morrison, Trevor W. 60 n.12
Moyers, Bill 122
MSNBC 77, 85, 100–7, 109, 146
Murphy, Tim 73

Nacos, Brigitte Lebens 96
Nagourney, Adam 94, 131
National Federation of Independent Business v. Sebelius 23, 44, 45, 48, 49, 54–7, 58, 59

National Public Radio 34
NBC: dropped plans 99; *Evening News* 79–81; HealthCare.gov 83; *Meet the Press* 33–7, 81, 97, 98–9; in modern media world 7
Nelson, Bill 76
New Deal 113, 117
new media norms 95–6
"new" vs. "old" media 50, 53
New York Post, The: "death panels" 127, 131–3; HealthCare.gov 79–81, 88 n.14; tax vs. penalty framing 49–50, 53–4, 57; and the toughness of presidential frames 143–4; use of name "Obamacare" 23, 24–7, 30–1
New York Times, The: "death panels" 131–3, 135; HealthCare.gov 79–81, 82, 83, 84; Johnson and the AMA 123–4; Kennedy's speech 119–20; in modern media world 6; policy promises 94, 100–7; refraction of presidential framing 146; "socialized medicine" 124–5, 127–9; tax vs. penalty framing 49–50, 53–4, 57, 58, 59; use of name "Obamacare" 23, 24–7, 29, 30–1, 38
novelty, new media favors 96
Nyhan, Brendan 131

Obama, Barack: address to Congress Sept. 9 2009 49; as aloof, and disengaged 77; avoiding penalty/tax issues 55; control over language 45; on "death panels" 130; on HealthCare.gov problems 68–9, 70, 71, 74–5, 78; on health-care reform 93, 113; interview with George Stephanopoulos 43–4; key advantages in framing 53; media characterizations of 77–8; on policy promises 99; "socialized medicine" 126; and storytelling 6; tax vs. penalty framing 61 n.19; on Twitter 70; on *Between Two Ferns* 65–6; use of name "Obamacare" 17–18, 19, 24, 33, 40 n.9
Obama, Michelle 2
"Obamacare" (name for Affordable Care Act) 17–42, 143
"Obama's Katrina" 81–5, 87, 144
objective journalism 96, 108–9, 115, 124, 127, 131
O'Brien, David M. 47, 125
"O'Care" 25

O'Donnell, Jayne 103
O'Donnell, Norah 34
"old" vs. "new" media 50, 53
opinion columns (op-eds) 25
opponents: as creators of name "Obamacare" 17, 18–19; and dropped plans 96–7, 106, 108–9; HealthCare.gov 66–7, 71–3, 76, 79, 81; impact on perceptions 134; resistance of "Obamacare" 142; role in framing 9–10; tax vs. penalty framing 53
Ornstein, Charles 71
"out of touch" narratives 67
Owen, Diana 8

Palin, Sarah 129, 130, 131, 133, 145
Parker, Ashley 99, 100
partisan media 8, 96, 100, 108, 127
Patrick, Deval 99
Patterson, Thomas E. 8, 49, 95, 96, 145
Paul, Rand 72, 73
PBS News Hour 54
Peake, Jeffery 6
Pear, Robert 72, 99
Pelosi, Nancy 98, 99, 105, 133
penalty/fine framing (vs. tax) 43–64
Pengelly, Martin 97
Perino, Dana 33
Persily, Nathaniel 44
Peters, Jeremy W. 49
Pew Research Center 5, 135
Pfeiffer, Dan 70, 130
Pickert, Kate 75
Plouffe, David 29, 40 n.8
policy content, rarity of coverage 50–8
policy promises 47–8, 56, 58, 93–112, 146
PolitiFact.com 95, 129, 133
polls 12 n.1, 33, 37, 45–6, 60 n.4, 68, 77, 86, 94, 107, 108, 134–5
Potter, Wendell 103
Preibus, Reince 57
presidency, views of 6–9
"President Passerby" 79
press: inhospitable environment for presidential messages 8, 21–2; press independence 7; and the Supreme Court 47
press conferences 74–5, 122
prestige press 6, 24, 25, 33, 50, 105
privacy 73, 86
problems, framing of 66–7
public leadership 6–9

public opinion: anti-socialist medicine 126; "death panels" 134–5; dropped plans/policy promises 94, 107–8; HealthCare.gov 76, 84–6; on health-care reform 44–5; and the name "Obamacare" 37–8; "socialized medicine" 129; and Supreme Court rulings 46–7
pundits 21, 96

qualitative inductive analysis 10
Quinnipiac University Poll. 107, 108
quotation marks, use of 24, 25

Reagan, Ronald 6, 21, 77, 78, 96, 116
"Reaganomics" 21
reelection efforts 19, 23
Reese, Stephen D. 9, 10
Reeve, Elspeth 18
refraction: conclusions on 145–6; defined 4, 9; and HealthCare.gov problems 67; liberal vs. conservative news 109 n.3; policy promises 102, 109; and popular participation 23; tax vs. penalty framing 55, 59
Reifler, Jason 131
Republicans: as creators of name "Obamacare" 18–19; "death panels" 129; and the Federal Government shut-down 68; HealthCare.gov 66–7, 70, 71–3, 79, 81, 86; policy promises 96–7, 101, 108–9; resistance of "Obamacare" 142; and "socialized medicine" 116; on the tax/ penalty issues 48; tax vs. penalty framing 53, 56, 57, 58, 59; use of name "Obamacare" 25
resilience: comparative approach 115, 135, 136; defined 3, 4, 7–8; frames fitting with norms of journalism 145; frames vs. silence 130; HealthCare.gov 66, 67, 75, 81, 86, 87; manifestations of 143–4; and the name "Obamacare" 23–33, 36, 38; and natural political allies 75; policy promises 101, 106; president cannot achieve framing resilience alone 22; tax vs. penalty framing 53, 58–9
responsibility, accepting 75, 78–9, 86
Reynolds, Alan 133
rhetoric: adopting opponents' 21; participation of citizens and presidential surrogates 22–3; policy promises 95,

108; rhetorical attack 18, 21; symbolic import of 45
Richard Prince's Journalisms 40 n.9
Roberts, Chief Justice John 44, 48, 54, 55, 56, 57, 59, 61 n.19, 82, 146
Romney, Mitt 18, 19, 25, 48–9, 57, 59, 97, 125
"Romneycare" 19
Roosevelt, Franklin Delano 6, 21, 113, 117, 118, 126, 135
Roosevelt, Teddy 6
Rose, Charlie 2
Rosen, Jay 131
Rosenberg, Gerald 47
Rottinghaus, Brandon 7, 8
Rowling, Charles M. 24
Roy, Avik 48
Rubio, Marco 56, 72

Saad, Lydia 108
Sabato, Larry J. 77
Sanders, Bernie 142
Santorum, Rick 25
satire 65, 150
Saturday Night Live 145
Scalia, Justice Antonin 49, 60 n.6, 60 n.8
Scalise, Steve 72
scandals 71
Schafer, Matthew L. 131, 135
Schaffner, Brian F. 10, 20
Schieffer, Bob 34
Schill, Dan 8, 9
Schnell, Frauke 9
Schulte Scott, Jeanne 39 n.2
Schultz, Ed 101–2
Schumacher-Matos, Edward 40 n.9
Scott, Dylan 109 n.3
scrutiny 8
Sebelius, Kathleen 69, 70, 71, 73, 74, 75, 77, 78, 145
Seidel, Stuart 40 n.9
Seinfeld, Jerry 87 n.1
Semple, Jr., Robert B. 123
Serafini, Marilyn Werber 18
Shaheen, Jeanne 76
Shapiro, Robert Y. 6, 21
Sheafer, Tamir 10
Shear, Michael D. 25, 49, 82, 84, 97, 100
Shimkus, John 97
short-term political goals vs. long-term national interests 7, 95

shutdown, government 68, 70, 93
side effects: conclusions on 145–6; defined 4, 9; dropped plans 105; and the name "Obamacare" 29, 37, 39; and popular participation 23
signature policies, need for naming of 20
Sill, Kaitlyn L. 47
Simas, David 74
Sink, Justin 40 n.10, 75
Smith, Renee M. 6
Sneed, Tierney 87 n.1
"socialism," health-care reform framed as 21, 27
"socialized medicine" 113–14, 115–35, 144
social media: and "death panels" 133–4, 136; for direct contact with public 8–9; for everyday governance 5–6; Facebook 129, 130, 133; new opportunities from 8; and the Obama Administration 8; upsurge in 5–6; YouTube 66, 74 *see also* Twitter
Social Security 18, 117, 126
Solicitor General 48
Somashekhar, Sandhya 76
sound bites 95
source reliability in news media 24
speed of news cycle 54–5, 86–7, 115, 142
spin 7
spreadability of reframing 38, 53, 143
"spreadable" marketing 22
Starr, Paul 125
Stephanopoulos, George 34, 43, 45, 53, 57, 84
Stewart, Jon 54, 150
storytelling 2, 4, 6
Stromer-Galley, Jennifer 9
Stuckey, Mary E. 8, 9, 21, 22, 45
Sullivan, Margaret 101
Sullivan, Nancy 40 n.9
Sullivan, Sean 108
Sun, Lena H 81
Sunday news shows 33–7, 38, 39
Supreme Court 23, 44, 45, 46–7, 48, 49, 54–7, 58, 59
Sussman, Dalia 131
symbolism 95

tabloid-style news 25, 50, 53, 127
Talking Points Memo 109 n.3
Tapper, Jake 72, 74
Tavenner, Marilyn 75

tax vs. penalty framing 43–64, 143, 145
"tech surge" 71
televised addresses 130
television, modernization/globalization of 7
Thee-Brenan, Megan 94
This Morning (CBS) 2
This Week (ABC) 33–7, 43, 47
Thompson, Dennis 45
Times, The see *New York Times, The*
Today Show 56
Todd, Chuck 77, 78, 88 n.13, 99
Tonight Show, The 87 n.1
town hall meetings 126
traditional news media, changes to 6
Truman, Harry 113–14, 116, 118, 121
trust in new media 134
trustworthiness 108
Tulis, Jeffrey 6
Twitter: and "death panels" 133–4; HealthCare.gov 70, 72, 84–5; and the name "Obamacare" 19; policy promises 98; resilience of framing 144

Udall, Mark 99
units of analysis 10
unpredictability of reactions 29
Upton, Fred 72, 97
Urbina, Ian 126
USA Today 97

Van Susteren, Greta 57
Vaughn, Justin S. 9
Verrilli, Donald 48, 60 n.9
Viebeck, Elise 45, 134
Vietnam War 8, 135
visual presentations 24
Vox polls 134

Wagstaff, Keith 79
Waldman, Paul 10, 55, 96, 109 n.3
Wallace, Chris 27, 33, 56
Wall Street Journal, The 60 n.7
"war on poverty" 20, 95
"war on terror" 7
Washington Post, The: "death panels" 131–3; HealthCare.gov 75, 78, 79–81, 83, 86; policy promises 100–7, 108; refraction of presidential framing 146; "socialized medicine" 127–9; tax vs. penalty framing 49–50, 57
Washington Times 83, 88 n.14
watchdog role of the press 96
Watergate 8
Waxman, Henry 76
Weaver, Christopher 74
Weekly Standard, The 81, 133
Weigel, David 100
Weiner, Robert N. 48
White House: communication strategies 75, 98, 101, 109; Office of Digital Strategy 22; official communications policies 40 n.10; website 47
Wilson, Woodrow 6, 118
Windt, Theodore 9
Wolf, Byron 99
Wolfsfeld, Gadi 10

Yan, Holly 74, 78
Yellin, Jessica 31
Young, Todd Christopher 73
younger demographics, reaching 65
YouTube 66, 74

Zaller, John R. 24, 147 n.1
Zarefsky, David 20, 21, 95
Zelizer, Julian E. 116